CHARLES LAMB
IN ESSAYS AND LETTERS

THE MACMILLAN COMPANY
NEW YORK · BOSTON · CHICAGO · DALLAS
ATLANTA · SAN FRANCISCO

MACMILLAN & CO., Limited
LONDON · BOMBAY · CALCUTTA
MELBOURNE

THE MACMILLAN COMPANY
OF CANADA, Limited
TORONTO

CHARLES LAMB
IN
ESSAYS AND LETTERS

Chosen and Edited

by

MAURICE GARLAND FULTON

NEW YORK

THE MACMILLAN COMPANY

1930

PREFACE

This volume offers a selection of the more generally enjoyed of the *Elia* essays, with suppletory extracts from Lamb's less-read but inimitable correspondence. Such yokefellows— the essays and the letters—lead one in a most agreeable way into acquaintance with that one of the *majores deii* of English prose regarding whom it has been said appropriately, "Charles Lamb was not a poet, or essayist, or critic—he was a person."

The hesitation many persons have about reading Lamb I have tried to overcome by building an easy avenue of approach. The way has been smoothed materially, I hope, by substituting a pseudo-autobiographic sequence for the appallingly discrete arrangement which seems canonical in editions of Lamb. Certain other stumbling-blocks peculiarly noticeable in the case of Lamb, such as obsolescences in language and inveterate allusiveness, I have sought to diminish by annotation, generous but not obtrusive in quantity or content.

M. G. F.

Roswell, New Mexico
July, 1930

CONTENTS

INTRODUCTORY

The rich inheritance in Charles Lamb's writings may be had upon easy terms by seeking to know him as an interesting and attractive personality. He is primarily an essayist, and, as such, is constantly revealing his intimate self. It has been aptly said of him that few writers ever made such confidants of their readers as did he. Though both the *Essays of Elia* and the *Last Essays of Elia* combine into a large miscellany, dealing with many different topics, yet there is hardly an essay in either volume that is not to a great extent a piece of biography.

In addition to the *Elia* essays, Lamb left another priceless legacy in the many letters he bestowed on his close friends. These supplement in valuable ways the revelation of himself in his more formal writing. If they did nothing else than testify that certain characteristics of the more wrought-out essays, sometimes thought to be pose or mannerism, are in reality the man himself, they would be helpful. To read the letters is to see Lamb's mind in "undress," as he expressed it, and to realize how natural and undesigned were the peculiarities of his attitude and manner.

Since DeQuincey in Lamb's own generation remarked that to appreciate him it was necessary to understand his character and temperament, there has continued a general agreement that acquaintance with Lamb's personality is the master-key with which to unlock the treasures of his writings. To facilitate doing this the selections in this book have been arranged so as to compose a kind of informal account of his career, but more particularly a revelation of his paradoxical personality. Before proceeding to this course of reading, it will be well for the reader to orient himself by means of the thumb-nail autobiography Lamb wrote, in whimsical vein, it is said, for the album of William Upcott, an industrious autograph collector of those days. After Lamb's death, this sketch was published in the *New Monthly Magazine* for April 1835.

AN AUTOBIOGRAPHICAL SKETCH

Charles Lamb, born in the Inner Temple, 10th February, 1775, educated in Christ's Hospital. Afterwards a clerk in the Accountant's office, East India House; pensioned off from that service, 1825, after thirty-three years of service; is now a gentleman at large, can remember few specialties in his life worth noting except that he once caught a swallow flying (*teste suâ manu*); below the middle stature, cast of face slightly Jewish, with no Judaic tinge in his complexional religion, stammers abominably, and is therefore more apt to discharge his occasional conversation in a quaint aphorism or a poor quibble than in set and edifying speeches; has consequently been libelled as a person always aiming at wit, which, as he told a dull fellow that charged him with it, is at least as good as aiming at dullness; a small eater but not drinker; confesses a partiality for the production of the juniper berry, was a fierce smoker of tobacco, but may be resembled to a volcano burnt out, emitting only now and then a casual puff. Has been guilty of obtruding upon the Public a Tale in Prose, called "Rosamund Gray," a dramatic sketch named "John Woodvil," a "Farewell Ode to Tobacco," with sundry other poems and light prose matter, collected in two slight crown octavos, and pompously christened his Works, tho' in fact they were his Recreations, and his true works may be found in the shelves of Leadenhall Street, filling some hundred folios. He is also the true Elia whose essays are extant in a little volume published a year or two since; and rather better known from that name without a meaning, than from anything he has done or can hope to do in his own. He was also the first to draw the Public attention to the old English dramatists in a work called "Specimens of English Dramatic Writers, who lived about the time of Shakespeare," published about fifteen years since. In short, all his merits and demerits to set forth would take to the end of Mr. Upcott's book, and then not be truly told. He died * 18—, much lamented.

Witness his hand, CHARLES LAMB.

*To any Body—Please fill up these blanks.

Hand in hand with this account of Lamb by himself may go an unpretentious appraisal of his accomplishment for English literature. This limpid paragraph of commentary is gleaned from its humble lodgement in the introduction to Professor Edward Everett Hale's collection entitled *English Essays*.

A GENIAL PARAGRAPH OF COMMENTARY

Of true essays, those called the *Essays of Elia* are the best examples in our literature. Elia was the name taken by Charles Lamb in a series of papers he wrote for the *London Magazine* in the years 1820 and following. Lamb was a quiet, retiring man who loved a few books and a few friends, and had no especial ambition to do great things or make a great name. He worked during easy business hours at the India house, and then was free to spend the rest of the day in reading and talking, in pleasant places, perhaps, or with pleasant people. When he wrote, he set down what he would otherwise have spoken; his letters sound very much as though he might be talking to some friend. And his essays are not very different in character from his letters, although they are just a little more confined to some subject. But, on the whole, it does not seem to have been very important to Lamb what he wrote about, nor was he indeed very careful how he wrote. His writings have so much of his own personality and character that generations of readers have been delighted with them. They are free, of a genial temper and a pure humour, and whether we are interested in the subject or not before we begin to read, we always end with a kinder and pleasanter feeling about it, and indeed about everything else.

CHARLES LAMB
IN ESSAYS AND LETTERS

CHARLES LAMB
IN
ESSAYS AND LETTERS

I

CHILDHOOD AND SCHOOL-TIME

Among the most generally pleasing of Lamb's essays are three or four telling of his early childhood and school days. As the child of John Lamb (clerk, servant, confidant, and advisor to Samuel Salt, a bencher of the Inner Temple and, for a time, member of Parliament), Charles Lamb was born on February 10, 1775, in a humble home at No. 2 Crown Row Office, Inner Temple. In the family were six brothers and sisters, only two of whom survived their childhood—John Lamb, the eldest, and Mary Lamb, the sister with whom the youngest, Charles Lamb, was so closely linked. In *The Old Benchers of the Inner Temple* Charles Lamb wrote not only an account of the surroundings of his earliest years, but also pen portraits both of his father, whom he disguises under the name Lovel, and of his father's employer, Samuel Salt.

THE OLD BENCHERS OF THE INNER TEMPLE

I was born, and passed the first seven years of my life, in the Temple. Its church, its halls, its gardens, its fountains, its river, I had almost said—for in those young years, what was this king of rivers to me but a stream that watered our pleasant places?—these are of my oldest recollections. I repeat, to this day, no verses to myself more frequently, or with kindlier emotion, than those of Spenser, where he speaks of this spot.

There when they came, whereas those bricky towers,
The which on Themmes brode aged back doth ride,
Where now the studious lawyers have their bowers,
There whylome wont the Templer knights to bide,
Till they decay'd through pride.

Indeed, it is the most elegant spot in the metropolis. What a transition for a countryman visiting London for the first time—the passing from the crowded Strand or Fleet-street, by unexpected avenues, into its magnificent ample squares, its classic green recesses! What a cheerful, liberal look hath that portion of it, which, from three sides, overlooks the greater garden; that goodly pile

Of building strong, albeit of Paper hight,

confronting with massy contrast, the lighter, older, more fantastically-shrouded one, named of Harcourt, with the cheerful Crown-office-row (place of my kindly engendure), right opposite the stately stream, which washes the garden-foot with her yet scarcely trade-polluted waters, and seems but just weaned from her Twickenham Naïades! a man would give something to have been born in such places. What a collegiate aspect has that fine Elizabethan hall, where the fountain plays, which I have made to rise and fall, how many times! to the astoundment of the young urchins, my contemporaries, who, not being able to guess at its recondite machinery, were almost tempted to hail the wondrous work as magic! What an antique air had the now almost effaced sun-dials, with their moral inscriptions, seeming coevals with that Time which they measured, and to take their revelations of its flight immediately from heaven, holding correspondence with the fountain of light! How would the dark line steal imperceptibly on, watched by the eye of childhood, eager to detect its movement, never catched, nice as an evanescent cloud, or the first arrests of sleep!

Ah! yet doth beauty like a dial hand
Steal from his figure, and no pace perceived!

What a dead thing is a clock, with its ponderous embowelments of lead and brass, its pert or solemn dulness of communication, compared with the simple altar-like structure and silent heart-language of the old dial! It stood as the garden god of Christian gardens. Why is it almost everywhere vanished? If its business-use be superseded by more elaborate inventions, its moral uses, its beauty, might have pleaded for its continuance. It spoke of moderate labours, of pleasures not protracted after sunset, of temperance, and good hours. It was the primitive clock, the horologe of the first world. Adam could scarce have missed it in Paradise. It was the measure appropriate for sweet plants and flowers to spring by, for the birds to apportion their silver warblings by, for flocks to pasture and be led to fold by. The shepherd "carved it out quaintly in the sun;" and, turning philosopher by the very occupation, provided it with mottoes more touching than tomb-stones. It was a pretty device of the gardener, recorded by Marvell, who, in the days of artificial gardening, made a dial out of herbs and flowers. I must quote his verses a little higher up, for they are full, as all his serious poetry was, of a witty delicacy. They will not come in awkwardly, I hope, in a talk of fountains and sun-dials. He is speaking of sweet garden scenes:—

What wondrous life is this I lead!
Ripe apples drop about my head.
The luscious clusters of the vine
Upon my mouth do crush their wine.
The nectarine, and curious peach,
Into my hands themselves do reach.
Stumbling on melons, as I pass,
Insnared with flowers, I fall on grass.
Meanwhile the mind from pleasure less
Withdraws into its happiness.

> The mind, that ocean, where each kind
> Does straight its own resemblance find;
> Yet it creates, transcending these,
> Far other worlds, and other seas;
> Annihilating all that's made
> To a green thought in a green shade.
> Here at the fountain's sliding foot
> Or at some fruit-tree's mossy root,
> Casting the body's vest aside,
> My soul into the boughs does glide;
> There, like a bird, it sits and sings,
> Then whets and claps its silver wings,
> And, till prepared for longer flight,
> Waves in its plumes the various light.
> How well the skilful gardener drew,
> Of flowers, and herbs, this dial new!
> Where, from above, the milder sun
> Does through a fragrant zodiac run:
> And, as it works, the industrious bee
> Computes its time as well as we.
> How could such sweet and wholesome hours
> Be reckoned, but with herbs and flowers?

The artificial fountains of the metropolis are, in like manner, fast vanishing. Most of them are dried up or bricked over. Yet, where one is left, as in that little green nook behind the South-Sea House, what a freshness it gives to the dreary pile! Four little winged marble boys used to play their virgin fancies, spouting out ever fresh streams from their innocent-wanton lips, in the square of Lincoln's-inn, when I was no bigger than they were figured. They are gone, and the spring choked up. The fashion, they tell me, is gone by, and these things are esteemed childish. Why not then gratify children, by letting them stand? Lawyers, I suppose, were children once. They are awakening images to them at least. Why must everything smack of man, and mannish? Is the world all grown up? Is childhood dead? Or is there not in the bosoms of the wisest and the best some of the child's heart left, to respond to its earliest enchantments? The figures were grotesque. Are the stiff-wigged living figures, that still flitter and chatter about that area, less Gothic in appearance? or is the splutter of their hot rhetoric one-half so refreshing and innocent as the little cool playful streams those exploded cherubs uttered?

They have lately gothicized the entrance to the Inner Temple-hall, and the library front; to assimilate them, I suppose, to the body of the hall, which they do not at all resemble. What is become of the winged horse that stood over the former? a stately arms! and who has removed those frescoes of the Virtues, which Italianized the end of the Paper-buildings?—my first hint of allegory! They must account to me for these things, which I miss so greatly.

The terrace is, indeed, left, which we used to call the parade; but the traces are passed away of the footsteps which made its pavement awful! It is become common and profane. The old benchers had it almost sacred to themselves, in the forepart of the day at least. They might not be sided or jostled. Their air and dress asserted the parade. You left wide spaces betwixt you, when you passed them. We walk on even terms with their successors. The roguish eye of J[eky]ll, ever ready to be delivered of a jest, almost invites a stranger to vie a repartee with it. But what insolent familiar durst have mated Thomas Coventry?—whose person was a quadrate, his step massy and elephantine, his face square as the lion's, his gait peremptory and path-keeping, indivertible from his way as a moving column, the scarecrow of his inferiors, the browbeater of equals and superiors, who made a solitude of children wherever he came, for they fled his insufferable presence, as they would have shunned an Elisha bear. His growl was as thunder in their ears, whether he spake to them in mirth or in rebuke; his invitatory notes being, indeed, of all, the most repulsive and horrid. Clouds of snuff, aggravating the natural terrors of his speech, broke from each majestic nostril, darkening the air. He took it, not by pinches, but a palmful at once, diving for it under the mighty flaps of his old-fashioned waistcoat pocket; his waistcoat red and angry, his coat dark rappee, tinctured by dye original, and by adjuncts, with buttons of obsolete gold. And so he paced the terrace.

By his side a milder form was sometimes to be seen; the pensive gentility of Samuel Salt. They were coevals, and had nothing but that and their benchership in common. In politics Salt was a whig, and Coventry a staunch tory. Many a sarcastic growl did the latter cast out—for Coventry had a rough spinous humour—at the political confederates of his associate, which rebounded from the gentle bosom of the latter like cannon-balls from wool. You could not ruffle Samuel Salt.

S. had the reputation of being a very clever man, and of excellent discernment in the chamber practice of the law. I suspect his knowledge did not amount to much. When a case of difficult disposition of money, testamentary or otherwise, came before him, he ordinarily handed it over with a few instructions to his man Lovel, who was a quick little fellow, and would despatch it out of hand by the light of natural understanding, of which he had an uncommon share. It was incredible what repute for talents S. enjoyed by the mere trick of gravity. He was a shy man; a child might pose him in a minute—indolent and procrastinating to the last degree. Yet men would give him credit for vast application, in spite of himself. He was not to be trusted with himself with impunity. He never dressed for a dinner party but he forgot his sword—they wore swords then—or some other necessary part of his equipage. Lovel had his eye upon him on all these

occasions, and ordinarily gave him his cue. If there was anything which he could speak unseasonably, he was sure to do
it.—He was to dine at a relative's of the unfortunate Miss
Blandy on the day of her execution;—and L., who had a
wary foresight of his probable hallucinations, before he set
out, schooled him with great anxiety, not in any possible
manner to allude to her story that day. S. promised faithfully
to observe the injunction. He had not been seated in the
parlour, where the company was expecting the dinner summons, four minutes, when, a pause in the conversation ensuing, he got up, looked out of the window, and pulling
down his ruffles—an ordinary motion with him—observed,
"it was a gloomy day," and added, "Miss Blandy must be
hanged by this time, I suppose." Instances of this sort were
perpetual. Yet S. was thought by some of the greatest men
of his time a fit person to be consulted, not alone in matters
pertaining to the law, but in the ordinary niceties and em-
barrassments of conduct—from force of manner entirely.
He never laughed. He had the same good fortune among the
female world,—was a known toast with the ladies, and one
or two are said to have died for love of him—I suppose,
because he never trifled or talked gallantly with them, or
paid them, indeed, hardly common attentions. He had a fine
face and person, but wanted, methought, the spirit that
should have shown them off with advantage to the women.
His eye lacked lustre.—Not so, thought Susan P[ierson];
who, at the advanced age of sixty, was seen, in the cold evening time, unaccompanied wetting the pavement of B[ed-
for]d Row, with tears that fell in drops which might be
heard, because her friend had died that day—he, whom she
had pursued with a hopeless passion for the last forty years—
a passion which years could not extinguish or abate; nor the
long resolved, yet gently enforced, puttings off of unrelent-

ing bachelorhood dissuade from its cherished purpose. Mild Susan P——, thou hast now thy friend in heaven!

Thomas Coventry was a cadet of the noble family of that name. He passed his youth in contracted circumstances, which gave him early those parsimonious habits which in after life never forsook him; so that, with one windfall or another, about the time I knew him he was master of four or five hundred thousand pounds; nor did he look, or walk, worth a moidore less. He lived in a gloomy house opposite the pump in Serjeants'-Inn, Fleet-street. J., the counsel, is doing self-imposed penance in it, for what reason I divine not, at this day. C. had an agreeable seat at North Cray, where he seldom spent above a day or two at a time in the summer; but preferred, during the hot months, standing at his window in this damp, close, well-like mansion, to watch, as he said, "the maids drawing water all day long." I suspect he had his within-door reasons for the preference. *Hic currus et arma fuêre.* He might think his treasures more safe. His house had the aspect of a strong box. C. was a close hunks— a hoarder rather than a miser—or, if a miser, none of the mad Elwes breed, who have brought discredit upon a character which cannot exist without certain admirable points of steadiness and unity of purpose. One may hate a true miser, but cannot, I suspect, so easily despise him. By taking care of the pence, he is often enabled to part with the pounds, upon a scale that leaves us careless generous fellows halting at an immeasurable distance behind. C. gave away 30,000*l.* at once in his lifetime to a blind charity. His housekeeping was severely looked after, but he kept the table of a gentleman. He would know who came in and who went out of his house, but his kitchen chimney was never suffered to freeze.

Salt was his opposite in this, as in all—never knew what he was worth in the world; and having but a competency for his rank, which his indolent habits were little calculated to improve, might have suffered severely if he had not had honest people about him. Lovel took care of everything. He was at once his clerk, his good servant, his dresser, his friend, his "flapper," his guide, stop-watch, auditor, treasurer. He did nothing without consulting Lovel, or failed in anything without expecting and fearing his admonishing. He put himself almost too much in his hands, had they not been the purest in the world. He resigned his title almost to respect as a master, if L. could ever have forgotten for a moment that he was a servant.

I knew this Lovel. He was a man of an incorrigible and losing honesty. A good fellow withal, and "would strike." In the cause of the oppressed he never considered inequalities, or calculated the number of his opponents. He once wrested a sword out of the hand of a man of quality that had drawn upon him, and pommelled him severely with the hilt of it. The swordsman had offered insult to a female—an occasion upon which no odds against him could have prevented the interference of Lovel. He would stand next day bareheaded to the same person, modestly to excuse his interference—for L. never forgot rank, where something better was not concerned. L. was the liveliest little fellow breathing, had a face as gay as Garrick's, whom he was said greatly to resemble (I have a portrait of him which confirms it), possessed a fine turn for humorous poetry—next to Swift and Prior—moulded heads in clay or plaster of Paris to admiration, by the dint of natural genius merely; turned cribbage-boards, and such small cabinet toys, to perfection; took a hand at quadrille or bowls with equal facility; made punch better than any man of his degree in England; had the merriest quips and conceits; and was altogether as brimful of rogueries and inventions as you could desire. He was a brother of the angle, moreover, and just such a free, hearty, honest companion as Mr. Izaak Walton would have chosen to go a fishing with. I saw him in his old age and the decay of his faculties, palsy-smitten, in the last sad stage of human weakness—"a remnant most forlorn of what he was,"—yet even then his eye would light up upon the mention of his favourite Garrick. He was greatest, he would say, in Bayes—"was upon the stage nearly throughout the whole performance, and as busy as a bee." At intervals, too, he would speak of his former life, and how he came up a little boy from Lincoln to go to service, and how his mother cried at parting with him, and how he returned, after some few years absence, in his smart new livery to see her, and she blest herself at the change, and could hardly be brought to believe that it was "her own bairn." And then, the excitement subsiding, he would weep, till I have wished that sad second-childhood might have a mother still to lay its head upon her lap. But the common mother of us all in no long time after received him gently into hers.

With Coventry and with Salt, in their walks upon the terrace, most commonly Peter Pierson would join, to make up a third. They did not walk linked arm-in-arm in those days— "as now our stout triumvirs sweep the streets,"—but generally with both hands folded behind them for state, or with one at least behind, the other carrying a cane. P. was a benevolent, but not a prepossessing man. He had that in his face which you could not term unhappiness; it rather implied an incapacity of being happy. His cheeks were colourless, even to whiteness. His look was uninviting, resembling (but without his sourness) that of our great philanthropist. I know that he *did* good acts, but I could never make out what he *was*. Contemporary with these, but subordinate, was Daines Barrington—another oddity—he walked burly and square—in imitation, I think, of Coventry—howbeit he attained not to the dignity of his prototype. Nevertheless, he did pretty well, upon the strength of being a tolerable antiquarian, and having a brother a bishop. When the account of his year's treasurership came to be audited, the following singular charge was unanimously disallowed by the bench: "Item, disbursed Mr. Allen, the gardener, twenty shillings, for stuff to poison the sparrows, by my orders." Next to him was old Barton— a jolly negation, who took upon him the ordering of the bills of fare for the parliament chamber, where the benchers dine —answering to the combination rooms at college—much to the easement of his less epicurean brethren. I know nothing more of him.—Then Read, and Twopenny—Read, good-humoured and personable—Twopenny, good-humoured, but thin, and felicitous in jests upon his own figure. If T. was thin, Wharry was attenuated and fleeting. Many must remember him (for he was rather of later date) and his singular gait, which was performed by three steps and a jump regularly succeeding. The steps were little efforts, like that of a child beginning to walk; the jump comparatively vigorous, as a foot to an inch. Where he learned this figure, or what occasioned it, I could never discover. It was neither graceful in itself, nor seemed to answer the purpose any better than common walking. The extreme tenuity of his frame, I suspect, set him upon it. It was a trial of poising. Twopenny would often rally him upon his leanness, and hail him as Brother Lusty; but W. had no relish of a joke. His features were spiteful. I have heard that he would pinch his cat's ears extremely, when anything had offended him. Jackson— the omniscient Jackson, he was called—was of this period. He had the reputation of possessing more multifarious knowledge than any man of his time. He was the Friar Bacon of the less literate portion of the Temple. I remember a pleasant passage of the cook applying to him, with much formality of apology, for instructions how to write down *edge* bone of beef in his bill of commons. He was supposed to know, if any man in the world did. He decided the orthography to be—as I have given it—fortifying his authority with such anatomical reasons as dismissed the manciple (for the time) learned and happy. Some do spell it yet, perversely, *aitch* bone, from a fanciful resemblance between its shape and that of the aspirate so denominated. I had almost forgotten Mingay with the iron hand—but he was somewhat later. He had lost his right hand by some accident, and supplied it with a grappling-hook, which he wielded with a tolerable adroitness. I detected the substitute before I was old enough to reason whether it were artificial or not. I remember the astonishment it raised in me. He was a blustering, loud-talking person; and I reconciled the phenomenon to my ideas as an emblem of power—somewhat like the horns in the forehead of Michael Angelo's Moses. Baron Maseres, who walks (or did till very lately) in the costume of the reign of George the Second, closes my imperfect recollections of the old benchers of the Inner Temple.

Fantastic forms, whither are ye fled? Or, if the like of you exist, why exist they no more for me? Ye inexplicable, half-understood appearances, why comes in reason to tear away the preternatural mist, bright or gloomy, that enshrouded you? Why make ye so sorry a figure in my relation, who made up to me—to my childish eyes—the mythology of the Temple? In those days I saw Gods, as "old men covered with a mantle," walking upon the earth. Let the dreams of classic idolatry perish,—extinct be the fairies and fairy trumpery of legendary fabling,—in the heart of childhood there will, for ever, spring up a well of innocent or wholesome superstition—the seeds of exaggeration will be busy there, and

vital from every-day forms educing the unknown and
the uncommon. In that little Goshen there will be light,
when the grown world flounders about in the darkness of
sense and materiality. While childhood, and while dreams,
reducing childhood, shall be left, imagination shall not have
spread her holy wings totally to fly the earth.

P.S.—I have done injustice to the soft shade of Samuel Salt.
See what it is to trust to imperfect memory, and the erring
notices of childhood! Yet I protest I always thought that he
had been a bachelor! This gentleman, R[andall] N[orris]
informs me, married young, and losing his lady in childbed,
within the first year of their union, fell into a deep melancholy, from the effects of which, probably, he never thoroughly recovered. In what a new light does this place his
rejection (O call it by a gentler name!) of mild Susan P——,
unravelling into beauty certain peculiarities of this very shy
and retiring character!—Henceforth let no one receive the
narratives of Elia for true records! They are, in truth, but
shadows of fact—verisimilitudes, not verities—or sitting but
upon the remote edges and outskirts of history. He is no such
honest chronicler as R. N., and would have done better perhaps to have consulted that gentleman, before he sent these
incondite reminiscences to press. But the worthy sub-treasurer—who respects his old and his new masters—would not
have been puzzled at the indecorous liberties of Elia. The
good man wots not, peradventure, of the licence which *Magazines* have arrived at in this plain-speaking age, or hardly
dreams of their existence beyond the *Gentleman's*—his fur-
thest monthly excursions in this nature having been long
confined to the holy ground of honest *Urban's* obituary. May
it be long before his own name shall help to swell those
columns of unenvied flattery!—Meantime, O ye New

Benchers of the Inner Temple, cherish him kindly, for he is himself the kindliest of human creatures. Should infirmities overtake him—he is yet in green and vigorous senility—make allowances for them, remembering that "ye yourselves are old." So many the Winged Horse, your ancient badge and cognizance, still flourish? so may future Hookers and Seldens illustrate your church and chambers! so may the sparrows, in default of more melodious quiristers, unpoisoned hop about your walks! so may the fresh-coloured and cleanly nursery-maid, who, by leave, airs her playful charge in your stately gardens, drop her prettiest blushing curtesy as ye pass, re-ductive of juvenescent emotion! so may the younkers of this generation eye you, pacing your stately terrace, with the same superstitious veneration, with which the child Elia gazed on the Old Worthies that solemnized the parade before ye!

Lamb's early schooling was at the academy of a Mr. William Bird. He has described this in a letter he was moved to write to Horn's *Every-Day Book*. A picture of a Captain Starkey, a former teacher at Mr. Bird's, had appeared in that publication, together with extracts from the unfortunate man's autobiogra-phy. Lamb promptly wrote the following reminiscential letter.

CAPTAIN STARKEY

To the Editor of "The Every Day Book"—

Dear Sir,—I read your account of the unfortunate Being, and his forlorn piece of self-history, with that smile of half-interest which the Annals of Insignificance excite, till I came to where he says, "I was bound apprentice to Mr. William Bird, an eminent writer and Teacher of Languages and Math-ematics," &c.—when I started as one does on the recognition of an old acquaintance in a supposed stranger. This then was that Starkey of whom I have heard my Sister relate so many

pleasant anecdotes; and whom, never having seen, I yet seem
almost to remember. For nearly fifty years she had lost all
sight of him—and behold the gentle Usher of her youth,
grown into an aged Beggar, dubbed with an opprobrious
title, to which he had no pretensions; an object, and a May
game! To what base purposes may we not return! What
may not have been the meek creature's sufferings—what his
wanderings—before he finally settled down in the comparative comfort of an old Hospitaller of the Almonry of Newcastle? And is poor Starkey dead?——

I was a scholar of that "eminent writer" that he speaks of;
but Starkey had quitted the school about a year before I
came to it. Still the odour of his merits had left a fragrancy
upon the recollection of the elder pupils. The school-room
stands where it did, looking into a discoloured dingy garden
in the passage leading from Fetter Lane into Bartlett's Buildings. It is still a School, though the main prop, alas! has
fallen so ingloriously; and bears a Latin inscription over the
entrance to the Lane, which was unknown in our humbler
times. Heaven knows what "languages" were taught in it
then; I am sure that neither my Sister nor myself brought
any out of it, but a little of our native English. By "mathematics," reader, must be understood "cyphering." It was in
fact a humble day-school, at which reading and writing were
taught to us boys in the morning, and the same slender erudition was communicated to the girls, our sisters, &c. in the
evening. Now Starkey presided, under Bird, over both estab-
lishments. In my time Mr. Cook, now or lately a respectable
Singer and Performer at Drury Lane Theatre, and Nephew
to Mr. Bird had succeeded him. I well remember Bird. He
was a squat, corpulant, middle-sized man, with something
of the gentleman about him, and that peculiar mild tone—
especially while he was inflicting punishment—which is so

much more terrible to children, than the angriest looks and gestures. Whippings were not frequent; but when they took place, the correction was performed in a private room adjoining, whence we could only hear the plaints, but saw nothing. This heightened the decorum and the solemnity. But the ordinary public chastisement was a bastinado, a stroke or two on the palm with that almost obsolete weapon now—the ferule. A ferule was a sort of flat ruler, widened at the inflicting end into a shape resembling a pear,—but nothing like so sweet—with a delectable hole in the middle, to raise blisters, like a cupping-glass. I have an intense recollection of that disused instrument of torture—and the malignancy, in proportion to the apparent mildness, with which its strokes were applied. The idea of a rod is accompanied with something ludicrous; but by no process can I look back upon this blister-raiser with anything but unmingled horror.—To make him look more formidable—if a pedagogue had need of these heightenings—Bird wore one of those flowered Indian gowns, formerly in use with schoolmasters; the strange figures upon which we used to interpret into hieroglyphics of pain and suffering. But boyish fears apart—Bird I believe was in the main a humane and judicious master.

O, how I remember our legs wedged in to those uncomfortable sloping desks, where we sat elbowing each other—and the injunctions to attain a free hand, unattainable in that position; the first copy I wrote after, with its moral lesson "Art improves Nature;" the still earlier pothooks, and the hangers some traces of which I fear may yet be apparent in this manuscript; the truant looks sidelong at the garden, which seemed a mockery of our imprisonment; the prize for best spelling, which had almost turned my head, and which to this day, I cannot reflect upon without a vanity, which I ought to be ashamed of—our little leaden inkstands, not separately subsisting, but sunk into the desks; the bright, punctually-washed morning fingers, darkening gradually with another and another inkspot; what a world of little associated circumstances, pains, and pleasures mingling their quotas of pleasure, arise at the reading of those simple words—"Mr. William Bird, an eminent Writer and Teacher of languages and mathematics, in Fetter Lane, Holborn!"

Poor Starkey, when young, had that peculiar stamp of old-fashionedness in his face, which makes it impossible for a beholder to predicate any particular age in the object. You can scarce make a guess between seventeen and seven and thirty. This antique case always seems to promise ill-luck, and penury. Yet it seems, he was not always the abject thing he came to. My Sister, who well remembers him, can hardly forgive Mr. Thomas Ransom for making an etching so unlike her idea of him, when he was a youthful teacher at Mr. Bird's school. Old age and poverty—a lifelong poverty she thinks, could at no time have so effaced the marks of native gentility, which were once so visible in a face, otherwise strikingly ugly, thin, and careworn. From her recollections of him, she thinks that he would have wanted bread, before he would have begged or borrowed a halfpenny. If any of the girls (she says) who were my schoolfellows should be reading, through their aged spectacles, tidings from the dead of their youthful friend Starkey, they will feel a pang, as I do, at ever having teased his gentle spirit. They were big girls, it seems, too old to attend his instructions with the silence necessary; and however old age, and a long state of beggary seem to have reduced his writing faculties to a state of imbecility, in those days, his language occasionally rose to the bold and figurative, for when he was in despair to stop their chattering, his ordinary phrase was, "Ladies, if you will not hold your peace, not all the powers in heaven can make you." Once he was missing for a day or two; he had run away. A little old unhappy-looking man brought him back—it was his father—and he did no business in the school that day, but sate moping in a corner, with his hands before his face; and the girls, his tormentors, in pity for his case, for the rest of that day forebore to annoy him. I had been there but a few months (adds she) when Starkey, who was the chief instructor of us girls, communicated to us as a profound secret, that the tragedy of "Cato" was shortly to be acted by the elder boys, and that we were to be invited to the representation. That Starkey lent a helping hand in fashioning the actors, she remembers; and but for his unfortunate person, he might have had some distinguished part in the scene to enact; as it was, he had the arduous task of prompter assigned to him, and his feeble voice was heard clear and distinct, repeating the text during the whole performance. She describes her recollections of the cast of characters even now with a relish. Martia, by the handsome Edgar Hickman, who afterwards went to Africa, and of whom she never afterwards heard tidings.—Lucia, by Master Walker, whose sister was her particular friend; Cato, by John Hunter, a masterly declaimer, but a plain boy, and shorter by the head than his two sons in the scene, &c.

In conclusion, Starkey appears to have been one of those mild spirits, which, not originally deficient in understanding, are crushed by penury into dejection and feebleness. He might have proved a useful adjunct, if not an ornament to Society, if Fortune had taken him into a very little fostering, but wanting that, he became a Captain—a by-word—and lived, and died, a broken bulrush.

As a child, Lamb was of nerves all compact and very imaginative. Like many another boy or girl of this type, the gift of an active imagination was sometimes a source of entertainment and release, as the essay *My First Play* clearly shows; but at other times it was an endowment that led into regions of torment, as Lamb shows in the essay *Witches, and Other Night Fears.*

MY FIRST PLAY

At the north end of Cross-court there yet stands a portal, of some architectual pretensions, though reduced to humble use, serving at present for an entrance to a printing-office. This old doorway, if you are young, Reader, you may not know was the identical pit entrance to old Drury—Garrick's Drury—all of it that is left. I never pass it without shaking some forty years from off my shoulders, recurring to the evening when I passed through it to see *my first play*. The afternoon had been wet, and the condition of our going (the elder folks and myself) was, that the rain should cease. With what a beating heart did I watch from the window the puddles, from the stillness of which I was taught to prognosticate the desired cessation! I seem to remember the last spurt, and the glee with which I ran to announce it.

We went with orders, which my godfather F[ields] had sent us. He kept the oil shop (now Davies's) at the corner of Featherstone-building, in Holborn. F. was a tall grave person, lofty in speech, and had pretensions above his rank. He associated in those days with John Palmer, the comedian, whose gait and bearing he seemed to copy; if John (which is quite as likely) did not rather borrow somewhat of his manner from my godfather. He was also known to, and visited by, Sheridan. It was to his house in Holborn that young Brinsley brought his first wife on her elopement with him from a boarding-school at Bath—the beautiful Maria Linley. My parents were present (over a quadrille table) when he arrived in the evening with his harmonious charge.—From either of these connections it may be inferred that my godfather could command an order for the then Drury-lane theatre at pleasure—and, indeed, a pretty liberal issue of those cheap billets, in Brinsley's easy autograph, I have heard him say was the sole remuneration which he had received for many years' nightly illumination of the orchestra and various avenues of that theatre—and he was content it should be so. The honour of Sheridan's familiarity—or supposed familiarity—was better to my godfather than money.

F. was the most gentlemanly of oilmen; grandiloquent, yet courteous. His delivery of the commonest matters of fact was Ciceronian. He had two Latin words almost constantly in his mouth (how odd sounds Latin from an oilman's lips!), which my better knowledge since has enabled me to correct. In strict pronunciation they should have been sounded *vice versâ*—but in those young years they impressed me with more awe than they would now do, read aright from Seneca or Varro—in his own peculiar pronunciation, monosyllabically elaborated, or Anglicized, into something like *verse verse*. By an imposing manner, and the help of these distorted syllables, he climbed (but that was little) to the highest parochial honours which St. Andrew's has to bestow.

He is dead—and thus much I thought due to his memory, both for my first orders (little wondrous talismans!—slight keys, and insignificant to outward sight, but opening to me more than Arabian paradises!) and, moreover, that by his testamentary beneficence I came into possession of the only landed property which I could ever call my own—situate near the road-way village of pleasant Puckeridge, in Hertfordshire. When I journeyed down to take possession, and planted foot on my own ground, the stately habits of the donor descended upon me, and I strode (shall I confess the vanity?) with larger paces over my allotment of three quarters of an acre, with its commodious mansion in the midst, with the feeling of an English freeholder that all betwixt sky and centre was my own. The estate has passed into more prudent hands, and nothing but an agrarian can restore it.

In those days were pit orders. Beshrew the uncomfortable manager who abolished them!—with one of these we went. I remember the waiting at the door—not that which is left—but between that and an inner door in shelter—O when shall I be such an expectant again!—with the cry of nonpareils, an indispensable play-house accompaniment in those days. As near as I can recollect, the fashionable pronunciation of the theatrical fruiteresses then was "Chase some oranges, chase some numparels, chase a bill of the play;"—chase *pro* chuse. But when we got in, and I beheld the green curtain that veiled a heaven to my imagination, which was soon to be disclosed—the breathless anticipations I endured! I had seen something like it in the plate prefixed to Troilus and Cressida, in Rowe's Shakspeare—the tent scene with Diomede—and a sight of that plate can always bring back in a measure the feeling of that evening.—The boxes at that time, full of well-dressed women of quality, projected over the pit; and the pilasters reaching down were adorned with a glistening substance (I know not what) under glass (as it seemed), resembling—a homely fancy—but I judged it to be sugar-candy—yet to my raised imagination, divested of its homelier qualities, it appeared a glorified candy!—The orchestra lights at length arose, those "fair Auroras!" Once the bell sounded. It was to ring out yet once again—and, incapable of the anticipation, I reposed my shut eyes in a sort of resignation upon the maternal lap. It rang the second time. The curtain drew up—I was not past six years old and the play was Artaxerxes!

I had dabbled a little in the Universal History—the ancient

part of it—and here was the court of Persia.—It was being admitted to a sight of the past. I took no proper interest in the action going on, for I understood not its import—but I heard the word Darius, and I was in the midst of Daniel. All feeling was absorbed in vision. Gorgeous vests, gardens, palaces, princesses, passed before me. I knew not players. I was in Persepolis for the time; and the burning idol of their devotion almost converted me into a worshipper. I was awe-struck, and believed those significations to be something more than elemental fires. It was all enchantment and a dream. No such pleasure has since visited me but in dreams. —Harlequin's Invasion followed; where, I remember, the transformation of the magistrates into reverend beldams seemed to me a piece of grave historic justice, and the tailor carrying his own head to be as sober a verity as the legend of St. Denys.

The next play to which I was taken was the Lady of the Manor, of which, with the exception of some scenery, very faint traces are left in my memory. It was followed by a pantomime, called Lun's Ghost—a satiric touch, I apprehend, upon Rich, not long since dead—but to my apprehension (too sincere for satire), Lun was as remote a piece of anti-quity as Lud—the father of a line of Harlequins—transmit-ting his dagger of lath (the wooden sceptre) through count-less ages. I saw the primeval Motley come from his silent tomb in a ghastly vest of white patchwork, like the appari-tion of a dead rainbow. So Harlequins (thought I) look when they are dead.

My third play followed in quick succession. It was the Way of the World. I think I must have sat at it as grave as a judge; for, I remember, the hysteric affectations of good Lady Wishfort affected me like some solemn tragic passion. Robin-son Crusoe followed; in which Crusoe, man Friday, and the parrot, were as good and authentic as in the story.—The clownery and pantaloonery of these pantomimes have clean passed out of my head. I believe, I no more laughed at them, than at the same age I should have been disposed to laugh at the grotesque Gothic heads (seeming to me then replete with devout meaning) that gape, and grin, in stone around the inside of the old Round Church (my church) of the Templars.

I saw these plays in the season 1781-2, when I was from six to seven years old. After the intervention of six or seven other years (for at school all play-going was inhibited) I again entered the doors of a theatre. That old Artaxerxes evening had never done ringing in my fancy. I expected the same feelings to come again with the same occasion. But we differ from ourselves less at sixty and sixteen, than the latter does from six. In that interval what had I not lost! At the first period I knew nothing, understood nothing, discriminated nothing. I felt all, loved all, wondered all—

Was nourished, I could not tell how—

I had left the temple a devotee, and was returned a rationalist. The same things were there materially; but the emblem, the reference, was gone!—The green curtain was no longer a veil, drawn between two worlds, the unfolding of which was to bring back past ages, to present a "royal ghost," but a certain quantity of green baize, which was to separate the audience for a given time from certain of their fellow-men who were to come forward and pretend those parts. The lights—the orchestra lights—came up a clumsy machinery. The first ring, and the second ring, was now but a trick of the prompter's bell—which had been, like the note of the cuckoo, a phantom of a voice, no hand seen or guessed at which ministered to its warning. The actors were men and women painted. I thought the fault was in them; but it was in myself, and the alteration which those many centuries— of six short twelvemonths—had wrought in me.—Perhaps it was fortunate for me that the play of the evening was but an indifferent comedy, as it gave me time to crop some un-reasonable expectations, which might have interfered with the genuine emotions with which I was soon after enabled to enter upon the first appearance to me of Mrs. Siddons in Isabella. Comparison and retrospection soon yielded to the present attraction of the scene; and the theatre became to me, upon a new stock, the most delightful of recreations.

WITCHES, AND OTHER NIGHT-FEARS

We are too hasty when we set down our ancestors in the gross for fools, for the monstrous inconsistencies (as they seem to us) involved in their creed of witchcraft. In the rela-tions of this visible world we find them to have been as rational, and shrewd to detect an historic anomaly, as our-selves. But when once the invisible world was supposed to be opened, and the lawless agency of bad spirits assumed, what measures of probability, of decency, of fitness, or pro-portion—of that which distinguishes the likely from the palpable absurd—could they have to guide them in the re-jection or admission of any particular testimony?—That maidens pined away, wasting inwardly as their waxen images consumed before a fire—that corn was lodged, and cattle lamed—that whirlwinds uptore in diabolic revelry the oaks of the forest—or that spits and kettles only danced a fearful-innocent vagary about some rustic's kitchen when no wind was stirring—were all equally probable where no law of agency was understood. That the prince of the powers of darkness, passing by the flower and pomp of the earth, should lay preposterous siege to the weak fantasy of indigent eld—has neither likelihood nor unlikelihood *à priori* to us, who have no measure to guess at his policy, or standard to estimate what rate those anile souls may fetch in the devil's market. Nor, when the wicked are expressly symbolised by a goat, was it to be wondered at so much, that *he* should come sometimes in that body, and assert his metaphor.—That the intercourse was opened at all between both worlds was perhaps the mistake—but that once assumed, I see no reason for disbelieving one attested story of this nature more than another on the score of absurdity. There is no law to judge of the lawless, or canon by which a dream may be criticised.

I have sometimes thought that I could not have existed in the days of received witchcraft; that I could not have slept in a village where one of those reputed hags dwelt. Our ancestors were bolder or more obtuse. Amidst the universal belief that these wretches were in league with the author of all evil, holding hell tributary to their muttering, no simple justice of the peace seems to have scrupled issuing, or silly headborough serving, a warrant upon them—as if they should subpœna Satan!—Prospero in his boat, with his books and wand about him, suffers himself to be conveyed away at the mercy of his enemies to an unknown island. He might have raised a storm or two, we think, on the passage. His acquiescence is in exact analogy to the non-resistance of witches to the constituted powers.—What stops the Fiend in Spenser from tearing Guyon to pieces—or who had made it a condition of his prey that Guyon must take assay of the glorious bait—we have no guess. We do not know the laws of that country.

From my childhood I was extremely inquisitive about witches and witch-stories. My maid, and more legendary aunt, supplied me with good store. But I shall mention the accident which directed my curiosity originally into this channel. In my father's book-closet the History of the Bible, by Stackhouse, occupied a distinguished station. The pictures with which it abounds—one of the ark, in particular, and another of Solomon's temple, delineated with all the fidelity of ocular admeasurement, as if the artist had been upon the spot—attracted my childish attention. There was a picture, too, of the Witch raising up Samuel, which I wish that I had never seen. We shall come to that hereafter. Stackhouse is in two huge tomes; and there was a pleasure in removing folios of that magnitude, which, with infinite straining, was as much as I could manage, from the situation which they occupied upon an upper shelf. I have not met with the work from that time to this, but I remember that it consisted of Old Testament stories, orderly set down, with the *objection* appended to each story, and the *solution* of the objection regularly tacked to that. The *objection* was a summary of whatever difficulties had been opposed to the credibility of the history, by the shrewdness of ancient or modern infidelity, drawn up with an almost complimentary excess of candour. The *solution* was brief, modest, and satisfactory. The bane and antidote were both before you. To doubts so put, and so quashed, there seemed to be an end for ever. The dragon lay dead, for the foot of the veriest babe to trample on. But—like as was rather feared than realized from that slain monster in Spenser—from the womb of those crushed errors young dragonets would creep, exceeding the prowess of so tender a Saint George as myself to vanquish. The habit of expecting objections to every passage, set me upon starting more objections, for the glory of finding a solution of my own for them. I became staggered and perplexed, a sceptic in long-coats. The pretty Bible stories which I had read, or heard read in church, lost their purity and sincerity of

impression, and were turned into so many historic or chrono-
logic theses to be defended against whatever impugners. I was
not to disbelieve them, but—the next thing to that—I was
to be quite sure that some one or other would or had disbe-
lieved them. Next to making a child an infidel, is the letting
him know that there are infidels at all. Credulity is the man's
weakness, but the child's strength. O, how ugly sound scriptural doubts from the mouth of a babe and a suckling!—
I should have lost myself in these mazes, and have pined
away, I think, with such unfit sustenance as these husks afforded, but for a fortunate piece of ill-fortune which about
this time befell me. Turning over the picture of the ark with
too much haste, I unhappily made a breach in its ingenious
fabric—driving my inconsiderate fingers right through the
two larger quadrupeds—the elephant and the camel—that
stare (as well they might) out of the two last windows next
the steerage in that unique piece of naval architecture. Stackhouse was henceforth locked up, and became an interdicted
treasure. With the book, the *objections* and *solutions* gradually cleared out of my head, and have seldom returned since
in any force to trouble me.—But there was one impression
which I had imbibed from Stackhouse, which no lock or bar
could shut out, and which was destined to try my childish
nerves rather more seriously.—That detestable picture!

I was dreadfully alive to nervous terrors. The night-time
solitude, and the dark, were my hell. The sufferings I endured in this nature would justify the expression. I never laid
my head on my pillow, I suppose, from the fourth to the
seventh or eighth year of my life—so far as memory serves
in things so long ago—without an assurance, which realized
its own prophecy, of seeing some frightful spectre. Be old
Stackhouse then acquitted in part, if I say, that to this picture of the Witch raising up Samuel—(O that old man cov-

ered with a mantle!)—I owe—not my midnight terrors, the hell of my infancy—but the shape and manner of their visitation. It was he who dressed up for me a hag that nightly sate upon my pillow—a sure bedfellow, when my aunt or my maid was far from me. All day long, while the book was permitted me, I dreamed waking over his delineation, and at night (if I may use so bold an expression) awoke into sleep, and found the vision true. I durst not, even in the day-light, once enter the chamber where I slept, without my face turned to the window, aversely from the bed where my witch-ridden pillow was.—Parents do not know what they do when they leave tender babes alone to go to sleep in the dark. The feeling about for a friendly arm—the hoping for a familiar voice—when they wake screaming—and find none to soothe them—what a terrible shaking it is to their poor nerves! The keeping them up till midnight, through candle-light and the unwholesome hours, as they are called,—would, I am satisfied, in a medical point of view, prove the better caution.—That detestable picture, as I have said, gave the fashion to my dreams—if dreams they were—for the scene of them was invariably the room in which I lay. Had I never met with the picture, the fears would have come self-pictured in some shape or other—

Headless bear, black man, or ape—

but, as it was, my imaginations took that form.—It is not book, or picture, or the stories of foolish servants, which create these terrors in children. They can at most but give them a direction. Dear little T[hornton H[unt], who of all children has been brought up with the most scrupulous exclusion of every taint of superstition—who was never allowed to hear of goblin or apparition, or scarcely to be told of bad men, or to read or hear of any distressing story—finds all this

world of fear, from which he has been so rigidly excluded
ab extra, in his own "thick-coming fancies;" and from his
little midnight pillow, this nurse-child of optimism will start
at shapes, unborrowed of tradition, in sweats to which the
reveries of the cell-damned murderer are tranquillity.

Gorgons, and Hydras, and Chimæras—dire stories of
Celæno and the Harpies—may reproduce themselves in the
brain of superstition—but they were there before. They are
transcripts, types—the archetypes are in us, and eternal. How
else should the recital of that, which we know in a waking
sense to be false, come to affect us at all?—or

> ——Names, whose sense we see not,
> Fray us with things that be not?

Is it that we naturally conceive terror from such objects, considered in their capacity of being able to inflict upon us
bodily injury—O, least of all! These terrors are of older
standing. They date beyond body—or, without the body,
they would have been the same. All the cruel, tormenting,
defined devils in Dante—tearing, mangling, choking, stifling,
scorching demons—are they one half so fearful to the spirit
of a man, as the simple idea of a spirit unembodied following
him—

> Like one that on a lonesome road
> Doth walk in fear and dread,
> And having once turn'd round, walks on
> And turns no more his head;
> Because he knows a frightful fiend
> Doth close behind him tread.

That the kind of fear here treated of is purely spiritual—
that it is strong in proportion as it is objectless upon earth
—that it predominates in the period of sinless infancy—are
difficulties, the solution of which might afford some probable

insight into our ante-mundane condition, and a peep at least into the shadowland of pre-existence.

My night fancies have long ceased to be afflictive. I confess an occasional nightmare; but I do not, as in early youth, keep a stud of them. Fiendish faces, with the extinguished taper, will come and look at me; but I know them for mockeries, even while I cannot elude their presence, and I fight and grapple with them. For the credit of my imagination, I am almost ashamed to say how tame and prosaic my dreams are grown. They are never romantic, seldom even rural. They are of architecture and of buildings—cities abroad, which I have never seen, and hardly have hoped to see. I have traversed, for the seeming length of a natural day, Rome, Amsterdam, Paris, Lisbon—their churches, palaces, squares, market-places, shops, suburbs, ruins, with an inexpressible sense of delight—a map-like distinctness of trace, and a daylight vividness of vision, that was all but being awake.— I have formerly travelled among the Westmoreland fells— my highest Alps,—but they are objects too mighty for the grasp of my dreaming recognition; and I have again and again awoke with ineffectual struggles of the inner eye, to make out a shape in any way whatever, of Helvellyn. Methought I was in that country, but the mountains were gone. The poverty of my dreams mortifies me. There is Coleridge, at his will can conjure up icy domes, and pleasure-houses for Kubla Khan, and Abyssinian maids, and songs of Abara, and caverns,

> Where Alph, the sacred river, runs,

to solace his night solitudes—when I cannot muster a fiddle. Barry Cornwall has his tritons and his nereids gambolling before him in nocturnal visions, and proclaiming sons born to Neptune—when my stretch of imaginative activity can hardly, in the night season, raise up the ghost of a fishwife. To set my failures in somewhat a mortifying light—it was after reading the noble Dream of this poet, that my fancy ran strong upon these marine spectra; and the poor plastic power, such as it is, within me set to work to humour my folly in a sort of dream that very night. Methought I was upon the ocean billows at some sea nuptials, riding and mounted high, with the customary train sounding their conchs before me (I myself, you may be sure, the *leading god*), and jollily we went careering over the main, till just where Ino Leucothea should have greeted me (I think it was Ino) with a white embrace, the billows gradually subsiding, fell from a sea roughness to a sea calm, and thence to a river motion, and that river (as happens in the familiarization of dreams) was no other than the gentle Thames, which landed me in the wafture of a placid wave or two, alone, safe and inglorious, somewhere at the foot of Lambeth palace.

The degree of the soul's creativeness in sleep might furnish no whimsical criterion of the quantum of poetical faculty resident in the same soul waking. An old gentleman, a friend of mine, and a humorist, used to carry this notion so far, that when he saw any stripling of his acquaintance ambitious of becoming a poet, his first question would be,—"Young man, what sort of dreams have you?" I have so much faith in my old friend's theory, that when I feel that idle vein returning upon me, I presently subside into my proper element of prose, remembering those eluding nereids, and that inauspicious inland landing.

In Lamb's childhood there were memorable seasons when he had glimpses of a life different from that which surrounded his home in the Temple. His grandmother, Mary Field, was housekeeper at the "old great house," as Lamb termed it, of the Plumer family, Blakesware, Hertfordshire, and Lamb was often privileged to visit her there. This large and elaborate homestead, with its old-fashioned architecture and furnishings conjoined with quiet, rural charm of the surrounding country, in producing on Lamb's childish imagination such a great impression, that it must be reckoned among the formative influences. "Nothing fills a child's mind like a large old mansion," he once wrote in a letter and attests the truth of this dictum in his own case in the essay *Blakesmoor in H[ertford]shire*.

BLAKESMOOR IN H[ERTFORD]SHIRE

I do not know a pleasure more affecting than to range at will over the deserted apartments of some fine old family mansion. The traces of extinct grandeur admit of a better passion than envy: and contemplations on the great and good, whom we fancy in succession to have been its inhabitants, weave for us illusions, incompatible with the bustle of modern occupancy, and vanities of foolish present aristocracy. The same difference of feeling, I think, attends us between entering an empty and a crowded church. In the latter it is chance but some present human frailty—an act of inattention on the part of some of the auditory—or a trait of affectation, or worse, vain glory, on that of the preacher, puts us by our best thoughts, disharmonising the place and the occasion. But would'st thou know the beauty of holiness?—go alone on some week-day, borrowing the keys of good Master Sexton, traverse the cool aisles of some country church: think of the piety that has kneeled there— the congregations, old and young, that have found consolation there—the meek pastor—the docile parishioner. With no disturbing emotions, no cross conflicting comparisons, drink in the tranquillity of the place, till thou thyself become as fixed and motionless as the marble effigies that kneel and weep around thee.

Journeying northward lately, I could not resist going some few miles out of my road to look upon the remains of an old great house with which I had been impressed in this way in infancy. I was apprised that the owner of it had lately pulled it down; still I had a vague notion that it could not all have perished,—that so much solidity with magnificence could not have been crushed all at once into the mere dust and rubbish which I found it.

The work of ruin had proceeded with a swift hand indeed, and the demolition of a few weeks had reduced it to—an antiquity.

I was astonished at the indistinction of everything. Where had stood the great gates? What bounded the court-yard? Whereabout did the out-houses commence? a few bricks only lay as representatives of that which was so stately and so spacious.

Death does not shrink up his human victim at this rate. The burnt ashes of a man weigh more in their proportion.

Had I seen these brick-and-mortar knaves at their process of destruction, at the plucking of every panel I should have felt the varlets at my heart. I should have cried out to them to spare a plank at least out of the cheerful storeroom, in whose hot window-seat I used to sit and read Cowley, with the grass-plat before, and the hum and flappings of that one solitary wasp that ever haunted it about me—it is in mine ears now, as oft as summer returns; or a panel of the yellow-room.

Why, every plank and panel of that house for me had magic in it. The tapestried bedrooms—tapestry so much better than painting—not adorning merely, but peopling the wainscots—at which childhood ever and anon would steal a look, shifting its coverlid (replaced as quickly) to exercise its tender courage in a momentary eye-encounter with those stern bright visages, staring reciprocally—all Ovid on the walls, in colours vivider than his descriptions. Actæon in mid sprout, with the unappeasable prudery of Diana; and the still more provoking and almost culinary coolness of Dan Phœbus, eel-fashion, deliberately divesting of Marsyas.

Then, that haunted room—in which old Mrs. Battle died—whereinto I have crept, but always in the day-time, with a passion of fear; and a sneaking curiosity, terror-tainted, to hold communication with the past.—*How shall they build it up again?*

It was an old deserted place, yet not so long deserted but that traces of the splendour of past inmates were everywhere apparent. Its furniture was still standing—even to the tarnished gilt leather battledores, and crumbling feathers of shuttlecocks in the nursery, which told that children had once played there. But I was a lonely child, and had the range at will of every apartment, knew every nook and corner, wondered and worshipped everywhere.

The solitude of childhood is not so much the mother of thought as it is the feeder of love, and silence, and admiration. So strange a passion for the place possessed me in those years, that, though there lay—I shame to say how few roods distant from the mansion—half hid by trees, what I judged some romantic lake, such was the spell which bound me to the house, and such my carefulness not to pass its strict and proper precincts, that the idle waters lay unexplored for me; and not till late in life, curiosity prevailing over elder devotion, I found, to my astonishment, a pretty brawling brook had been the Lacus Incognitus of my infancy. Variegated views, extensive prospects—and those at no great distance from the house—I was told of such—what were they to me, being out of the boundaries of my Eden?—So far from a wish to roam, I would have drawn, methought, still closer the fences of my chosen prison; and have been hemmed in by a yet securer cincture of those excluding garden walls. I could have exclaimed with the garden-loving poet—

> Bind me, ye woodbines, in your twines;
> Curl me about, ye gadding vines;
> And oh so close your circles lace,
> That I may never leave this place;
> But, lest your fetters prove too weak
> Ere I your silken bondage break,
>   Do you, O brambles, chain me too,
>   And, courteous briars, nail me through.

I was here as in a lonely temple. Snug firesides—the low-built roof—parlours ten feet by ten—frugal boards, and all the homeliness of home—these were the condition of my birth—the wholesome soil which I was planted in. Yet, without impeachment to their tenderest lessons, I am not sorry to have had glances of something beyond; and to have taken, if but a peep, in childhood, at the contrasting accidents of a great fortune.

To have the feeling of gentility, it is not necessary to have been born gentle. The pride of ancestry may be had on cheaper terms than to be obliged to an importunate race of ancestors and the coatless antiquary in his unemblazoned cell, revolving the long line of a Mowbray's or De Clifford's pedigree, at those sounding names may warm himself into as gay a vanity as those who do inherit them. The claims of birth are ideal merely, and what herald shall go about to strip me of an idea? Is it trenchant to their swords? can it be hacked off as a spur can? or torn away like a tarnished garter?

What, else, were the families of the great to us? what pleasure should we take in their tedious genealogies, or their capitulatory brass monuments? What to us the uninterrupted current of their bloods, if our own did not answer within us to a cognate and correspondent elevation?

Or, wherefore, else, O tattered and diminished 'Scutcheon that hung upon the time-worn walls of thy princely stairs, BLAKESMOOR! have I in childhood so oft stood poring upon thy mystic characters—thy emblematic supporters, with their prophetic "Resurgam"—till, every dreg of peasantry purging off, I received into myself Very Gentility? Thou wert first in my morning eyes; and of nights, hast detained my steps from bedward, till it was but a step from gazing at thee to dreaming on thee.

This is the only true gentry by adoption; the veritable change of blood, and not as empirics have fabled, by transfusion.

Who it was by dying that had earned the splendid trophy, I know not, I inquired not; but its fading rags, and colours cobweb-stained, told that its subject was of two centuries back.

And what if my ancestor at that date was some Damœtas, —feeding flocks, not his own, upon the hills of Lincoln— did I in less earnest vindicate to myself the family trappings of this once proud Ægon? repaying by a backward triumph the insults he might possibly have heaped in his life-time upon my poor pastoral progenitor.

If it were presumption so to speculate, the present owners of the mansion had least reason to complain. They had long forsaken the old house of their fathers for a newer trifle; and I was left to appropriate to myself what images I could pick up, to raise my fancy, or to soothe my vanity.

I was the true descendant of those old W——s; and not

the present family of that name, who had fled the old waste places.

Mine was that gallery of good old family portraits, which as I have gone over, giving them in fancy my own family name, one—and then another—would seem to smile, reaching forward from the canvas, to recognise the new relationship; while the rest looked grave, as it seemed, at the vacancy in their dwelling, and thoughts of fled posterity.

That Beauty, with the cool blue pastoral drapery, and a lamb—that hung next the great bay window—with the bright yellow H——shire hair, and eye of watchet hue—so like my Alice!—I am persuaded she was a true Elia—Mildred Elia, I take it.

Mine too, BLAKESMOOR, was thy noble Marble Hall, with its mosaic pavements, and its Twelve Cæsars—stately busts in marble—ranged round: of whose countenances, young reader of faces as I was, the frowning beauty of Nero, I remember, had most of my wonder; but the mild Galba had my love. There they stood in the coldness of death, yet freshness of immortality. Mine too, thy lofty Justice Hall, with its one chair of authority, high-backed and wickered, once the terror of luckless poacher, or self-forgetful maiden —so common since, that bats have roosted in it.

Mine too,—whose else?—thy costly fruit-garden, with its sun-baked southern wall; the ampler pleasure-garden, rising backwards from the house in triple terraces, with flower-pots now of palest lead, save that a speck here and there, saved from the elements, bespake their pristine state to have been gilt and glittering; the verdant quarters backwarder still; and, stretching still beyond, in old formality, thy firry wilderness, the haunt of the squirrel, and the day-long murmuring wood-pigeon, with that antique image in the centre, God or Goddess I wist not; but child of Athens or old Rome paid never a sincerer worship to Pan or to Sylvanus in their native groves, than I to that fragmental mystery.

Was it for this, that I kissed my childish hands too fervently in your idol-worship, walks and windings of BLAKESMOOR! for this, or what sin of mine, has the plough passed over your pleasant places? I sometimes think that as men, when they die, do not die all, so of their extinguished habitations there may be a hope—a germ to be revivified.

When Charles Lamb was seven years old, his father's employer, Samuel Salt, obtained for him admission to the famous school in London for poor boys, called Christ's Hospital. In the same year, young Samuel Taylor Coleridge also came to the school from his home at Ottery St. Mary, and between the future author of *The Rime of the Ancient Mariner* and gentle, nervous, stammering Charles Lamb there sprang up immediately a friendship that lasted for more than fifty years and was one of the happiest influences in their lives. Lamb has written of the old schooldays in *Christ's Hospital Five-and-Thirty Years Ago*. For the sake of innocent mystification, he has chosen to write as if he were Coleridge.

CHRIST'S HOSPITAL FIVE-AND-THIRTY YEARS AGO

In Mr. Lamb's "Works," published a year or two since, I find a magnificent eulogy on my old school, such as it was, or now appears to him to have been, between the year 1782 and 1789. It happens, very oddly, that my own standing at Christ's was nearly corresponding with his; and, with all gratitude to him for his enthusiasm for the cloisters, I think he has contrived to bring together whatever can be said in praise of them, dropping all the other side of the argument most ingeniously.

I remember L. at school; and can well recollect that he had some peculiar advantages, which I and others of his school-fellows had not. His friends lived in town, and were near at hand; and he had the privilege of going to see them, almost as often as he wished, through some invidious distinction, which was denied to us. The present worthy sub-treasurer to the Inner Temple can explain how that happened. He had his tea and hot rolls in a morning, while we were battening upon our quarter of a penny loaf—our *crug*—moistened with attenuated small beer, in wooden piggins, smacking of the pitched leathern jack it was poured from. Our Monday's milk porritch, blue and tasteless, and the pease soup of Saturday, coarse and choking, were enriched for him with a slice of "extraordinary bread and butter," from the hot-loaf of the Temple. The Wednesday's mess of millet, somewhat less repugnant—(we had three banyan to four meat days in the week)—was endeared to his palate with a lump of double-refined, and a smack of ginger (to make it go down the more glibly) or the fragrant cinnamon. In lieu of our *half-pickled* Sundays, or *quite fresh* boiled beef on Thursdays (strong as *caro equina*), with detestable marigolds floating in the pail to poison the broth—our scanty mutton scrags on Fridays—and rather more savoury, but grudging, portions of the same flesh, rotten-roasted or rare, on the Tuesdays (the only dish which excited our appetites, and disappointed our stomachs, in almost equal proportion)—he had his hot plate of roast veal, or the more tempting griskin (exotics unknown to our palates), cooked in the paternal kitchen (a great thing), and brought him daily by his maid or aunt! I remember the good old relative (in whom love forbade pride) squatting down upon some odd stone in a by-nook of the cloisters, disclosing the viands (of higher regale than those cates which the ravens ministered to the Tishbite);

and the contending passions of L. at the unfolding. There was love for the bringer; shame for the thing brought, and the manner of its bringing; sympathy for those who were too many to share in it; and, at top of all, hunger (eldest, strongest of the passions!) predominant, breaking down the stony fences of shame, and awkwardness, and a troubling over-consciousness.

I was a poor friendless boy. My parents, and those who should care for me, were far away. Those few acquaintances of theirs, which they could reckon upon being kind to me in the great city, after a little forced notice, which they had the grace to take of me on my first arrival in town, soon grew tired of my holiday visits. They seemed to them to recur too often, though I thought them few enough; and, one after another, they all failed me, and I felt myself alone among six hundred playmates.

O the cruelty of separating a poor lad from his early homestead! The yearnings which I used to have towards it in those unfledged years! How, in my dreams, would my native town (far in the west) come back, with its church, and trees, and faces! How I would wake weeping, and in the anguish of my heart exclaim upon sweet Calne in Wiltshire!

To this late hour of my life, I trace impressions left by the recollection of those friendless holidays. The long warm days of summer never return but they bring with them a gloom from the haunting memory of those *whole-day leaves*, when, by some strange arrangement, we were turned out, for the livelong day, upon our own hands, whether we had friends to go to, or none. I remember those bathing-excursions to the New River, which L. recalls with such relish, better, I think, than he can—for he was a home-seeking lad, and did not much care for such water-pastimes: —How merrily we would sally forth into the fields; and strip under the first warmth of the sun; and wanton like young dace in the streams; getting us appetites for noon, which those of us that were penniless (our scanty morning crust long since exhausted) had not the means of allaying—while the cattle, and the birds, and the fishes, were at feed about us, and we had nothing to satisfy our cravings—the very beauty of the day, and the exercise of the pastime, and the sense of liberty, setting a keener edge upon them!—How faint and languid, finally, we would return, towards night-fall, to our desired morsel, half-rejoicing, half-reluctant, that the hours of our uneasy liberty had expired!

It was worse in the days of winter, to go prowling about the streets objectless—shivering at cold windows of print-shops, to extract a little amusement; or haply, as a last resort, in the hope of a little novelty, to pay a fifty-times repeated visit (where our individual faces should be as well known to the warden as those of his own charges) to the Lions in the Tower—to whose levée, by courtesy immemorial, we had a prescriptive title to admission.

L's governor (so we called the patron who presented us to the foundation) lived in a manner under his paternal roof. Any complaint which he had to make was sure of being attended to. This was understood at Christ's, and was an effectual screen to him against the severity of masters, or worse tyranny of the monitors. The oppressions of these young brutes are heart-sickening to call to recollection. I have been called out of my bed, and *waked for the purpose,* in the coldest winter nights—and this not once, but night after night—in my shirt, to receive the discipline of a leathern thong, with eleven other sufferers, because it pleased my callow overseer, when there has been any talking heard after we were gone to bed, to make the six last beds in the dormitory, where the youngest children of us slept, answerable for an offence they neither dared to commit, nor had the power to hinder.—The same execrable tyranny drove the younger part of us from the fires, when our feet were perishing with snow; and, under the cruellest penalties, forbade the indulgence of a drink of water, when we lay in sleepless summer nights, fevered with the season, and the day's sports.

There was one H[odges], who, I learned in after days, was seen expiating some maturer offence in the hulks. (Do I flatter myself in fancying that this might be the planter of that name, who suffered—at Nevis, I think, or St. Kitts, —some few years since? My friend Tobin was the benevolent instrument of bringing him to the gallows.) This petty Nero actually branded a boy, who had offended him, with a red-hot iron; and nearly starved forty of us, with exacting contributions, to the one half of our bread, to pamper a young ass, which, incredible as it may seem, with the connivance of the nurse's daughter (a young flame of his) he had contrived to smuggle in, and keep upon the leads of the *ward*, as they called our dormitories. This game went on for better than a week, till the foolish beast, not able to fare well but he must cry roast meat—happier than Caligula's minion, could he have kept his own counsel—but, foolisher, alas! than any of his species in the fables—waxing fat, and kicking, in the fulness of bread, one unlucky minute would needs proclaim his good fortune to the world below; and, laying out his simple throat, blew such a ram's horn blast, as (toppling down the walls of his own Jericho) set concealment any longer at defiance. The client was dismissed, with certain attentions, to Smithfield; but I never understood that the patron underwent any censure on the occasion. This was in the stewardship of L.'s admired Perry.

Under the same *facile* administration, can L. have forgotten the cool impunity with which the nurses used to carry away, openly, in open platters, for their own tables, one out of two of every hot joint, which the careful matron had been seeing scrupulously weighed out for our dinners? These things were daily practised in that magnificent apartment, which L. (grown connoisseur since, we presume) praises so highly for the grand paintings "by Verrio and others," with which it is "hung round and adorned." But the sight of sleek well-fed blue-coat boys in pictures was, at that time, I believe, little consolatory to him, or us, the living ones, who saw the better part of our provisions carried away before our faces by harpies; and ourselves reduced (with the Trojan in the hall of Dido)

To feed our mind with idle portraiture.

L. has recorded the repugnance of the school to *gags,* or the fat of fresh beef boiled; and sets it down to some superstition. But these unctuous morsels are never grateful to young palates (children are universally fat-haters) and in strong, coarse, boiled meats, *unsalted,* are detestable. A *gag-eater* in our time was equivalent to a *goul,* and held in equal detestation. ——suffered under the imputation:

. . . . 'Twas said
He ate strange flesh.

He was observed, after dinner, carefully to gather up the remnants left at his table (not many, nor very choice fragments, you may credit me)—and, in an especial manner, these disreputable morsels, which he would convey away, and secretly stow in the settle that stood at his bedside. None saw when he ate them. It was rumoured that he privately devoured them in the night. He was watched, but no traces of such midnight practices were discoverable. Some reported, that, on leave-days, he had been seen to carry out of the bounds a large blue-check handkerchief, full of something. This then must be the accursed thing. Conjecture next was at work to imagine how he could dispose of it. Some said he sold it to the beggars. This belief generally prevailed. He went about moping. None spake to him. No one would play with him. He was excommunicated; put out of the pale of the school. He was too powerful a boy to be beaten, but he underwent every mode of that negative punishment, which is more grievous than many stripes. Still he persevered. At length he was observed by two of his schoolfellows, who were determined to get at the secret, and had traced him one leave-day for that purpose, to enter a large worn-out building, such as there exist specimens of in Chancery-lane, which are let out to various scales of pauperism, with open door, and a common staircase. After him they silently slunk in, and followed by stealth up four flights, and saw him tap at a poor wicket, which was opened by an aged woman, meanly clad. Suspicion was now ripened into certainty. The informers had secured their victim. They had him in their toils. Accusation was formally preferred, and retribution most signal was looked for. Mr. Hathaway, the then steward (for this happened a little after my time), with that patient sagacity which tempered all his conduct, determined to investigate the matter, before he proceeded to sentence. The result was, that the supposed mendicants, the receivers or purchasers of the mysterious scraps, turned out to be the parents of——, an honest couple come to decay,—whom this seasonable supply had, in all probability, saved from mendicancy: and that this young stork, at the expense of his own good name, had all this while been only feeding the old birds!—The governors on this occasion, much to their honour, voted a present relief to the family of——, and presented him with a silver medal. The lesson which the steward read upon RASH JUDGMENT, on the occasion of publicly delivering the medal to——, I believe, would not be lost upon his auditory.—I had left school then, but I well remember——. He was a tall, shambling youth, with a cast in his eye, not at all calculated to conciliate hostile prejudices. I have since seen him carrying a baker's basket. I think I heard he did not do quite so well by himself as he had done by the old folks.

I was a hypochondriac lad; and the sight of a boy in fetters, upon the day of my first putting on the blue clothes, was not exactly fitted to assuage the natural terrors of initiation. I was of tender years, barely turned of seven; and had only read of such things in books, or seen them but in dreams. I was told he had *run away*. This was the punishment for the first offence.—As a novice I was soon after taken to see the dungeons. These were little, square, Bedlam cells, where a boy could just lie at his length upon straw and a blanket—a mattress, I think, was afterwards substituted—with a peep of light, let in askance, from a prison-orifice at top, barely enough to read by. Here the poor boy was locked in by himself all day, without sight of any but the porter who brought him his bread and water—who *might not speak to him;*—or of the beadle, who came twice a week to call him out to receive his periodical chastisement, which was almost welcome, because it separated him for a brief interval from solitude:—and here he was shut up by himself of *nights,* out of the reach of any sound, to suffer whatever horrors the weak nerves, and superstition incident to his time of life, might subject him to. This was the penalty for the second offence. Wouldst thou like, Reader, to see what became of him in the next degree?

The culprit, who had been a third time an offender, and whose expulsion was at this time deemed irreversible, was brought forth, as at some solemn *auto-da-fé*, arrayed in uncouth and most appalling attire; all traces of his late "watchet-weeds" carefully effaced, he was exposed in a jacket, resembling those which London lamplighters formerly delighted in, with a cap of the same. The effect of this divestiture was such as the ingenious devisers of it could have anticipated. With his pale and frighted features, it was as if some of those disfigurements in Dante had seized upon him. In this disguisement he was brought into the hall (*L.'s favourite state-room*), where awaited him the whole number of his schoolfellows, whose joint lessons and sports he was thenceforth to share no more; the awful presence of the steward, to be seen for the last time; of the executioner beadle, clad in his state robe for the occasion; and of two faces more, of direr import, because never but in these extremities visible. These were governors; two of them, by choice, or charter, were always accustomed to officiate at these *Ultima Supplicia;* not to mitigate (so at least we understood it), but to enforce the uttermost stripe. Old Bamber Gascoigne, and Peter Aubert, I remember, were colleagues on one occasion, when the beadle turning rather pale, a glass of brandy was ordered to prepare him for the mysteries. The scourging was, after the old Roman fashion, long and stately. The lictor accompanied the criminal quite round the hall. We were generally too faint with attending to the previous disgusting circumstances, to make accurate report with our eyes of the degree of corporal suffering inflicted. Report, of course, gave out the back knotty and livid. After scouring, he was made over, in his *San Benito,* to his friends, if he had any (but commonly such poor runagates were friendless), or to his parish officer, who, to enhance the effect of the scene, had his station allotted to him on the outside of the hall gate.

These solemn pageantries were not played off so often as
to spoil the general mirth of the community. We had plenty
of exercise and recreation *after* school hours; and, for myself,
I must confess, that I was never happier than *in* them. The
Upper and Lower Grammar Schools were held in the same
room; and an imaginary line only divided their bounds.
Their character was as different as that of the inhabitants
on the two sides of the Pyrenees.   The Rev. James Boyer was
the Upper Master, but the Rev. Matthew Field presided over
that portion of the apartments, of which I had the good
fortune to be a member. We lived a life as careless as birds.
We talked and did just what we pleased, and nobody mo-
lested us. We carried an accidence, or a grammar, for form;
but, for any trouble it gave us, we might take two years in
getting through the verbs deponent, and another two in forgetting all that we had learned about them. There was now
and then the formality of saying a lesson, but if you had
not learned it, a brush across the shoulders (just enough to
disturb a fly) was the sole remonstrance. Field never used
the rod; and in truth he wielded the cane with no great
goodwill—holding it "like a dancer." It looked in his hands
rather like an emblem than an instrument of authority; and
an emblem, too, he was ashamed of. He was a good easy man,
that did not care to ruffle his own peace, nor perhaps set any
great consideration upon the value of juvenile time. He came
among us, now and then, but often staid away whole days
from us; and when he came, it made no difference to us—
he had his private room to retire to, the short time he staid,
to be out of the sound of our noise. Our mirth and uproar
went on. We had classics of our own, without being beholden to "insolent Greece or haughty Rome," that passed
current among us—Peter Wilkins—the Adventures of the
Hon. Captain Robert Boyle—the Fortunate Blue-coat Boy—

and the like. Or we cultivated a turn for mechanic or scientific operations; making little sun-dials of paper; or weaving those ingenious parentheses, called *cat-cradles*; or making dry peas to dance upon the end of a tin pipe; or studying the art military over that laudable game "French and English," and a hundred other such devices to pass away the time— mixing the useful with the agreeable—as would have made the souls of Rousseau and John Locke chuckle to have seen us.

Matthew Field belonged to that class of modest divines who affect to mix in equal proportion the *gentleman,* the *scholar,* and the *Christian;* but, I know not how, the first ingredient is generally found to be the predominating dose in the composition. He was engaged in gay parties, or with his courtly bow at some episcopal levée, when he should have been attending upon us. He had for many years the classical charge of a hundred children, during the four or five first years of their education; and his very highest form seldom proceeded further than two or three of the introductory fables of Phædrus. How things were suffered to go on thus, I cannot guess. Boyer, who was the proper person to have remedied these abuses, always affected, perhaps felt, a delicacy in interfering in a province not strictly his own. I have not been without my suspicions, that he was not altogether displeased at the contrast we presented to his end of the school. We were a sort of Helots to his young Spartans. He would sometimes, with ironic deference, send to borrow a rod of the Under Master, and then, with Sardonic grin, observe to one of his upper boys, "how neat and fresh the twigs looked." While his pale students were battering their brains over Xenophon and Plato, with a silence as deep as that enjoined by the Samite, we were enjoying ourselves at our ease in our little Goshen. We saw a little into the secrets of his discipline, and the prospect did but the more reconcile us to our lot. His thunders rolled innocuous for us; his storms came near, but never touched us; contrary to Gideon's miracle, while all around were drenched, our fleece was dry. His boys turned out the better scholars; we, I suspect, have the advantage in temper. His pupils cannot speak of him without something of terror allaying their gratitude; the remembrance of Field comes back with all the soothing images of indolence, and summer slumbers, and work like play, and innocent idleness, and Elysian exemptions, and life itself a "playing holiday."

Though sufficiently removed from the jurisdiction of Boyer, we were near enough (as I have said) to understand a little of his system. We occasionally heard sounds of the *Ululantes,* and caught glances of Tartarus. B. was a rabid pedant. His English style was crampt to barbarism. His Easter anthems (for his duty obliged him to those periodical flights) were grating as scrannel pipes.—He would laugh, ay, and heartily, but then it must be at Flaccus's quibble about *Rex*——or at the *tristis severitas in vultu,* or *inspicere in patinas;* of Terence—thin jests, which at their first broaching could hardly have had *vis* enough to move a Roman muscle.—He had two wigs, both pedantic, but of differing omen. The one serene, smiling, fresh powdered, betokening a mild day. The other, an old discoloured, unkempt, angry caxon, denoting frequent and bloody execution. Woe to the school, when he made his morning appearance in his *passy,* or *passionate wig.* No comet expounded surer.—J. B. had a heavy hand. I have known him double his knotty fist at a poor trembling child (the maternal milk hardly dry upon its lips) and with a "Sirrah, do you presume to set your wits at me?"—Nothing was more common than to see him make a headlong entry into the school-room, from his inner recess, or library, and, with turbulent eye, singling out a lad, roar out, "Odd's my life, Sirrah," (his favourite adjuration) "I have a great mind to whip you,"—then, with as sudden a retracting impulse, fling back into his lair—and, after a cooling lapse of some minutes (during which all but the culprit had totally forgotten the context) drive headlong out again, piecing out his imperfect sense, as if it had been some Devil's Litany, with the expletory yell—"*and I* WILL, *too.*"—In his gentler moods, when the *rabidus furor* was assuaged, he had resort to an ingenious method, peculiar, from what I have heard, to himself, of whipping the boy, and reading the Debates, at the same time; a paragraph, and a lash between; which in those times, when parliamentary oratory was most at a height and flourishing in these realms, was not calculated to impress the patient with a veneration for the diffuser graces of rhetoric.

Once, and but once, the uplifted rod was known to fall ineffectual from his hand—when droll squinting W——— having been caught putting the inside of the master's desk to a use for which the architect had clearly not designed it, to justify himself, with great simplicity averred, that *he did not know that the thing had been forewarned*. This exquisite irrecognition of any law antecedent to the *oral* or *declaratory*, struck so irresistibly upon the fancy of all who heard it (the pedagogue himself not excepted) that remission was unavoidable.

L. has given credit to B.'s great merits as an instructor. Coleridge, in his literary life, has pronounced a more intelligible and ample encomium on them. The author of the Country Spectator doubts not to compare him with the ablest teachers of antiquity. Perhaps we cannot dismiss him better than with the pious ejaculation of C.—when he heard that his old master was on his death-bed—"Poor J. B.!—

may all his faults be forgiven; and may he be wafted to bliss by little cherub boys, all head and wings, with no *bottoms* to reproach his sublunary infirmities."

Under him were many good and sound scholars bred.— First Grecian of my time was Lancelot Pepys Stevens, kindest of boys and men, since Co-grammar-master (and inseparable companion) with Dr. T[rollop]e. What an edifying spectacle did this brace of friends present to those who remembered the anti-socialities of their predecessors!—You never met the one by chance in the street without a wonder, which was quickly dissipated by the almost immediate subappearance of the other. Generally arm-in-arm, these kindly coadjutors lightened for each other the toilsome duties of their profession, and when in advanced age, one found it convenient to retire, the other was not long in discovering that it suited him to lay down the fasces also. Oh, it is pleasant, as it is rare, to find the same arm linked in yours at forty, which at thirteen helped it to turn over the *Cicero De Amicitiâ*, or some tale of Antique Friendship, which the young heart even then was burning to anticipate!—Co-Grecian with S. was Th[ornton], who has since executed with ability various diplomatic functions at the Northern courts. Th——was a tall, dark, saturnine youth, sparing of speech, with raven locks.—Thomas Fanshaw Middleton followed him (now Bishop of Calcutta), a scholar and a gentleman in his teens. He has the reputation of an excellent critic; and is author (besides the Country Spectator) of a Treatise on the Greek Article, against Sharpe.—M. is said to bear his mitre high in India, where the *regni novitas* (I dare say) sufficiently justifies the bearing. A humility quite as primitive as that of Jewel or Hooker might not be exactly fitted to impress the minds of those Anglo-Asiatic diocesans with a reverence for home institutions, and the church which those fathers watered. The manners of M. at school, though firm, were mild and unassuming.—Next to M. (if not senior to him) was Richards, author of the Aboriginal Britons, the most spirited of the Oxford Prize Poems; a pale, studious Grecian.—Then followed poor S[cott], ill-fated M[aunde]! of these the Muse is silent.

> Finding some of Edward's race
> Unhappy, pass their annals by.

Come back into memory, like as thou wert in the day-spring of thy fancies, with hope like a fiery column before thee—the dark pillar not yet turned—Samuel Taylor Coleridge—Logician, Metaphysician, Bard!—How have I seen the casual passer through the Cloisters stand still, entranced with admiration (while he weighed the disproportion between the *speech* and the *garb* of the young Mirandula), to hear thee unfold, in thy deep and sweet intonations, the mysteries of Jamblichus, or Plotinus (for even in those years thou waxedst not pale at such philosophic draughts), or reciting Homer in his Greek, or Pindar——while the walls of the old Grey Friars reechoed to the accents of the *inspired charity-boy!*—Many were the "wit-combats" (to dally awhile with the words of old Fuller) between him and C. V. Le G[rice], "which two I behold like a Spanish great galleon, and an English man of war: Master Coleridge, like the former, was built far higher in learning, solid, but slow in his performances; C. V. L., with the English man of war, lesser in bulk, but lighter in sailing, could turn with all tides, tack about, and take advantage of all winds, by the quickness of his wit and invention."

Nor shalt thou, their compeer, be quickly forgotten, Allen, with the cordial smile, and still more cordial laugh, with which thou wert wont to make the old Cloisters shake, in

thy cognition of some poignant jest of theirs; or the anticipation of some more material, and peradventure practical one,
of thine own Extinct are those smiles, with that beautiful
countenance, with which (for thou wert the *Nireus formo-
sus* of the school), in the days of thy maturer waggery, thou
didst disarm the wrath of infuriated town-damsel, who, in-
censed by provoking pinch, turning tigress-like round, suddenly converted by thy angel-look, exchanged the half-
formed terrible "*bl———,*" for a gentler greeting—"*bless thy
handsome face!*"

Next follow two, who ought to be now alive, and the
friends of Elia—the junior Le G[rice] and F[avell]; who
impelled, the former by a roving temper, the latter by too
quick a sense of neglect—ill capable of enduring the slights
poor Sizars are sometimes subject to in our seats of learning
—exchanged their Alma Mater for the camp; perishing, one
by climate, and one on the plains of Salamanca:—Le G———,
sanguine, volatile, sweet-natured; F———, dogged, faithful,
anticipative of insult, warm-hearted, with something of the
old Roman height about him.

Fine, frank-hearted Fr[anklin], the present master of
Hertford, with Marmaduke T[hompson)] mildest of Mis-
sionaries—and both my good friends still—close the catalogue of Grecians in my time.

II

EARLY MANHOOD: THE SHADOW OF TRAGEDY

At Christ's Hospital, Lamb received a good classical education. His school days were probably the happiest of his life, and when they came to an end, it was hard indeed for him to part from Coleridge, Le Grice, and others, endeared to him by seven years of close association. Coleridge was going on to Oxford for a college education, but for Lamb there was to be no such opportunity. He realized, as he afterwards wrote in one of the essays, that he was to be "defrauded in his young years of the sweet food of academic institution" by the poverty of his family. It was necessary, that as soon as he was able to help, he should get some sort of position in the business world.

At the age of fifteen or so, with the help of Thomas Coventry, one of his friends among The Old Benchers, he found a place in the office of a London merchant, Joseph Paice, whose delicacy he so finely depicts in the essay *Modern Gallantry*.

MODERN GALLANTRY

In comparing modern with ancient manners, we are pleased to compliment ourselves upon the point of gallantry; a certain obsequiousness, or deferential respect, which we are supposed to pay to females, as females.

I shall believe that this principle actuates our conduct, when I can forget, that in the nineteenth century of the era from which we date our civility, we are but just beginning to leave off the very frequent practice of whipping females in public, in common with the coarsest male offenders.

I shall believe it to be influential, when I can shut my eyes to the fact that in England women are still occasionally—hanged.

I shall believe in it, when actresses are no longer subject to be hissed off a stage by gentlemen.

I shall believe in it, when Dorimant hands a fishwife across the kennel; or assists the apple-woman to pick up her wandering fruit, which some unlucky dray has just dissipated.

I shall believe in it, when the Dorimants in humbler life, who would be thought in their way notable adepts in this refinement, shall act upon it in places where they are not known, or think themselves not observed—when I shall see the traveller for some rich tradesman part with his admired box-coat, to spread it over the defenceless shoulders of the poor woman, who is passing to her parish on the roof of the same stage-coach with him, drenched in the rain—when I shall no longer see a woman standing up in the pit of a London theatre, till she is sick and faint with the exertion, with men about her, seated at their ease, and jeering at her distress; till one, that seems to have more manners or conscience than the rest, significantly declares "she should be welcome to his seat, if she were a little younger and handsomer." Place this dapper warehouseman, or that rider, in a circle of their own female acquaintance, and you shall confess you have not seen a politer-bred man in Lothbury.

Lastly, I shall begin to believe that there is some such principle influencing our conduct, when more than one-half of the drudgery and coarse servitude of the world shall cease to be performed by women.

Until that day comes, I shall never believe this boasted point to be anything more than a conventional fiction; a pageant got up between the sexes, in a certain rank, and at a certain time of life, in which both find their account equally.

I shall be even disposed to rank it among the salutary fictions of life, when in polite circles I shall see the same attentions paid to age as to youth, to homely features as to handsome, to coarse complexions as to clear—to the woman, as she is a woman, not as she is a beauty, a fortune, or a title.

I shall believe it to be something more than a name, when a well-dressed gentleman in a well-dressed company can advert to the topic of *female old age* without exciting, and intending to excite, a sneer:—when the phrases "antiquated virginity," and such a one has "overstood her market," pronounced in good company, shall raise immediate offence in man, or woman, that shall hear them spoken.

Joseph Paice, of Bread-street-hill, merchant, and one of the Directors of the South-Sea company—the same to whom Edwards, the Shakspeare commentator, has addressed a fine sonnet—was the only pattern of consistent gallantry I have met with. He took me under his shelter at an early age, and bestowed some pains upon me. I owe to his precepts and example whatever there is of the man of business (and that is not much) in my composition. It was not his fault that I did not profit more. Though bred a Presbyterian, and brought up a merchant, he was the finest gentleman of his time. He had not *one* system of attention to females in the drawing-room, and *another* in the shop, or at the stall. I do not mean that he made no distinction. But he never lost sight of sex, or overlooked it in the casualties of a disadvantageous situation. I have seen him stand bareheaded—smile if you please—to a poor servant-girl, while she has been inquiring of him the way to some street—in such a posture of unforced civility, as neither to embarrass her in the acceptance, nor himself in the offer, of it. He was no dangler, in the common acceptation of the word, after women: but he reverenced and upheld, in every form in which it came before him, *womanhood*. I have seen him—nay, smile not—tenderly escorting a market-woman, whom he had encountered in a shower, exalting his umbrella over her poor basket of fruit, that it might receive no damage, with as much carefulness as if she had been a countess. To the reverend form of Female Eld he would yield the wall (though it were to an ancient beggar-woman) with more ceremony than we can afford to show our grandams. He was the Preux Chevalier of Age; the Sir Calidore, or Sir Tristan, to those who have no Calidores or Tristans to defend them. The roses, that had long faded thence, still bloomed for him in those withered and yellow cheeks.

He was never married, but in his youth he paid his addresses to the beautiful Susan Winstanley—old Winstanley's daughter of Clapton—who dying in the early days of their courtship, confirmed in him the resolution of perpetual bachelorship. It was during their short courtship, he told me, that he had been one day treating his mistress with a profusion of civil speeches—the common gallantries—to which kind of thing she had hitherto manifested no repugnance—but in this instance with no effect. He could not obtain from her a decent acknowledgment in return. She rather seemed to resent his compliments. He could not set it down to caprice, for the lady had always shown herself above that littleness. When he ventured on the following day, finding her a little better humoured, to expostulate with her on her coldness of yesterday, she confessed, with her usual frankness, that she had no sort of dislike to his attentions; that she could even endure some high-flown compliments; that a young woman placed in her situation had a right to expect all sorts of civil things said to her; that she hoped she could digest a dose of adulation, short of insincerity, with as little

injury to her humility as most young women; but that—
a little before he had commenced his compliments—she had
overheard him by accident, in rather rough language, rating
a young woman, who had not brought home his cravats
quite to the appointed time, and she thought to herself, "As
I am Miss Susan Winstanley, and a young lady—a reputed
beauty, and known to be a fortune,—I can have my choice
of the finest speeches from the mouth of this very fine
gentleman who is courting me—but if I had been poor Mary
Such-a-one (*naming the milliner*),—and had failed of bringing home the cravats to the appointed hour—though perhaps
I had sat up half the night to forward them—what sort of
compliments should I have received then?—And my
woman's pride came to my assistance; and I thought, that
if it were only to do *me* honour, a female, like myself, might
have received handsomer usage; and I was determined not
to accept any fine speeches to the compromise of that sex,
the belonging to which was after all my strongest claim
and title to them."

I think the lady discovered both generosity, and a just way
of thinking, in this rebuke which she gave her lover; and I
have sometimes imagined, that the uncommon strain of
courtesy, which through life regulated the actions and behaviour of my friend towards all of womankind indiscriminately, owed its happy origin to this seasonable lesson from
the lips of his lamented mistress.

I wish the whole female world would entertain the same
notion of these things that Miss Winstanley showed. Then
we should see something of the spirit of consistent gallantry;
and no longer witness the anomaly of the same man—a
pattern of true politness to a wife—of cold contempt, or
rudeness, to a sister—the idolater of his female mistress—
the disparager and despiser of his no less female aunt, or

unfortunately—still female—maiden cousin. Just so much respect as a woman derogates from her own sex, in whatever condition placed—her handmaid, or dependent—she deserves to have diminished from herself on that score; and probably will feel the diminution, when youth, and beauty, and advantages, not inseparable from sex, shall lose of their attraction. What a woman should demand of a man in courtship, or after it, is first—respect for her as she is a woman;—and next to that—to be respected by him above all other women. But let her stand upon her female character as upon a foundation; and let the attentions, incident to individual preference, be so many pretty additaments and ornaments—as many, and as fanciful, as you please—to that main structure. Let her first lesson be—with sweet Susan Winstanley—to *reverence her sex*.

In 1791 Lamb obtained a position in the South-Sea House, where were the offices of one of the large exporting and importing companies of England. His stay there was short, for through the influence of that friend of the family, Samuel Salt, he secured a better position as an accountant in the offices of the East India Company. Though his salary was meager at the start, Lamb became from this time on, the chief support of the family.

In an essay called the *South-Sea House*, Lamb has given a description of the "humourous" clerks at his first place of business, but of his life there very little else is known. Though he did not write a parallel account of the East India House, where he worked for thirty-three years, many of the details undoubtedly could be transferred from the South-Sea House to the East India House.

THE SOUTH-SEA HOUSE

Reader, in thy passage from the Bank—where thou hast been receiving thy half-yearly dividends (supposing thou

art a lean annuitant like myself)—to the Flower Pot, to
secure a place for Dalston, or Shacklewell, or some other shy
suburban retreat northerly,—didst thou never observe a
melancholy-looking, handsome, brick and stone edifice, to
the left, where Threadneedle-street abuts upon Bishopsgate?
I dare say thou hast often admired its magnificent portals
ever gaping wide, and disclosing to view a grave court, with
cloisters and pillars, with few or no traces of goers-in or
comers-out—a desolation something like Balclutha's.

This was once a house of trade,—a centre of busy interests. The throng of merchants was here—the quick pulse
of gain—and here some forms of business are still kept up,
though the soul be long since fled. Here are still to be seen
stately porticoes; imposing staircases; offices roomy as the
state apartments in palaces—deserted, or thinly peopled with
a few straggling clerks; the still more sacred interiors of
court and committee rooms, with venerable faces of beadles,
door-keepers,—directors seated in form on solemn days (to
proclaim a dead dividend) at long worm-eaten tables, that
have been mahogany, with tarnished gilt-leather coverings,
supporting massy silver ink-stands long since dry;—the
oaken wainscots hung with pictures of deceased governors
and sub-governors, of Queen Anne, and the two first mon-
archs of the Brunswick dynasty;—huge charts, which sub-
sequent discoveries have antiquated;—dusty maps of Mexico,
dim as dreams,—and soundings of the Bay of Panama! The
long passages hung with buckets, appended, in idle row, to
walls, whose substance might defy any, short of the last,
conflagration:—with vast ranges of cellerage after all,
where dollars and pieces of eight once lay, an "unsunned
heap," for Mammon to have solaced his solitary heart withal,
—long since dissipated, or scattered into air at the blast of
the breaking of that famous BUBBLE.

Such is the SOUTH-SEA HOUSE. At least such it was forty years ago, when I knew it,—a magnificent relic! What alterations may have been made in it since, I have had no opportunities of verifying. Time, I take for granted, has not freshened it. No wind has resuscitated the face of the sleeping waters. A thicker crust by this time stagnates upon it. The moths that were then battening upon its obsolete ledgers and day-books, have rested from their depredations, but other light generations have succeeded, making fine fretwork among their single and double entries. Layers of dust have accumulated (a superfœtation of dirt!) upon the old layers that seldom used to be disturbed, save by some curious finger, now and then, inquisitive to explore the mode of book-keeping in Queen Anne's reign; or, with less hallowed curiosity, seeking to unveil some of the mysteries of that tremendous HOAX, whose extent the petty peculators of our day look back upon with the same expression of incredulous admiration and hopeless ambition of rivalry as would become the puny face of modern conspiracy contemplating the Titan size of Vaux's superhuman plot.

Peace to the names of the BUBBLE! Silence and destitution are upon thy walls, proud house, for a memorial!

Situated as thou art, in the very heart of stirring and living commerce,—amid the fret and fever of speculation—with the Bank, and the 'Change, and the India-house about thee, in the heyday of present prosperity, with their important faces, as it were, insulting thee, their *poor neighbour out of business*—to the idle and merely contemplative,—to such as me, old house! there is a charm in thy quiet:—a cessation—a coolness from business—an indolence almost cloistral—which is delightful! With what reverence have I paced thy great bare rooms and courts at eventide! They spoke of the past:—the shade of some dead accountant, with visionary pen in ear, would flit by me, stiff as in life. Living accounts and accountants puzzle me. I have no skill in figuring. But thy great dead tomes, which scarce three degenerate clerks of the present day could lift from their enshrining shelves—with their old fantastic flourishes and decorative rubric interlacings—their sums in triple columniations, set down with formal superfluity of ciphers—with pious sentences at the beginning, without which our religious ancestors never ventured to open a book of business, or bill of lading—the costly vellum covers of some of them almost persuading us that we are got into some *better library,*—are very agreeable and edifying spectacles. I can look upon these defunct dragons with complacency. Thy heavy odd-shaped ivory-handled penknives (our ancestors had everything on a larger scale than we have hearts for) are as good as anything from Herculaneum. The pounce-boxes of our days have gone retrograde.

The very clerks which I remember in the South-Sea House —I speak of forty years back—had an air very different from those in the public offices that I have had to do with since. They partook of the genius of the place!

They were mostly (for the establishment did not admit of superfluous salaries) bachelors. Generally (for they had not much to do) persons of a curious and speculative turn of mind. Old-fashioned, for a reason mentioned before. Humourists, for they were of all descriptions; and, not having been brought together in early life (which has a tendency to assimilate the members of corporate bodies to each other), but, for the most part, placed in this house in ripe or middle age, they necessarily carried into it their separate habits and oddities, unqualified, if I may so speak, as into a common stock. Hence they formed a sort of Noah's ark. Odd fishes. A lay-monastery. Domestic retainers in a great house, kept

more for show than use. Yet pleasant fellows, full of chat—
and not a few among them had arrived at considerable
proficiency on the German flute.

The cashier at that time was one Evans, a Cambro-Briton.
He had something of the choleric complexion of his countrymen stamped on his visage, but was a worthy, sensible man
at bottom. He wore his hair, to the last, powdered and
frizzed out, in the fashion which I remember to have been
seen in caricatures of what were termed, in my young days,
Maccaronies. He was the last of that race of beaux. Melancholy as a gibcat over his counter all the forenoon, I think I
see him making up his cash (as they call it) with tremulous
fingers, as if he feared every one about him was a defaulter;
in his hypochondry, ready to imagine himself one; haunted
at least, with the idea of the possibility of his becoming one:
his tristful visage clearing up a little over his roast neck of
veal at Anderton's at two (where his picture still hangs,
taken a little before his death by desire of the master of the
coffee-house which he had frequented for the last five and
twenty years), but not attaining the meridian of its anima-
tion till evening brought on the hour of tea and visiting.
The simultaneous sound of his well-known rap at the door
with the stroke of the clock announcing six, was a topic of
never-failing mirth in the families which this dear old
bachelor gladdened with his presence. Then was his *forte,* his
glorified hour! How would he chirp and expand over a
muffin! How would he dilate into secret history! His
countryman Pennant himself, in particular, could not be
more eloquent than he in relation to old and new London—
the site of old theatres, churches, streets gone to decay—
where Rosamond's pond stood—the Mulberry-gardens—and
the Conduit in Cheap,—with many a pleasant anecdote,
derived from paternal tradition, of those grotesque figures

which Hogarth has immortalized in his picture of *Noon*,—
the worthy descendants of those heroic confessors, who,
flying to this country from the wrath of Louis the Fourteenth and his dragoons, kept alive the flame of pure religion
in the sheltering obscurities of Hog-lane and the vicinity
of the Seven Dials!

Deputy, under Evans, was Thomas Tame. He had the air
and stoop of a nobleman. You would have taken him for
one, had you met him in one of the passages leading to
Westminster-hall. By stoop, I mean that gentle bending of
the body forwards, which, in great men, must be supposed
to be the effect of an habitual condescending attention to
the applications of their inferiors. While he held you in
converse, you felt strained to the height in the colloquy.
The conference over, you were at leisure to smile at the
comparative insignificance of the pretensions which had just
awed you. His intellect was of the shallowest order. It did
not reach to a saw or a proverb. His mind was in its original
state of white paper. A sucking babe might have posed
him. What was it then? Was he rich? Alas, no! Thomas
Tame was very poor. Both he and his wife looked outwardly
gentlefolks, when I fear all was not well at all times within.
She had a neat, meagre person, which it was evident she had
not sinned in over-pampering; but in its veins was noble
blood. She traced her descent, by some labyrinth of relationship, which I never thoroughly understood,—much less can
explain with any heraldic certainty at this time of day,—to
the illustrious, but unfortunate, house of Derwentwater.
This was the secret of Thomas's stoop. This was the thought
—the sentiment—the bright solitary star of your lives,—ye
mild and happy pair,—which cheered you in the night of
intellect, and in the obscurity of your station! This was to
you instead of riches, instead of rank, instead of glittering

attainments: and it was worth them all together. You insulted none with it; but, while you wore it as a piece of
defensive armour only, no insult likewise could reach you
through it. *Decus et solamen.*

Of quite another stamp was the then accountant, John
Tipp. He neither pretended to high blood, nor in good truth
cared one fig about the matter. He "thought an accountant
the greatest character in the world, and himself the greatest
accountant in it." Yet John was not without his hobby. The
fiddle relieved his vacant hours. He sang, certainly, with
other notes than to the Orphean lyre. He did, indeed, scream
and scrape most abominably. His fine suite of official rooms
in Threadneedle-street, which, without anything very substantial appended to them, were enough to enlarge a man's
notions of himself that lived in them (I know not who is the
occupier of them now), resounded fortnightly to the notes
of a concert of "sweet breasts," as our ancestors would have
called them, culled from club-rooms, and orchestras—chorus
singers—first and second violoncellos—double basses—and
clarionets,—who ate his cold mutton, and drank his punch,
and praised his ear. He sate like Lord Midas among them.
But at the desk Tipp was quite another sort of creature.
Thence all ideas that were purely ornamental, were banished.
You could not speak on anything romantic without rebuke.
Politics were excluded. A newspaper was thought too refined
and abstracted. The whole duty of man consisted in writing
off dividend warrants. The striking of the annual balance
in the company's books (which, perhaps, differed from the
balance of last year in the sum of 25*l.* 1*s.* 6*d.*) occupied his
days and nights for a month previous. Not that Tipp was
blind to the deadness of *things* (as they called them in the
city) in his beloved house, or did not sigh for a return of the
old stirring days when South-Sea hopes were young—(he

was indeed equal to the wielding of any of the most intricate accounts of the most flourishing company in these or those days):—but to a genuine accountant the difference of proceeds is as nothing. The fractional farthing is as dear to his heart as the thousands which stand before it. He is the true actor who, whether his part be a prince or a peasant, must act it with like intensity. With Tipp form was everything. His life was formal. His actions seemed ruled with a ruler. His pen was not less erring than his heart. He made the best executor in the world: he was plagued with incessant executorships accordingly, which excited his spleen and soothed his vanity in equal ratios. He would swear (for Tipp swore) at the little orphans, whose rights he would guard with a tenacity like the grasp of the dying hand that commended their interests to his protection. With all this there was about him a sort of timidity (his few enemies used to give it a worse name)—a something which, in reverence to the dead, we will place, if you please, a little on this side of the heroic. Nature certainly had been pleased to endow John Tipp with a sufficient measure of the principle of self-preservation. There is a cowardice which we do not despise, because it has nothing base or treacherous in its elements; it betrays itself, not you: it is mere temperament; the absence of the romantic and the enterprising; it sees a lion in the way, and will not, with Fortinbras, "greatly find quarrel in a straw," when some supposed honour is at stake. Tipp never mounted the box of a stage-coach in his life; or leaned against the rails of a balcony; or walked upon the ridge of a parapet; or looked down a precipice; or let off a gun; or went upon a water-party; or would willingly let you go if he could have helped it: neither was it recorded of him, that for lucre, or for intimidation, he ever forsook friend or principle.

Whom next shall we summon from the dusty dead, in whom common qualities become uncommon? Can I forget thee, Henry Man, the wit, the polished man of letters, the *author,* of the South-Sea House? who never enteredst thy office in a morning or quittedst it in midday (what didst *thou* in an office?) without some quirk that left a sting! Thy gibes and thy jokes are now extinct, or survive but in two forgotten volumes, which I had the good fortune to rescue from a stall in Barbican, not three days ago, and found thee terse, fresh, epigrammatic, as alive. Thy wit is a little gone by in these fastidious days—thy topics are staled by the "new-born gauds" of the time:—but great thou used to be in Public Ledgers, and in Chronicles, upon Chatham, and Shelburne, and Rockingham, and Howe, and Burgoyne, and Clinton, and the war which ended in the tearing from Great Britain her rebellious colonies,—and Keppel, and Wilkes, and Sawbridge, and Bull, and Dunning, and Pratt, and Richmond,—and such small politics.——

A little less facetious, and a great deal more obstreperous, was fine rattling, rattleheaded Plumer. He was descended,— not in a right line, Reader (for his lineal pretensions, like his personal, favoured a little of the sinister bend) from the Plumers of Hertfordshire. So tradition gave him out; and certain family features not a little sanctioned the opinion. Certainly old Walter Plumer (his reputed author) had been a rake in his day, and visited much in Italy, and had seen the world. He was uncle, bachelor-uncle, to the fine old whig still living, who has represented the county in so many successive parliaments, and has a fine old mansion near Ware. Walter flourished in George the Second's days, and was the same who was summoned before the House of Commons about a business of franks, with the old Duchess of Marlborough. You may read of it in Johnson's Life of Cave.

Cave came off cleverly in that business. It is certain our Plumer did nothing to discountenance the rumour. He rather seemed pleased whenever it was, with all gentleness, insinuated. But, besides his family pretensions, Plumer was an engaging fellow, and sang gloriously.——

Not so sweetly sang Plumer as thou sangest, mild, childlike, pastoral M[aynard]; a flute's breathing less divinely whispering than thy Arcadian melodies, when, in tones worthy of Arden, thou didst chant that song sung by Amiens to the banished Duke, which proclaims the winter wind more lenient than for a man to be ungrateful. Thy sire was old surly M[aynard], the unapproachable churchwarden of Bishopsgate. He knew not what he did, when he begat thee, like spring, gentle offspring of blustering winter: —only unfortunate in thy ending, which should have been mild, conciliatory, swan-like.——

Much remains to sing. Many fantastic shapes rise up, but they must be mine in private:—already I have fooled the reader to the top of his bent; else could I omit that strange creature Woollett, who existed in trying the question, and *bought litigations!*—and still stranger, inimitable, solemn Hepworth, from whose gravity Newton might have deduced the law of gravitation. How profoundly would he nib a pen —with what deliberation would he wet a wafer!——

But it is time to close—night's wheels are rattling fast over me—it is proper to have done with this solemn mockery.

Reader, what if I have been playing with thee all this while—peradventure the very *names,* which I have summoned up before thee, are fantastic—insubstantial—like Henry Pimpernel, and old John Naps of Greece:——

Be satisfied that something answering to them has had a being. Their importance is from the past.

For many years Lamb's life was one of monotonous drudgery and heavy cares. Insanity was hereditary in the family, and patient and hardworking Mary Lamb became its victim. Some twelve years older than Charles, she had been to him almost a mother, and he loved and leaned upon her as upon one stronger and wiser than himself. We can judge in what agony of spirit he wrote in September, 1796, the letter below which tells how his sister, in a sudden fit of madness, had stabbed her mother to the heart, wounded her almost imbecile father, and might have added other victims to the tragedy if Lamb had not snatched the knife from her hand.

LETTER TO COLERIDGE

September 27th, 1796.

My dearest Friend,—White, or some of my friends, or the public papers, by this time may have informed you of the terrible calamities that have fallen on our family. I will only give you the outlines:—My poor dear, dearest sister, in a fit of insanity, has been the death of her own mother. I was at hand only time enough to snatch the knife out of her grasp. She is at present in a madhouse, from whence I fear she must be moved to an hospital. God has preserved to me my senses: I eat, and drink, and sleep, and have my judgment, I believe, very sound. My poor father was slightly wounded, and I am left to take care of him and my aunt. Mr. Norris, of the Bluecoat School, has been very kind to us, and we have no other friend; but, thank God, I am very calm and composed, and able to do the best that remains to do. Write as religious a letter as possible, but no mention of what is gone and done with. With me "the former things are passed away," and I have something more to do than to feel.

God Almighty have us all in His keeping!   C. LAMB.

Mention nothing of poetry. I have destroyed every vestige of past vanities of that kind. Do as you please, but if you publish, publish mine (I give free leave) without name or initial, and never send me a book, I charge you.

Your own judgment will convince you not to take any notice of this yet to your dear wife. You look after your family; I have my reason and strength left to take care of mine. I charge you, don't think of coming to see me. Write. I will not see you if you come. God Almighty love you all and all of us!

C. Lamb.

The spirit in which this young man of twenty-two faced the terrible crisis is to be seen in another letter to Coleridge which followed a few days later. He realized that the care of the whole family had fallen upon him, and he took up the burden quietly and bravely.

LETTER TO COLERIDGE

October 3, 1796.

My dearest Friend—Your letter was an inestimable treasure to me. It will be a comfort to you, I know, to know that our prospects are somewhat brighter. My poor dear, dearest sister, the unhappy and unconscious instrument of the Almighty's judgments on our house, is restored to her senses,—to a dreadful sense and recollection of what has past, awful to her mind, and impressive (as it must be to the end of life), but tempered with religious resignation and the reasonings of a sound judgment, which, in this early stage, knows how to distinguish between a deed committed in a transient fit of frenzy and the terrible guilt of a mother's murder. I have seen her. I found her this morning, calm and serene; far, very far from an indecent forgetful serenity:

she has a most affectionate and tender concern for what has happened. Indeed, from the beginning—frightful and hopeless as her disorder seemed—I had confidence enough in her strength of mind and religious principle, to look forward to a time when *even she* might recover tranquillity.

God be praised, Coleridge! wonderful as it is to tell, I have never once been otherwise than collected and calm; even on the dreadful day, and in the midst of the terrible scene, I preserved a tranquillity which bystanders may have construed into indifference—a tranquillity not of despair. Is it folly or sin in me to say that it was a religious principle that *most* supported me? I allow much to other favourable circumstances. I felt that I had something else to do than to regret. On that first evening my aunt was lying insensible— to all appearance like one dying; my father, with his poor forehead plaistered over from a wound he had received from a daughter, dearly loved by him, and who loved him no less dearly; my mother a dead and murdered corpse in the next room; yet was I wonderfully supported. I closed not my eyes in sleep that night, but lay without terrors and without despair. I have lost no sleep since. I had been long used not to rest in things of sense,—had endeavoured after a comprehension of mind, unsatisfied with the "ignorant present time;" and *this* kept me up. I had the whole weight of the family thrown on me; for my brother, little disposed (I speak not without tenderness for him) at any time to take care of old age and infirmities, had now, with his bad leg, an exemption from such duties, and I was now left alone.

One little incident may serve to make you understand my way of managing my mind: Within a day or two after the fatal one, we dressed for dinner a tongue, which we had had salted for some weeks in the house. As I sat down, a feeling like remorse struck me: this tongue poor Mary got for me; and can I partake of it now, when she is far away? A thought occurred and relieved me:—if I give into this way of feeling, there is not a chair, a room, an object in our rooms, that will not awaken the keenest griefs. I must rise above such weaknesses. I hope this was not want of true feeling. I did not let this carry me, though, too far. On the very second day (I date from the day of horrors), as is usual in such cases, there were a matter of twenty people, I do think, supping in our room: they prevailed on me to eat *with them* (for to eat I never refused.) They were all making merry in the room! Some had come from friendship, some from busy curiosity, and some from interest. I was going to partake with them, when my recollection came that my poor dead mother was lying in the next room—the very next room;—a mother who, through life, wished nothing but her children's welfare. Indignation, the rage of grief, something like remorse, rushed upon my mind. In an agony of emotion I found my way mechanically to the adjoining room, and fell on my knees by the side of her coffin, asking forgiveness of Heaven, and sometimes of her, for forgetting her so soon. Tranquillity returned, and it was the only violent emotion that mastered me. I think it did me good.

I mention these things because I hate concealment, and love to give a faithful journal of what passes within me. Our friends have been very good. Sam Le Grice, who was then in town, was with me the first three or four days, and was as a brother to me; gave up every hour of his time, to the very hurting of his health and spirits, in constant attendance and humouring my poor father; talked with him, read to him, played at cribbage with him (for so short is the old man's recollection, that he was playing at cards as though nothing had happened, while the coroner's inquest was sitting over the way!) Samuel wept tenderly when he went away, for his mother wrote him a very severe letter on his loitering so long in town, and he was forced to go. Mr. Norris, of Christ's Hospital, has been as a father to me— Mrs. Norris as a mother; though we had few claims on them. A gentleman, brother to my godmother, from whom we never had right or reason to expect any such assistance, sent my father twenty pounds; and to crown all these God's blessings to our family at such a time, an old lady, a cousin of my father and aunt's, a gentlewoman of fortune, is to take my aunt and make her comfortable for the short remainder of her days. My aunt is recovered, and as well as ever, and highly pleased at thoughts of going—and has generously given up the interest of her little money (which was formerly paid my father for her board) wholely and solely to my sister's use. Reckoning this, we have, Daddy and I, for our two selves and an old maid-servant to look after him, when I am out, which will be necessary, 170*l* (or 180*l* rather) a-year, out of which we can spare 50*l* or 60*l* at least for Mary while she stays at Islington, where she must and shall stay during her father's life, for his and her comfort. I know John will make speeches about it, but she shall not go into an hospital. The good lady of the madhouse, and her daughter, an elegant, sweet-behaved young lady, love her, and are taken with her amazingly; and I know from her own mouth she loves them, and longs to be with them as much. Poor thing, they say she was but the other morning saying she knew she must go to Bethlem for life; that one of her brothers would have it so, but the other would wish it not, but be obliged to go with the stream; that she had often as she passed Bethlem thought it likely, "here it may be my fate to end my days," conscious of a certain flightiness in her poor head oftentimes, and mindful of more than one severe illness of that nature before. A legacy of 100*l*, which my father will have at Christmas, and this 20*l* I mentioned before, with what is in the house, will much more than set us clear. If my father, an old servant-maid, and I, can't live, and live comfortably, on 130*l* or 120*l* a-year, we ought to burn by slow fires; and I almost would, that Mary might not go into an hospital. Let me not leave one unfavourable impression on your mind respecting my brother. Since this has happened, he has been very kind and brotherly; but I fear for his mind: he has taken his ease in the world, and is not fit himself to struggle with difficulties, nor has much accustomed himself to throw himself into their way; and I know his language is already, "Charles, you must take care of yourself; you must not abridge yourself of a single pleasure you have been used to," etc., etc., and in that style of talking. But you, a necessarian, can respect a difference of mind, and love what *is amiable* in a character not perfect. He has been very good; but I fear for his mind. Thank God, I can unconnect myself with him, and shall manage all my father's moneys in future myself, if I take charge of Daddy, which poor John has not even hinted a wish, at any future time even, to share with me. The lady at this madhouse assures me that I may dismiss immediately both doctor and apothecary, retaining occasionally a composing draught or so for a while; and there is a less expensive establishment in her house, where she will not only have a room and nurse to herself, for 50*l* or guineas a-year—the outside would be 60*l*. You know, by economy, how much more even I shall be able to spare for her comforts. She will I fancy, if she stays, make one of the family, rather than of the patients; and the old and young ladies I like exceedingly, and she loves dearly; and they, as the saying is, take to her very extraordinarily, if it is extraordinary that people

who see my sister should love her. Of all the people I ever
saw in the world, my poor sister was most and thoroughly
devoid of the least tincture of selfishness. I will enlarge upon
her qualities, poor dear, dearest soul, in a future letter, for
my own comfort, for I understand her thoroughly; and, if
I mistake not, in the most trying situation that a human
being can be found in, she will be found—(I speak not with
sufficient humility, I fear), but humanly and foolishly speaking, she will be found, I trust, uniformly great and amiable.
God keep her in her present mind!—to whom be thanks and
praise for all His dispensations to mankind.

C. Lamb.

These mentioned good fortunes and change of prospects
had almost brought my mind over to the extreme, the very
opposite to despair. I was in danger of making myself too
happy. Your letter brought me back to a view of things
which I had entertained from the beginning. I hope (for
Mary I can answer)—but I hope that *I* shall through life
never have less recollection nor a fainter impression of what
has happened than I have now. 'Tis not a light thing, nor
meant by the Almighty to be received lightly. I must be
serious, circumspect, and deeply religious through life; and
by such means may *both* of us escape madness in future, if it
so please the Almighty.

Send me word how it fares with Sara. I repeat it, your
letter was, and will be, an inestimable treasure to me. You
have a view of what my situation demands of me, like my
own view, and I trust a just one.

Coleridge, continue to write; but do not forever offend
me by talking of sending me cash. Sincerely on my soul,
we do not want it. God love you both!

I will write again very soon. Do you write directly.

A few months later and the old father was dead. The elder brother, John Lamb, had a responsible and lucrative position in the business world, but he troubled himself as little as possible about the welfare of the family. Lamb has described him with considerable frankness, but at the same time, with a great deal of affection, in the essay, *My Relations*. The name has been changed from John Lamb to James Elia.

MY RELATIONS

I am arrived at that point of life, at which a man may account it a blessing, as it is a singularity, if he have either of his parents surviving. I have not that felicity—and sometimes think feelingly of a passage in "Browne's Christian Morals," where he speaks of a man that hath lived sixty or seventy years in the world. "In such a compass of time," he says, "a man may have a close apprehension what it is to be forgotten, when he hath lived to find none who could remember his father, or scarcely the friends of his youth, and may sensibly see with what a face in no long time OBLIVION will look upon himself."

I had an aunt, a dear and good one. She was one whom single blessedness had soured to the world. She often used to say that I was the only thing in it which she loved; and, when she thought I was quitting it, she grieved over me with mother's tears. A partiality quite so exclusive my reason cannot altogether approve. She was from morning till night poring over good books, and devotional exercises. Her favourite volumes were, "Thomas à Kempis," in Stanhope's translation; and a Roman Catholic Prayer Book, with the *matins* and *complines* regularly set down,—terms which I was at that time too young to understand. She persisted in reading them, although admonished daily concerning their Papistical tendency; and went to church every Sabbath, as a good

Protestant should do. These were the only books she studied; though, I think at one period of her life, she told me, she had read with great satisfaction the "Adventures of an Unfortunate Nobleman." Finding the door of the chapel in Essex-street open one day—it was in the infancy of that heresy—she went in, liked the sermon, and the manner of worship, and frequented it at intervals for some time after. She came not for doctrinal points, and never missed them. With some little asperities in her constitution, which I have above hinted at, she was a steadfast, friendly being, and a fine *old Christian*. She was a woman of strong sense, and a shrewd mind—extraordinary at a *repartee;* one of the few occasions of her breaking silence—else she did not much value wit. The only secular employment I remember to have seen her engaged in was the splitting of French beans, and dropping them into a China basin of fair water. The odour of those tender vegetables to this day comes back upon my sense, redolent of soothing recollections. Certainly it is the most delicate of culinary operations.

Male aunts, as somebody calls them, I had none—to remember. By the uncle's side I may be said to have been born an orphan. Brother, or sister, I never had any—to know them. A sister, I think, that should have been Elizabeth, died in both our infancies. What a comfort, or what a care, may I not have missed in her!—But I have cousins, sprinkled about in Hertfordshire—besides *two,* with whom I have been all my life in habits of the closest intimacy, and whom I may term cousins *par excellence*. These are James and Bridget Elia. They are older than myself by twelve, and ten, years; and neither of them seems disposed, in matters of advice and guidance, to waive any of the prerogatives which primogeniture confers. May they continue still in the same mind; and when they shall be seventy-five, and seventy-three, years old

(I cannot spare them sooner), persist in treating me in my grand climacteric precisely as a stripling, or younger brother!

James is an inexplicable cousin. Nature hath her unities, which not every critic can penetrate; or, if we feel, we cannot explain them. The pen of Yorick and of none since his, could have drawn J. E. entire—those fine Shandean lights and shades, which make up his story. I must limp after in my poor antithetical manner, as the fates have given me grace and talent. J. E. then—to the eye of a common observer at least—seemeth made up of contradictory principles. The genuine child of impulse, the frigid philosopher of prudence —the phlegm of my cousin's doctrine, is invariably at war with his temperament, which is high sanguine. With always some fire-new project in his brain, J. E. is the systematic opponent of innovation, and crier down of everything that has not stood the test of age and experiment. With a hundred fine notions chasing one another hourly in his fancy, he is startled at the least approach to the romantic in others; and, determined by his own sense in everything, commends *you* to the guidance of common sense on all occasions.—With a touch of the eccentric in all which he does, or says, he is only anxious that *you* should not commit yourself by doing anything absurd or singular. On my once letting slip at table, that I was not fond of a certain popular dish, he begged me at any rate not to *say* so—for the world would think me mad. He disguises a passionate fondness for works of high art (whereof he hath amassed a choice collection), under the pretext of buying only to sell again—that his enthusiasm may give no encouragement to yours. Yet, if it were so, why does that piece of tender, pastoral Domenichino hang still by his wall?—is the ball of his sight much more dear to him?—or what picture-dealer can talk like him?

Whereas mankind in general are observed to warp their

speculative conclusions to the bent of their individual humours, *his* theories are sure to be in diametrical opposition to his constitution. He is courageous as Charles of Sweden, upon instinct; chary of his person upon principle, as a travelling Quaker. He has been preaching up to me, all my life, the doctrine of bowing to the great—the necessity of forms, and manner, to a man's getting on in the world. He himself never aims at either, that I can discover,—and has a spirit that would stand upright in the presence of the Cham of Tartary. It is pleasant to hear him discourse of patience—extolling it as the truest wisdom—and to see him during the last seven minutes that his dinner is getting ready. Nature never ran up in her haste a more restless piece of workmanship than when she moulded this impetuous cousin—and Art never turned out a more elaborate orator than he can display himself to be, upon his favourite topic of the advantages of quiet and contentedness in the state, whatever it be, that we are placed in. He is triumphant on this theme, when he has you safe in one of those short stages that ply for the western road, in a very obstructing manner, at the foot of John Murray's street—where you get in when it is empty, and are expected to wait till the vehicle hath completed her just freight—a trying three quarters of an hour to some people. He wonders at your fidgetiness,—"where could we be better than we are, *thus sitting, thus consulting?*"—"prefers, for his part, a state of rest to locomotion,"—with an eye all the while upon the coachman,—till at length, waxing out of all patience, at *your want of it*, he breaks out into a pathetic remonstrance at the fellow for detaining us so long over the time which he had professed, and declares peremptorily, that "the gentleman in the coach is determined to get out, if he does not drive on that instant."

Very quick at inventing an argument, or detecting a

sophistry, he is incapable of attending *you* in any chain of arguing. Indeed he makes wild work with logic; and seems to jump at most admirable conclusions by some process not at all akin to it. Consonantly enough to this, he hath been heard to deny, upon certain occasions, that there exists such a faculty at all in man as *reason;* and wondereth how man came first to have a conceit of it—enforcing his negation with all the might of *reasoning* he is master of. He has some speculative notions against laughter, and will maintain that laughing is not natural to *him*—when peradventure the next moment his lungs shall crow like Chanticleer. He says some of the best things in the world, and declareth that wit is his aversion. It was he who said, upon seeing the Eton boys at play in their grounds—*What a pity to think that these fine ingenuous lads in a few years will all be changed into frivolous Members of Parliament!*

His youth was fiery, glowing, tempestuous—and in age he discovereth no symptom of cooling. This is that which I admire in him. I hate people who meet Time halfway. I am for no compromise with that inevitable spoiler. While he lives, J. E. will take his swing.—It does me good, as I walk towards the street of my daily avocation, on some fine May morning, to meet him marching in a quite opposite direction, with a jolly handsome presence, and shining sanguine face, that indicates some purchase in his eyes—a Claude—or a Hobbima—for much of his enviable leisure is consumed at Christie's, and Phillips's—or where not, to pick up pictures, and such gauds. On these occasions he mostly stoppeth me, to read a short lecture on the advantage a person like me possesses above himself, in having his time occupied with business which he *must* do—assureth me that he often feels it hang heavy on his hands—wishes he had fewer holidays—and goes off—Westward Ho!—chanting a tune, to Pall Mall—perfectly convinced that he has convinced me—while I proceed in my opposite direction tuneless.

It is pleasant, again, to see this Professor of Indifference doing the honours of his new purchase, when he has fairly housed it. You must view it in every light, till *he* has found the best—placing it at this distance, and at that, but always suiting the focus of your sight to his own. You must spy at it through your fingers, to catch the aërial perspective—though you assure him that to you the landscape shows much more agreeable without that artifice. Woe be to the luckless wight who does not only not respond to his rapture, but who should drop an unseasonable intimation of preferring one of his anterior bargains to the present!—The last is always his best hit—his "Cynthia of the minute."—Alas! how many a mild Madonna have I known to *come in*—a Raphael!—keep its ascendency for a few brief moons—then, after certain inter-medial degradations, from the front drawing-room to the back gallery, thence to the dark parlour,—adopted in turn by each of the Carracci, under successive lowering ascriptions of filiation, mildly breaking its fall—consigned to the obliv-ious lumber-room, *go out* at last a Lucca Giordano, or plain Carlo Maratti! —which things when I beheld—musing upon the chances and mutabilities of fate below hath made me to reflect upon the altered condition of great personages, or that woeful Queen of Richard the Second—

> ———— set forth in pomp,
> She came adorned hither like sweet May;
> Sent back like Hallowmass or shortest day.

With great love for *you*, J. E. hath but a limited sympathy with what you feel or do. He lives in a world of his own, and makes slender guesses at what passes in your mind. He never pierces the marrow of your habits. He will tell an old established play-goer, that Mr. Such-a-one, or So-and-so (naming one of the theatres), is a very lively comedian—as a piece of news! He advertised me but the other day of some pleasant green lanes which he had found out for me, *knowing me to be a great walker,* in my own immediate vicinity—who have haunted the identical spot any time these twenty years!— He has not much respect for that class of feelings which goes by the name of sentimental. He applies the definition of real evil to bodily sufferings exclusively—and rejecteth all others as imaginary. He is affected by the sight, or the bare supposition, of a creature in pain, to a degree which I have never witnessed out of womankind. A constitutional acuteness to this class of sufferings may in part account for this. The animal tribe in particular he taketh under his especial protection. A broken-winded or spur-galled horse is sure to find an advocate in him. An overloaded ass is his client for ever. He is the apostle to the brute kind—the never-failing friend of those who have none to care for them. The contemplation of a lobster boiled, or eels skinned *alive,* will wring him so, that "all for pity he could die." It will take the savour from his palate, and the rest from his pillow, for days and nights. With the intense feeling of Thomas Clarkson, he wanted only the steadiness of pursuit, and unity of purpose, of that "true yoke-fellow with Time," to have effected as much for the *Animal,* as *he* hath done for the *Negro Creation.* But my uncontrollable cousin is but imperfectly formed for purposes which demand co-operation. He cannot wait. His amelioration-plans must be ripened in a day. For this reason he has cut but an equivocal figure in benevolent societies, and combinations for the alleviation of human sufferings. His zeal constantly makes him to outrun, and put out, his coadjutors. He thinks of relieving,—while they think of debating. He was black-balled out of a society for the

Relief of *   *   *   * because the fervour of his humanity toiled beyond the formal apprehension and creeping processes of his associates. I shall always consider this distinction as a patent of nobility in the Elia family!

Do I mention these seeming inconsistencies to smile at, or upbraid, my unique cousin? Marry, heaven, and all good manners, and the understanding that should be between kinsfolk, forbid!—With all the strangeness of this *strangest of the Elias*—I would not have him in one jot or tittle other than he is; neither would I barter or exchange my wild kinsman for the most exact, regular, and every way consistent kinsman breathing.

In my next, Reader, I may perhaps give you some account of my cousin Bridget—if you are not already surfeited with cousins—and take you by the hand, if you are willing to go with us, on an excursion which we made a summer or two since, in search of *more cousins*—

Through the green plains of pleasant Hertfordshire.

Of Mary Lamb, the sister so loved and tenderly cared for, and of the life that the two led when she was not in an insane asylum, the essays tell us much. The essay entitled *Mackery End, in Hertfordshire* presents an interesting picture of this life, Mary Lamb appearing as Elia's cousin, Bridget Elia. Such excursions as the essay describes were one of the means Lamb and his sister used to relieve the monotony and strain of their lives.

MACKERY END, IN HERTFORDSHIRE

Bridget Elia has been my housekeeper for many a long year. I have obligations to Bridget, extending beyond the period of memory. We house together, old bachelor and maid, in a sort of double singleness; with such tolerable comfort, upon the whole, that I, for one, find in myself no sort of disposition to go out upon the mountains, with the rash king's offspring, to bewail my celibacy. We agree pretty well in our tastes and habits—yet so, as "with a difference." We are generally in harmony, with occasional bickerings—as it should be among near relations. Our sympathies are rather understood than expressed; and once, upon my dissembling a tone in my voice more kind than ordinary, my cousin burst into tears, and complained that I was altered. We are both great readers in different directions. While I am hanging over (for the thousandth time) some passage in old Burton, or one of his strange contemporaries, she is abstracted in some modern tale, or adventure, whereof our common reading-table is daily fed with assiduously fresh supplies. Narrative teases me. I have little concern in the progress of events. She must have a story—well, ill, or indifferently told —so there be life stirring in it, and plenty of good or evil accidents. The fluctuations of fortune in fiction—and almost in real life—have ceased to interest, or operate but dully upon me. Out-of-the-way humours and opinions—heads with some diverting twist in them—the oddities of authorship, please me most. My cousin has a native disrelish of anything that sounds odd or bizarre. Nothing goes down with her that is quaint, irregular, or out of the road of common sympathy. She "holds Nature more clever." I can pardon her blindness to the beautiful obliquities of the Religio Medici; but she must apologize to me for certain disrespectful insinuations, which she has been pleased to throw out latterly, touching the intellectuals of a dear favourite of mine, of the last century but one—the thrice noble, chaste, and virtuous,—but again somewhat fantastical, and original brain'd, generous Margaret Newcastle.

It has been the lot of my cousin, oftener perhaps than I

could have wished, to have had for her associates and mine, free-thinkers—leaders, and disciples, of novel philosophies and systems; but she neither wrangles with, nor accepts, their opinions. That which was good and venerable to her, when a child, retains its authority over her mind still. She never juggles or plays tricks with her understanding.

We are both of us inclined to be a little too positive; and I have observed the result of our disputes to be almost uniformly this—that in matters of fact, dates, and circumstances, it turns out, that I was in the right, and my cousin in the wrong. But where we have differed upon moral points; upon something proper to be done, or let alone; whatever heat of opposition, or steadiness of conviction, I set out with, I am sure always, in the long-run, to be brought over to her way of thinking.

I must touch upon the foibles of my kinswoman with a gentle hand, for Bridget does not like to be told of her faults. She hath an awkward trick (to say no worse of it) of reading in company: at which times she will answer *yes* or *no* to a question, without fully understanding its purport—which is provoking, and derogatory in the highest degree to the dignity of the putter of the said question. Her presence of mind is equal to the most pressing trials of life, but will sometimes desert her upon trifling occasions. When the purpose requires it, and is a thing of moment, she can speak to it greatly; but in matters which are not stuff of the conscience, she hath been known sometimes to let slip a word less seasonably.

Her education in youth was not much attended to; and she happily missed all that train of female garniture which passeth by the name of accomplishments. She was tumbled early, by accident or design, into a spacious closet of good old English reading, without much selection or prohibition, and browsed at will upon that fair and wholesome pasturage.

Had I twenty girls, they should be brought up exactly in this fashion. I know not whether their chance in wedlock might not be diminished by it, but I can answer for it, that it makes (if the worst come to the worst) most incomparable old maids.

In a season of distress, she is the truest comforter; but in the teasing accidents and minor perplexities, which do not call out the *will* to meet them, she sometimes maketh matters worse by an excess of participation. If she does not always divide your trouble, upon the pleasanter occasions of life she is sure always to treble your satisfaction. She is excellent to be at a play with, or upon a visit; but best, when she goes a journey with you.

We made an excursion together a few summers since, into Hertfordshire, to beat up the quarters of some of our less-known relations in that fine corn country.

The oldest thing I remember is Mackery End, or Mackarel End, as it is spelt, perhaps more properly, in some old maps of Hertfordshire; a farm-house,—delightfully situated within a gentle walk from Wheathampstead. I can just remember having been there, on a visit to a great-aunt, when I was a child, under the care of Bridget; who, as I have said, is older than myself by some ten years. I wish that I could throw into a heap the remainder of our joint existences, that we might share them in equal division. But that is impossible. The house was at that time in the occupation of a substantial yeoman, who had married my grandmother's sister. His name was Gladman. My grandmother was a Bruton, married to a Field. The Gladmans and the Brutons are still flourishing in that part of the county, but the Fields are almost extinct. More than forty years had elapsed since the visit I speak of; and, for the greater portion of that period, we had lost sight of the other two branches also. Who or what sort of persons inherited Mackery End—kindred or strange folk—we were afraid almost to conjecture, but determined some day to explore.

By somewhat a circuitous route, taking the noble park at Luton in our way from Saint Albans, we arrived at the spot of our anxious curiosity about noon. The sight of the old farmhouse, though every trace of it was effaced from my recollection, affected me with a pleasure which I had not experienced for many a year. For though *I* had forgotten it, *we* had never forgotten being there together, and we had been talking about Mackery End all our lives, till memory on my part became mocked with a phantom of itself, and I thought I knew the aspect of a place, which, when present, O how unlike it was to *that* which I had conjured up so many times instead of it!

Still the air breathed balmily about it; the season was in the "heart of June," and I could say with the poet,

> But thou, that didst appear so fair
>   To fond imagination,
> Dost rival in the light of day
>   Her delicate creation!

Bridget's was more a waking bliss than mine, for she easily remembered her old acquaintance again—some altered features, of course, a little grudged at. At first, indeed, she was ready to disbelieve for joy; but the scene soon re-confirmed itself in her affections—and she traversed every outpost of the old mansion, to the wood-house, the orchard, the place where the pigeon-house had stood (house and birds were alike flown)—with a breathless impatience of recognition, which was more pardonable perhaps than decorous at the age of fifty odd. But Bridget in some things is behind her years.

The only thing left was to get into the house—and that

was a difficulty which to me singly would have been insur-
mountable; for I am terribly shy in making myself known
to strangers and out-of-date kinsfolk. Love, stronger than
scruple, winged my cousin in without me; but she soon returned with a creature that might have sat to a sculptor for
the image of Welcome. It was the youngest of the Gladmans;
who, by marriage with a Bruton, had become mistress of the
old mansion. A comely brood are the Brutons. Six of them,
females, were noted as the handsomest young women in the
county. But this adopted Bruton, in my mind, was better
than they all—more comely. She was born too late to have
remembered me. She just recollected in early life to have
had her cousin Bridget once pointed out to her, climbing a
stile. But the name of kindred, and of cousinship, was
enough. Those slender ties, that prove slight as gossamer in
the rending atmosphere of a metropolis, bind faster, as we
found it, in hearty, homely, loving Hertfordshire. In five
minutes we were as thoroughly acquainted as if we had been
born and bred up together; were familiar, even to the calling
of each other by our Christian names. So Christians should
call one another. To have seen Bridget and her—it was like
the meeting of the two scriptural cousins! There was a grace
and dignity, an amplitude of form and stature, answering to
her mind, in this farmer's wife, which would have shined in a
palace—or so we thought it. We were made welcome by husband and wife equally—we, and our friend that was with us.
—I had almost forgotten him—but B[arron] F[ield] will
not so soon forget that meeting, if peradventure he shall read
this on the far distant shores where the Kangaroo haunts.
The fatted calf was made ready, or rather was already so,
as if in anticipation of our coming; and, after an appropriate
glass of native wine, never let me forget with what honest
pride this hospitable cousin made us proceed to Wheathamp-

stead, to introduce us (as some new-found rarity) to her mother and sister Gladmans, who did indeed know something more of us, at a time when she almost knew nothing.—With what corresponding kindness we were received by them also —how Bridget's memory, exalted by the occasion, warmed into a thousand half-obliterated recollections of things and persons, to my utter astonishment, and her own—and to the astoundment of B. F. who sat by, almost the only thing that was not a cousin there,—old effaced images of more than half-forgotten names and circumstances still crowding back upon her, as words written in lemon come out upon exposure to a friendly warmth,—when I forget all this, then may my country cousins forget me; and Bridget no more remember, that in the days of weakling infancy I was her tender charge—as I have been her care in foolish manhood since— in those pretty pastoral walks, long ago, about Mackery End, in Hertfordshire.

Lamb realized that he must give up all hopes of marrying and having wife and children of his own. In his younger days, he had fallen in love with a girl whose identity is vague, but whom Lamb called "Alice W———n" in the essays. In *Dream-Children; A Reverie,* Lamb reverts to this incident, and shows that although he had set himself to lead a bachelor life, there were moments of longing for what might have been.

DREAM-CHILDREN: A REVERIE

Children love to listen to stories about their elders, when *they* were children; to stretch their imagination to the conception of a traditionary great-uncle, or grandame, whom they never saw. It was in this spirit that my little ones crept about me the other evening to hear about their great-grandmother Field, who lived in a great house in Norfolk (a hundred times bigger than that in which they and papa lived) which had been the scene—so at least it was generally believed in that part of the country—of the tragic incidents which they had lately become familiar with from the ballad of the Children in the Wood. Certain it is that the whole story of the children and their cruel uncle was to be seen fairly carved out in wood upon the chimney-piece of the great hall, the whole story down to the Robin Redbreasts; till a foolish rich person pulled it down to set up a marble one of modern invention in its stead, with no story upon it. Here Alice put out one of her dear mother's looks, too tender to be called upbraiding. Then I went on to say, how religious and how good their great-grandmother Field was, how beloved and respected by everybody, though she was not indeed the mistress of this great house, but had only charge of it (and yet in some respects she might be said to be the mistress of it too) committed to her by the owner, who preferred living in a newer and more fashionable mansion which he had purchased somewhere in the adjoining county; but still she lived in it in a manner as if it had been her own, and kept up the dignity of the great house in a sort while she lived, which afterwards came to decay, and was nearly pulled down, and all its old ornaments stripped and carried away to the owner's other house, where they were set up, and looked as awkward as if some one were to carry away the old tombs they had seen lately at the Abbey, and stick them up in Lady C.'s tawdry gilt drawing-room. Here John smiled, as much as to say, "that would be foolish indeed." And then I told how, when she came to die, her funeral was attended by a concourse of all the poor, and some of the gentry too, of the neighbourhood for many miles round, to show their respect for her memory, because she had been such a good and religious woman; so good indeed that she knew all the Psaltery by heart, ay, and a great part of the Testament besides. Here little Alice spread her hands. Then I told what a tall, upright, graceful person their great-grandmother Field once was; and how in her youth she was esteemed the best dancer— here Alice's little right foot played an involuntary movement, till, upon my looking grave, it desisted—the best dancer, I was saying, in the county, till a cruel disease, called a cancer, came, and bowed her down with pain; but it could never bend her good spirits, or make them stoop, but they were still upright, because she was so good and religious. Then I told how she was used to sleep by herself in a lone chamber of the great lone house; and how she believed that an apparition of two infants was to be seen at midnight gliding up and down the great staircase near where she slept, but she said "those innocents would do her no harm;" and how frightened I used to be, though in those days I had my maid to sleep with me, because I was never half so good or religious as she —and yet I never saw the infants. Here John expanded all his eyebrows and tried to look courageous. Then I told how good she was to all her grandchildren, having us to the great house in the holy-days, where I in particular used to spend many hours by myself, in gazing upon the old busts of the Twelve Cæsars, that had been Emperors of Rome, till the old marble heads would seem to live again, or I to be turned into marble with them; how I never could be tired with roaming about that huge mansion, with its vast empty rooms, with their worn-out hangings, fluttering tapestry, and carved oaken panels, with the gilding almost rubbed out—sometimes in the spacious old-fashioned gardens, which I had almost to myself, unless when now and then a solitary gardening man would cross me—and how the nectarines and peaches hung upon the walls, without my ever offering to pluck them, because they were forbidden fruit, unless now and then, and because I had more pleasure in strolling about among the old melancholy-looking yew-trees, or the firs, and picking up the red berries, and the fir-apples, which were good for nothing but to look at—or in lying about upon the fresh grass, with all the fine garden smells around me—or basking in the orangery, till I could almost fancy myself ripening too along with the oranges and the limes in that grateful warmth—or in watching the dace that darted to and fro in the fishpond, at the bottom of the garden, with here and there a great sulky pike hanging midway down the water in silent state, as if it mocked at their impertinent friskings,—I had more pleasure in these busy-idle diversions than in all the sweet flavours of peaches, nectarines, oranges, and such-like common baits of children. Here John slyly deposited back upon the plate a bunch of grapes, which, not unobserved by Alice, he had meditated dividing with her, and both seemed willing to relinquish them for the present as irrelevant. Then, in somewhat a more heightened tone, I told how, though their great-grandmother Field loved all her grandchildren, yet in an especial manner she might be said to love their uncle, John L[amb], because he was so handsome and spirited a youth, and a king to the rest of us; and, instead of moping about in solitary corners, like some of us, he would mount the most mettlesome horse he could get, when but an imp no bigger than themselves, and make it carry him half over the county in a morning, and join the hunters when there were any out—and yet he loved the old great house and gardens too, but had too much spirit to be always pent up within their boundaries—and how their uncle grew up to man's estate as brave as he was handsome, to the admiration of everybody, but of their great-grandmother Field most especially; and how he used to carry me upon his

back when I was a lame-footed boy—for he was a good bit
older than me—many a mile when I could not walk for pain;
—and how in after life he became lame-footed too, and I did
not always (I fear) make allowances enough for him when
he was impatient and in pain, nor remember sufficiently
how considerate he had been to me when I was lame-footed;
and how when he died, though he had not been dead an hour,
it seemed as if he had died a great while ago, such a distance
there is betwixt life and death; and how I bore his death as I
thought pretty well at first, but afterwards it haunted and
haunted me; and though I did not cry or take it to heart as
some do, and as I think he would have done if I had died, yet
I missed him all day long, and knew not till then how much
I had loved him. I missed his kindness, and I missed his cross-
ness, and wished him to be alive again, to be quarrelling with
him (for we quarrelled sometimes), rather than not have him
again, and was as uneasy without him, as he, their poor uncle,
must have been when the doctor took off his limb. Here the
children fell a crying, and asked if their little mourning
which they had on was not for uncle John, and they looked
up, and prayed me not to go on about their uncle, but to tell
them some stories about their pretty dead mother. Then I told
how for seven long years, in hope sometimes, sometimes in
despair, yet persisting ever, I courted the fair Alice W[in
terto]n; and, as much as children could understand, I explained to them what coyness, and difficulty, and denial,
meant in maidens—when suddenly turning to Alice, the soul
of the first Alice looked out at her eyes with such a reality
of re-presentment, that I became in doubt which of them
stood there before me, or whose that bright hair was; and
while I stood gazing, both the children gradually grew fainter
to my view, receding, and still receding, till nothing at last
but two mournful features were seen in the uttermost dis-

tance, which, without speech, strangely impressed upon me the effects of speech: "We are not of Alice, nor of thee, nor are we children at all. The children of Alice call Bartrum father. We are nothing; less than nothing, and dreams. We are only what might have been, and must wait upon the tedious shores of Lethe millions of ages before we have existence, and a name"——and immediately awaking, I found myself quietly seated in my bachelor arm-chair, where I had fallen asleep, with the faithful Bridget unchanged by my side—but John L. (or James Elia) was gone for ever.

In later life, when his responsibilities had become somewhat lightened and his income somewhat increased, Lamb felt that he might perhaps marry. His interest in the theater had led to a great admiration for Miss Fanny Kelly, one of the leading actresses of those days. That Lamb had been for a long while an admirer of her acting and character is shown by the essay *Barbara S*——, which relates an incident in the life of Miss Kelly, who had made her first appearance at the Drury Lane Theater at the age of seven. Some months later he made her an offer of marriage by letter, which she, however, declined. The brave way in which Lamb took this disappointment is revealed in his answer to Miss Kelly.

BARBARA S——

On the noon of the 14th of November, 1743 or 4, I forget which it was, just as the clock had struck one, Barbara S——, with her accustomed punctuality, ascended the long rambling staircase, with awkward interposed landing-places, which led to the office, or rather a sort of box with a desk in it, whereat sat the then Treasurer of (what few of our readers may remember) the old Bath Theatre. All over the island it was the custom, and remains so I believe to this day, for the players to receive their weekly stipend on the Saturday. It was not much that Barbara had to claim.

The little maid had just entered her eleventh year; but her important station at the theatre, as it seemed to her, with the benefits which she felt to accrue from her pious application of her small earnings, had given an air of womanhood to her steps and to her behaviour. You would have taken her to have been at least five years older.

Till latterly she had merely been employed in choruses, or where children were wanted to fill up the scene. But the manager, observing a diligence and adroitness in her above her age, had for some few months past intrusted to her the performance of whole parts. You may guess the self-consequence of the promoted Barbara. She had already drawn tears in young Arthur; had rallied Richard with infantine petulance in the Duke of York; and in her turn had rebuked that petulance when she was Prince of Wales. She would have done the elder child in Morton's pathetic afterpiece to the life; but as yet the "Children in the Wood" was not.

Long after this little girl was grown an aged woman, I have seen some of these small parts, each making two or three pages at most, copied out in the rudest hand of the then prompter, who doubtless transcribed a little more carefully and fairly for the grown-up tragedy ladies of the establishment. But such as they were, blotted and scrawled, as for a child's use, she kept them all; and in the zenith of her after reputation it was a delightful sight to behold them bound up in costliest Morocco, each single—each small part making a *book*—with fine clasps, gilt-splashed, etc. She had conscientiously kept them as they had been delivered to her; not a blot had been effaced or tampered with. They were precious to her for their affecting remembrancings. They were her principia, her rudiments; the elementary atoms; the little steps by which she pressed forward to perfection. "What," she would say, "could Indian rubber, or a pumice stone, have done for these darlings?"

I am in no hurry to begin my story—indeed I have little or none to tell—so I will just mention an observation of hers connected with that interesting time.

Not long before she died I had been discoursing with her on the quantity of real present emotion which a great tragic performer experiences during acting. I ventured to think, that though in the first instance such players must have possessed the feelings which they so powerfully called up in others, yet by frequent repetition those feelings must become deadened in great measure, and the performer trust to the memory of past emotion, rather than express a present one. She indignantly repelled the notion, that with a truly great tragedian the operation, by which such effects were produced upon an audience, could ever degrade itself into what was purely mechanical. With much delicacy, avoiding to instance in her *self*-experience, she told me, that so long ago as when she used to play the part of the Little Son to Mrs. Porter's Isabella (I think it was), when that impressive actress has been bending over her in some heart-rending colloquy, she has felt real hot tears come trickling from her, which, to use her powerful expression) have perfectly scalded her back.

I am not quite so sure that it was Mrs. Porter; but it was some great actress of that day. The name is indifferent; but the fact of the scalding tears I most distinctly remember.

I was always fond of the society of players, and am not sure that an impediment in my speech (which certainly kept me out of the pulpit), even more than certain personal disqualifications, which are often got over in that profession, did not prevent me at one time of life from adopting it. I have had the honour (I must ever call it) once to have been admitted to the tea-table of Miss Kelly. I have played at serious whist with Mr. Liston. I have chatted with ever good-humoured Mrs. Charles Kemble. I have conversed as friend to friend with her accomplished husband. I have been indulged with a classical conference with Macready; and with a sight of the Player-picture-gallery, at Mr. Mathews's, when the kind owner, to remunerate me for my love of the old actors (whom he loves so much), went over it with me, supplying to his capital collection, what alone the artist could not give them—voice; and their living motion. Old tones, half-faded, of Dodd, and Parsons, and Baddeley, have lived again for me at his bidding. Only Edwin he could not restore to me. I have supped with——; but I am growing a coxcomb.

As I was about to say—at the desk of the then treasurer of the old Bath Theatre—not Diamond's—presented herself the little Barbara S——.

The parents of Barbara had been in reputable circumstances. The father had practised, I believe, as an apothecary in the town. But his practice, from causes which I feel my own infirmity too sensibly that way to arraign—or perhaps from that pure infelicity which accompanies some people in their walk through life, and which it is impossible to lay at the door of imprudence—was now reduced to nothing. They were in fact in the very teeth of starvation, when the manager, who knew and respected them in better days, took the little Barbara into his company.

At the period I commenced with, her slender earnings were the sole support of the family, including two younger sisters. I must throw a veil over some mortifying circumstances. Enough to say, that her Saturday's pittance was the only chance of a Sunday's (generally their only) meal of meat.

One thing I will only mention, that in some child's part, where in her theatrical character she was to sup off a roast fowl (O joy to Barbara!) some comic actor, who was for the night caterer for this dainty—in the misguided humour of his part, threw over the dish such a quantity of salt (O grief and pain of heart to Barbara!) that when he crammed a portion of it into her mouth, she was obliged sputteringly to reject it; and what with the shame of her ill-acted part, and pain of real appetite at missing such a dainty, her little heart sobbed almost to breaking, till a flood of tears, which the well-fed spectators were totally unable to comprehend, mercifully relieved her.

This was the little starved, meritorious maid, who stood before old Ravenscroft, the treasurer, for her Saturday's payment.

Ravenscroft was a man, I have heard many old theatrical people besides herself say, of all men least calculated for a treasurer. He had no head for accounts, paid away at random, kept scarce any books, and summing up at the week's end, if he found himself a pound or so deficient, blest himself that it was no worse.

Now Barbara's weekly stipend was a bare half-guinea.— By mistake he popped into her hand a—whole one.

Barbara tripped away.

She was entirely unconscious at first of the mistake: God knows, Ravenscroft would never have discovered it.

But when she had got down to the first of those uncouth landing-places, she became sensible of an unusual weight of metal pressing her little hand.

Now mark the dilemma.

She was by nature a good child. From her parents and those about her, she had imbibed no contrary influence. But then they had taught her nothing. Poor men's smoky cabins are not always porticoes of moral philosophy. This little maid had no instinct to evil, but then she might be said to have no fixed principle. She had heard honesty commended, but never dreamed of its application to herself. She thought of it as something which concerned grown up people,—men and women. She had never known temptation, or thought of preparing resistance against it.

Her first impulse was to go back to the old treasurer, and explain to him his blunder. He was already so confused with age, besides a natural want of punctuality, that she would have had some difficulty in making him understand it. She saw *that* in an instant. And then it was such a bit of money! and then the image of a larger allowance of butcher's meat on their table the next day came across her, till her little eyes glistened, and her mouth moistened. But then Mr. Ravenscroft had always been so good-natured, had stood her friend behind the scenes, and even recommended her promotion to some of her little parts. But again the old man was reputed to be worth a world of money. He was supposed to have fifty pounds a year clear of the theatre. And then came staring upon her the figures of her little stockingless and shoeless sisters. And when she looked at her own neat cotton stockings, which her situation at the theatre had made it indispensable for her mother to provide for her, with hard straining and pinching from the family stock, and thought how glad she should be to cover their poor feet with the same—and how then they could accompany her to rehearsals, which they had hitherto been precluded from doing, by reason of their unfashionable attire,—in these thoughts she reached the second landing-place—the second, I mean, from the top—for there was still another left to traverse.

Now virtue support Barbara!

And that never-failing friend *did* step in—for at that moment a strength not her own, I have heard her say, was revealed to her—a reason above reasoning—and without her own agency, as it seemed (for she never felt her feet to move), she found herself transported back to the individual desk she had just quitted, and her hand in the old hand of Ravenscroft, who in silence took back the refunded treasure, and who had been sitting (good man) insensible to the lapse of minutes, which to her were anxious ages; and from that moment a deep peace fell upon her heart, and she knew the quality of honesty.

A year or two's unrepining application to her profession brightened up the feet, and the prospects, of her little sisters, set the whole family upon their legs again, and released her from the difficulty of discussing moral dogmas upon a landing-place.

I have heard her say, that it was a surprise, not much short of mortification to her, to see the coolness with which the old man pocketed the difference, which had caused her such mortal throes.

This anecdote of herself I had in the year 1800, from the mouth of the late Mrs. Crawford, then sixty-seven years of age (she died soon after); and to her struggles upon this childish occasion I have sometimes ventured to think her indebted for that power of rending the heart in the representation of conflicting emotions, for which in after years she was considered as little inferior (if at all so in the part of Lady Randolph) even to Mrs. Siddons.

LETTER TO MISS KELLY

20 July, 1819.

Dear Miss Kelly,—We had the pleasure, *pain* I might better call it, of seeing you last night in the new Play. It was a most consummate piece of Acting, but what a task for you to undergo! at a time when your heart is sore from real sorrow! it has given rise to a train of thinking, which I cannot suppress.

Would to God you were released from this way of life; that you could bring your mind to consent to take your lot with us, and throw off for ever the whole burden of your Profession. I neither expect or wish you to take notice of this which I am writing, in your present over occupied and hurried state.—But to think of it at your leisure. I have quite income enough, if that were all, to justify for me making such a proposal, with what I may call even a handsome provision for my survivor. What you possess of your own would naturally be appropriated to those, for whose sakes chiefly you have made so many hard sacrifices. I am not so foolish as not to know that I am a most unworthy match for such a one as you, but you have for years been a principal object in my mind. In many a sweet assumed character I have learned to love you, but simply as F. M. Kelly I love you better than them all. Can you quit these shadows of existence, and come and be a reality to us? can you leave off harassing yourself to please a thankless multitude, who know nothing of you, and begin at last to live to yourself and your friends?

As plainly and frankly as I have seen you give or refuse assent in some feigned scene, so frankly do me the justice to answer me. It is impossible I should feel injured or aggrieved by your telling me at once, that the proposal does not suit you. It is impossible that I should even think of molesting you with idle importunity and persecution after your mind once firmly spoken—but happier, far happier, could I have leave to hope a time might come, when our friends might be your friends; our interests yours; our book-knowledge, if in that inconsiderable particular we have any little advantage, might impart something to you, which you would every day have it in your power ten thousand fold to repay by the added cheerfulness and joy which you could not fail to bring as a dowry into whatever family should have the honor and happiness of receiving *you*, the most welcome accession that could be made to it.

In haste, but with entire respect and deepest affection, I subscribe myself

C. LAMB.

LETTER TO MISS KELLY

July 20th, 1819.

Dear Miss Kelly—*Your injunctions shall be obeyed to a tittle*. I feel myself in a lackadaisacal no-how-ish kind of a humour. I believe it is the rain, or something. I had thought to have written seriously, but I fancy I succeed best in epistles of mere fun; puns & *that* nonsense. You will be good friends with us, will you not? let what has past "break no bones" between us. You will not refuse us them next time we send for them?

Yours very truly,   C. L.

Do you observe the delicacy of not signing my full name? N. B. Do not paste that last letter of mine into your Book.

The brother and sister made various efforts to increase their very scanty income by means of literary work. For about three years Lamb contributed facetious paragraphs to the morning papers at the rate of sixpence a joke. Recollections of this attempt at a "supplementary livelihood" led afterwards to the writing of the essay *Newspapers Thirty-five Years Ago*.

NEWSPAPERS THIRTY-FIVE YEARS AGO

Dan Stuart once told us, that he did not remember that he ever deliberately walked into the Exhibition at Somerset

House in his life. He might occasionally have escorted a party of ladies across the way that were going in; but he never went in of his own head. Yet the office of the Morning Post newspaper stood then just where it does now—we are carrying you back, Reader, some thirty years or more—with its gilt-globe-topt front facing that emporium of our artists' grand Annual Exposure. We sometimes wish that we had observed the same abstinence with Daniel.

A word or two of D.S. He ever appeared to us one of the finest-tempered of Editors. Perry, of the Morning Chronicle, was equally pleasant, with a dash, no slight one either, of the courtier. S. was frank, plain, and English all over. We have worked for both these gentlemen.

It is soothing to contemplate the head of the Ganges; to trace the first little bubblings of a mighty river,

> With holy reverence to approach the rocks,
> Whence glide the streams renowned in ancient song.

Fired with a perusal of the Abyssinian Pilgrim's exploratory ramblings after the cradle of the infant Nilus, we well remember on one fine summer holyday (a "whole day's leave" we called it at Christ's Hospital) sallying forth at rise of sun, not very well provisioned either for such an undertaking, to trace the current of the New River—Middletonian stream!—to its scaturient source, as we had read, in meadows by fair Amwell. Gallantly did we commence our solitary quest—for it was essential to the dignity of a DISCOVERY, that no eye of schoolboy, save our own, should beam on the detection. By flowery spots, and verdant lanes skirting Hornsey, Hope trained us on in many a baffling turn; endless, hopeless meanders, as it seemed; or as if the jealous waters had *dodged* us, reluctant to have the humble spot of their nativity revealed; till spent, and nigh famished, before set of the same sun, we sate down somewhere by Bowes Farm near Tottenham, with a tithe of our proposed labours only yet accomplished; sorely convinced in spirit, that that Brucian enterprise was as yet too arduous for our young shoulders.

Not more refreshing to the thirsty curiosity of the traveller is the tracing of some mighty waters up to their shallow fontlet, than it is to a pleased and candid reader to go back to the inexperienced essays, the first callow flights in authorship, of some established name in literature; from the Gnat which preluded to the Æneid, to the Duck which Samuel Johnson trod on.

In those days, every Morning Paper, as an essential retainer to its establishment, kept an author, who was bound to furnish daily a quantum of witty paragraphs. Sixpence a joke—and it was thought pretty high too—was Dan Stuart's settled remuneration in these cases. The chat of the day—scandal, but, above all, *dress*—furnished the material. The length of no paragraph was to exceed seven lines. Shorter they might be, but they must be poignant.

A fashion of *flesh,* or rather *pink*-coloured hose for the ladies, luckily coming up at the juncture when we were on our probation for the place of Chief Jester to S.'s Paper, established our reputation in that line. We were pronounced a "capital hand." O the conceits which we varied upon *red* in all its prismatic differences! from the trite and obvious flower of Cytherea, to the flaming costume of the lady that has her sitting upon "many waters." Then there was the collateral topic of ankles. What an occasion to a truly chaste writer, like ourself, of touching that nice brink, and yet never tumbling over it, of a seemingly ever approximating something "not quite proper;" while, like a skilful posture-master, balancing betwixt decorums and their opposites, he keeps the line, from which a hair's-breadth deviation is destruction; hovering in the confines of light and darkness, or where "both seem either;" a hazy uncertain delicacy; Autolycus-like in the Play, still putting off his expectant auditory with "Whoop, do me no harm, good man!" But above all, that conceit arrided us most at that time, and still tickles our midriff to remember, where, allusively to the flight of Astræa—*ultima Cælestûm terras reliquit*—we pronounced —in reference to the stockings still—that MODESTY TAKING HER FINAL LEAVE OF MORTALS, HER LAST BLUSH WAS VIS-IBLE IN HER ASCENT TO THE HEAVENS BY THE TRACT OF THE GLOWING INSTEP. This might be called the crowning conceit: and was esteemed tolerable writing in those days.

But the fashion of jokes, with all other things, passes away; as did the transient mode which had so favoured us. The ankles of our fair friends in a few weeks began to reassume their whiteness, and left us scarce a leg to stand upon. Other female whims followed, but none, methought, so pregnant, so invitatory of shrewd conceits, and more than single meanings.

Somebody has said, that to swallow six cross-buns daily consecutively for a fortnight, would surfeit the stoutest digestion. But to have to furnish as many jokes daily, and that not for a fortnight, but for a long twelvemonth, as we were constrained to do, was a little harder exaction. "Man goeth forth to his work until the evening"—from a reasonable hour in the morning, we presume it was meant. Now, as our main occupation took us up from eight till five every day in the City; and as our evening hours, at that time of life, had generally to do with anything rather than business, it follows, that the only time we could spare for this manu-factory of jokes—our supplementary livelihood, that supplied us in every want beyond mere bread and cheese—was exactly that part of the day which (as we have heard of No Man's Land) may be fitly denominated No Man's Time; that is, no time in which a man ought to be up, and awake, in. To speak more plainly, it is that time, of an hour, or an hour and a half's duration, in which a man, whose occasions call him up so preposterously, has to wait for his breakfast.

O those headaches at dawn of day, when at five, or half-past five in summer, and not much later in the dark seasons, we were compelled to rise, having been perhaps not above four hours in bed——(for we were no go-to-beds with the lamb, though we anticipated the lark ofttimes in her rising—we like a parting cup at midnight, as all young men did before these effeminate times, and to have our friends about us—we were not constellated under Aquarius that watery sign, and therefore incapable of Bacchus, cold, washy, blood-less—we were none of your Basilian watersponges (nor had taken our degrees at Mount Ague—we were right toping Capulets, jolly companions, we and they)—but to have to get up, as we said before, curtailed of half our fair sleep, fasting, with only a dim vista of refreshing Bohea in the distance—to be necessitated to rouse ourselves at the detest-able rap of an old hag of a domestic, who seemed to take a diabolical pleasure in her announcement that it was "time to rise;" and whose chappy knuckles we have often yearned to amputate, and string them up at our chamber door, to be a terror to all such unseasonable rest-breakers in fu-ture——

"Facil" and sweet, as Virgil sings, had been the "descend-ing" of the over-night, balmy the first sinking of the heavy head upon the pillow; but to get up, as he goes on to say,

—revocare gradus, superasque evadere ad auras—

and to get up moreover to make jokes with malice prepended —there was the "labour," there the "work."

No Egyptian taskmaster ever devised a slavery like to that,

our slavery. No fractious operants ever turned out for half the tyranny which this necessity exercised upon us. Half a dozen jests in a day (bating Sundays too), why, it seems nothing! We make twice the number every day in our lives as a matter of course, and claim no Sabbatical exemptions. But then they come into our head. But when the head has to go out to them—when the mountain must go to Mahomet——

Reader, try it for once, only for one short twelvemonth.

It was not every week that a fashion of pink stockings came up; but mostly, instead of it, some rugged untractable subject; some topic impossible to be contorted into the risible; some feature, upon which no smile could play; some flint, from which no process of ingenuity could procure a scintillation. There they lay; there your appointed tale of brickmaking was set before you, which you must finish, with or without straw, as it happened. The craving dragon—*the Public*—like him in Bel's Temple—must be fed, it expected its daily rations; and Daniel, and ourselves, to do us justice, did the best we could on this side bursting him.

While we were wringing out coy sprightlinesses for the Post, and writhing under the toil of what is called "easy writing," Bob Allen, our *quondam* schoolfellow, was tapping his impracticable brains in a like service for the Oracle. Not that Robert troubled himself much about wit. If his paragraphs had a sprightly air about them, it was sufficient. He carried this nonchalance so far at last, that a matter of intelligence, and that no very important one, was not seldom palmed upon his employers for a good jest; for example sake —"*Walking yesterday morning casually down Snow Hill, who should we meet but Mr. Deputy Humphreys! we rejoice to add, that the worthy Deputy appeared to enjoy a good state of health. We do not remember ever to have seen him look better.*" This gentleman so surprisingly met upon Snow Hill, from some peculiarities in gait or gesture, was a constant butt for mirth to the small paragraph-mongers of the day; and our friend thought that he might have his fling at him with the rest. We met A. in Holborn shortly after this extraordinary rencounter, which he told with tears of satisfaction in his eyes, and chuckling at the anticipated effects of its announcement next day in the paper. We did not quite comprehend where the wit of it lay at the time; nor was it easy to be detected, when the thing came out advantaged by type and letterpress. He had better have met anything that morning than a Common Council Man. His services were shortly after dispensed with, on the plea that his paragraphs of late had been deficient in point. The one in question, it must be owned, had an air, in the opening especially, proper to awaken curiosity; and the sentiment, or moral, wears the aspect of humanity and good neighbourly feeling. But somehow the conclusion was not judged altogether to answer to the magnificent promise of the premises. We traced our friend's pen afterwards in the True Briton, the Star, the Traveller,—from all which he was successively dismissed, the Proprietors having "no further occasion for his services." Nothing was easier than to detect him. When wit failed, or topics ran low, there constantly appeared the following— "*It is not generally known that the three Blue Balls at the Pawnbrokers' shops are the ancient arms of Lombardy. The Lombards were the first money-brokers in Europe.*" Bob has done more to set the public right on this important point of blazonry, than the whole College of Heralds.

The appointment of a regular wit has long ceased to be a part of the economy of a Morning Paper. Editors find their own jokes, or do as well without them. Parson Este, and Topham, brought up the set custom of "witty paragraphs" first in the World. Boaden was a reigning paragraphist in his day, and succeeded poor Allen in the Oracle. But, as we said, the fashion of jokes passes away; and it would be difficult to discover in the Biographer of Mrs. Siddons, any traces of that vivacity and fancy which charmed the whole town at the commencement of the present century. Even the pre-lusive delicacies of the present writer—the curt "Astræan allusion"—would be thought pedantic and out of date, in these days.

From the office of the Morning Post (for we may as well exhaust our Newspaper Reminiscences at once) by change of property in the paper, we were transferred, mortifying ex-change! to the office of the Albion Newspaper, late Rack-strow's Museum, in Fleet-street. What a transition—from a handsome apartment, from rosewood desks and silver ink-stands, to an office—no office, but a *den* rather, but just re-deemed from the occupation of dead monsters, of which it seemed redolent—from the centre of loyalty and fashion, to a focus of vulgarity and sedition; Here in murky closet, inadequate from its square contents to the receipt of the two bodies of Editor and humble paragraph-maker, together at one time, sat in the discharge of his new Editorial func-tions (the "Bigod" of Elia) the redoubted John Fenwick.

F., without a guinea in his pocket, and having left not many in the pockets of his friends whom he might com-mand, had purchased (on tick, doubtless) the whole and sole Editorship, Proprietorship, with all the rights and titles (such as they were worth) of the Albion from one Lovell; of whom we know nothing, save that he had stood in the pillory for a libel on the Prince of Wales. With this hopeless concern—for it had been sinking ever since its commence-ment, and could now reckon upon not more than a hundred subscribers—F. resolutely determined upon pulling down the

Government in the first instance, and making both our fortunes by way of corollary. For seven weeks and more did this infatuated Democrat go about borrowing seven-shilling pieces, and lesser coin, to meet the daily demands of the Stamp Office, which allowed no credit to publications of that side in politics. An outcast from politer bread, we attached our small talents to the forlorn fortunes of our friend. Our occupation now was to write treason.

Recollections of feelings—which were all that now remained from our first boyish heats kindled by the French Revolution, when if we were misled, we erred in the company of some who are accounted very good men now—rather than any tendency at this time to Republican doctrines—assisted us in assuming a style of writing, while the paper lasted, consonant in no very undertone to the right earnest fanaticism of F. Our cue was now to insinuate, rather than recommend, possible abdications. Blocks, axes, Whitehall tribunals, were covered with flowers of so cunning a periphrasis—as Mr. Bayes says, never naming the *thing* directly—that the keen eye of an Attorney-General was insufficient to detect the lurking snake among them. There were times, indeed, when we sighed for our more gentleman-like occupation under Stuart. But with change of masters it is every change of service. Already one paragraph, and another, as we learned afterwards from a gentleman at the Treasury, had begun to be marked at that office, with a view of its being submitted at least to the attention of the proper Law Officers—when an unlucky, or rather lucky epigram from our pen, aimed at Sir J[ame]s M[ackintos]h, who was on the eve of departing for India to reap the fruits of his apostasy, as F. pronounced it (it is hardly worth particularizing), happening to offend the nice sense of Lord, (or, as he then delighted to be called, Citizen Stanhope), deprived F. at once of the last hopes of a guinea from the last patron that had stuck by us; and breaking up our establishment, left us to the safe, but somewhat mortifying, neglect of the Crown Lawyers.—It was about this time, or a little earlier, that Dan Stuart made that curious confession to us, that he had "never deliberately walked into an Exhibition at Somerset House in his life."

III

LOVER OF THE SIGHTS AND SOUNDS OF "ENCHANTING LONDON"

Lamb's position as a bookkeeper in the East India House kept him and his sister residents of London. During the thirty-three years that Lamb continued in this position, they frequently changed their place of abode in the city. Mary's malady made them undesirable tenants, and we find brother and sister in not less than eleven lodgings between 1796 and 1834. For a time they were settled at 4 Inner Temple Lane, and Talfourd, Lamb's friend and earliest biographer, gives it as his opinion that those years were among the happiest of Lamb's mature years. In a letter to his friend, Manning, then in China, he gives a picture of these lodgings.

LETTER TO MANNING

Jan. 2nd, 1810.

Dear Manning,—When I last wrote to you I was in lodgings. I am now in chambers, No. 4, Inner Temple Lane, where I should be happy to see you any evening. Bring any of your friends, the Mandarins, with you. I have two sitting-rooms: I call them so *par excellence*, for you may stand, or loll, or lean, or try any posture in them, but they are best for sitting; not squatting down Japanese fashion, but the more decorous use of the——which European usage has consecrated. I have two of these rooms on the third floor, and five sleeping, cooking, &c. rooms, on the fourth floor. In my best room is a choice collection of the works of Hogarth, an

English painter of some humour. In my next best are shelves containing a small but well-chosen library. My best room commands a court, in which there are trees and a pump, the water of which is excellent cold, with brandy, and not very insipid without. Here I hope to set up my rest, and not quit till Mr. Powell, the undertaker, gives me notice that I may have possession of my last lodging. He lets lodgings for single gentlemen. I sent you a parcel of books by my last, to give you some idea of the state of European literature. There comes with this two volumes, done up as letters, of minor poetry, a sequel to "Mrs. Leicester;" the best you may suppose mine; the next best are my coadjutor's. You may amuse yourself in guessing them out; but I must tell you mine are but one-third in quantity of the whole. So much for a very delicate subject. It is hard to speak of one's self, &c. Holcroft had finished his life when I wrote to you, and Hazlitt has since finished his life; I do not mean his own life, but he has finished a life of Holcroft, which is going to press. Tuthill is Dr. Tuthill, I continue Mr. Lamb. I have published a little book for children on titles of honour; and to give them some idea of the difference of rank and gradual rising, I have made a little scale, supposing myself to receive the following various accessions of dignity from the king, who is the fountain of honour—As at first, 1, Mr. C. Lamb; 2, C. Lamb, Esq.; 3, Sir C. Lamb, Bart.; 4, Baron Lamb, of Stamford; 5, Viscount Lamb; 6, Earl Lamb; 7, Marquis Lamb; 8, Duke Lamb. It would look like quibbling to carry it on further, and especially as it is not necessary for children to go beyond the ordinary titles of subregal dignity in our own country; otherwise I have sometimes in my dreams imagined myself still advancing, as 9th, King Lamb; 10th, Emperor Lamb; 11th, Pope Innocent; higher than which is nothing upon earth. Puns I have not made many, (nor punch much), since the date of my last; one I cannot help relating. A constable in Salisbury Cathedral was telling me that eight people dined at the top of the spire of the cathedral; upon which I remarked, that they must be very sharp set. But in general I cultivate the reasoning part of my mind more than the imaginative. I am stuffed out so with eating turkey for dinner, and another turkey for supper yesterday, (Turkey in Europe and Turkey in Asia,) that I can't jog on. It is New Year here; that is, it was New Year half a-year back, when I was writing this. Nothing puzzles me more than time and space; and yet nothing puzzles me less, for I never think about them. The Persian ambassador is the principal thing talked of now. I sent some people to see him worship the sun on Primrose Hill, at half-past six in the morning, 28th November; but he did not come, which makes me think the old fire-worshippers are a sect almost extinct in Persia. The Persian ambassador's name is Shaw Ali Mirza. The common people call him Shaw Nonsense. While I think of it, I have put three letters, besides my own three, into the India post for you, from your brother, sister, and some gentleman whose name I forget. Will they, have they, did they come safe? The distance you are at, cuts up tenses by the root. I think you said you did not know Kate * * * * * * * * *. I express her by nine stars, though she is but one. You must have seen her at her father's. Try and remember her. Coleridge is bringing out a paper in weekly Numbers, called the Friend, which I would send if I could; but the difficulty I had in getting the packets of books out to you before, deters me; and you'll want some thing new to read when you come home. It is chiefly intended to puff off Wordsworth's poetry; but there are some noble things in it by the by. Except Kate, I have had no vision of excellence this year, and she passed by like the Queen on her coronation day; you don't know whether you saw her or not. Kate is fifteen: I go about moping, and sing the old pathetic ballad I used to like in my youth—

> "She's sweet fifteen,
> I'm *one year more*."

Mrs. Bland sang it in boy's clothes the first time I heard it. I sometimes think the lower notes in my voice are like Mrs. Bland's. That glorious singer, Braham, one of my lights, is fled. He was for a season. He was a rare composition of the Jew, the gentleman, and the angel; yet all these elements mixed up so kindly in him, that you could not tell which preponderated; but he is gone, and one Phillips is engaged instead. Kate is vanished, but Miss B—— is always to be met with!

> Queens drop away, while blue-legg'd Maukin thrives;
> And courtly Mildred dies while country Madge survives.

That is not my poetry, but Quarles's; but haven't you observed that the rarest things are the least obvious? Don't show any body the names in this letter. I wrote confidentially, and wish this letter to be considered as *private*. Hazlitt has written a *grammar* for Godwin. Godwin sells it bound up with a treatise of his own on language; but the *grey mare is the better horse*. I don't allude to Mrs. [Godwin], but to the word *grammar*, which comes near to *grey mare*, if you observe, in sound. That figure is called paronomasia in Greek. I am sometimes happy in it. An old woman begged of me for charity. "Ah! sir," said she, "I have seen better days." "So have I, good woman," I replied; but I meant, literally, days not so rainy and overcast as that on which she begged: she meant more prosperous days. Mr. Dawe is made associate of the Royal Academy. By what law of association I can't guess, Mrs. Holcroft, Miss Holcroft, Mr. and Mrs. Godwin,

Mr. and Mrs. Hazlitt, Mrs. Martin and Louisa, Mrs. Lum, Capt. Burney, Mrs. Burney, Martin Burney, Mr. Rickman, Mrs. Rickman, Dr. Stoddart, William Dollin, Mr. Thompson, Mr. and Mrs. Norris, Mr. Fenwick, Mrs. Fenwick, Miss Fenwick, a man that saw you at our house one day, and a lady that heard me speak of you; Mrs. Buffam that heard Hazlitt mention you, Dr. Tuthill, Mrs. Tuthill, Colonel Harwood, Mrs. Harwood, Mr. Collier, Mrs. Collier, Mr. Sutton, Nurse, Mr. Fell, Mrs. Fell, Mr. Marshall, are very well, and occasionally inquire after you.

I remain yours ever,

CH. LAMB.

Some glimpses of the life led by Lamb and his sister at 4 Inner Temple Lane may be had from the essay, *Old China*. A more appropriate title might have been the "Pleasures of Moderate Poverty," for, though Lamb's purse was never plethoric, yet his life was full of varied pleasures and interests.

OLD CHINA

I have an almost feminine partiality for old china. When I go to see any great house, I inquire for the china-closet, and next for the picture-gallery. I cannot defend the order of preference, but by saying that we have all some taste or other, of too ancient a date to admit of our remembering distinctly that it was an acquired one. I can call to mind the first play, and the first exhibition, that I was taken to; but I am not conscious of a time when china jars and saucers were introduced into my imagination.

I had no repugnance then—why should I now have?—to those little, lawless, azure-tinctured grotesques, that, under the notion of men and women, float about, uncircumscribed

by any element, in that world before perspective—a china
tea-cup.

I like to see my old friends—whom distance cannot diminish—figuring up in the air (so they appear to our optics),
yet on *terra firma* still—for so we must in courtesy interpret
that speck of deeper blue, which the decorous artist, to prevent absurdity, had made to spring up beneath their sandals.

I love the men with women's faces, and the women, if
possible, with still more womanish expressions.

Here is a young and courtly Mandarin, handing tea to a
lady from a salver—two miles off. See how distance seems to
set off respect! And here the same lady, or another—for likeness is identity on tea-cups—is stepping into a little fairy
boat, moored on the hither side of this calm garden river,
with a dainty mincing foot, which in a right angle of inci-
dence (as angles go in our world) must infallibly land her
in the midst of a flowery mead—a furlong off on the other
side of the same strange stream!

Farther on—if far or near can be predicated of their world
—see horses, trees, pagodas, dancing the hays.

Here—a cow and rabbit couchant, and coextensive—so
objects show, seen through the lucid atmosphere of fine
Cathay.

I was pointing out to my cousin last evening, over our
Hyson (which we are old-fashioned enough to drink unmixed still of an afternoon), some of these *speciosa miracula*
upon a set of extraordinary old blue china (a recent purchase) which we were now for the first time using; and could
not help remarking, how favourable circumstances had been
to us of late years, that we could afford to please the eye
sometimes with trifles of this sort—when a passing sentiment
seemed to overshade the brows of my companion. I am quick
at detecting these summer clouds in Bridget.

"I wish the good old times would come again," she said, "when we were not quite so rich. I do not mean that I want to be poor; but there was a middle state"—so she was pleased to ramble on,—"in which I am sure we were a great deal happier. A purchase is but a purchase, now that you have money enough and to spare. Formerly it used to be a triumph. When we coveted a cheap luxury (and, O! how much ado I had to get you to consent in those times!), we were used to have a debate two or three days before, and to weigh the *for* and *against*, and think what we might spare it out of, and what saving we could hit upon, that should be an equivalent. A thing was worth buying then, when we felt the money that we paid for it.

"Do you remember the brown suit, which you made to hang upon you, till all your friends cried shame upon you, it grew so threadbare—and all because of that folio Beaumont and Fletcher, which you dragged home late at night from Barker's in Covent-garden? Do you remember how we eyed it for weeks before we could make up our minds to the purchase, and had not come to a determination till it was near ten o'clock of the Saturday night, when you set off from Islington, fearing you should be too late—and when the old bookseller with some grumbling opened his shop, and by the twinkling taper (for he was setting bedwards) lighted out the relic from his dusty treasures—and when you lugged it home, wishing it were twice as cumbersome—and when you presented it to me—and when we were exploring the perfectness of it (*collating* you called it)—and while I was repairing some of the loose leaves with paste, which your impatience would not suffer to be left till daybreak—was there no pleasure in being a poor man? or can those neat black clothes which you wear now, and are so careful to keep brushed, since we have become rich and finical, give you

half the honest vanity with which you flaunted it about in
that overworn suit—your old corbeau—for four or five
weeks longer than you should have done, to pacify your
conscience for the mighty sum of fifteen—or sixteen shillings was it?—a great affair we thought it then—which you
had lavished on the old folio. Now you can afford to buy
any book that pleases you, but I do not see that you ever
bring me home any nice old purchases now.

"When you came home with twenty apologies for laying
out a less number of shillings upon that print after Lionardo,
which we christened the 'Lady Blanch;' when you looked at
the purchase, and thought of the money—and thought of the
money, and looked again at the picture—was there no pleasure in being a poor man? Now, you have nothing to do but
to walk into Colnaghi's, and buy a wilderness of Lionardos.
Yet do you?

"Then, do you remember our pleasant walks to Enfield,
and Potter's bar, and Waltham, when we had a holyday—
holydays and all other fun are gone now we are rich—and
the little handbasket in which I used to deposit our day's
fare of savoury cold lamb and salad—and how you would pry
about at noontide for some decent house, where we might go
in and produce our store—only paying for the ale that you
must call for—and speculate upon the looks of the landlady,
and whether she was likely to allow us a tablecloth—and
wish for such another honest hostess as Izaak Walton has
described many a one on the pleasant banks of the Lea,
when he went a fishing—and sometimes they would prove
obliging enough, and sometimes they would look grudgingly
upon us—but we had cheerful looks still for one another, and
would eat our plain food savourily, scarcely grudging Piscator
his Trout Hall? Now—when we go out for a day's pleasuring, which is seldom, moreover, we *ride* part of the way

and go into a fine inn, and order the best of dinners, never debating the expense—which, after all, never has half the relish of those chance country snaps, when we were at the mercy of uncertain usage, and a precarious welcome.

"You are too proud to see a play anywhere now but in the pit. Do you remember where it was we used to sit, when we saw the battle of Hexham, and the Surrender of Calais, and Bannister and Mrs. Bland in the Children in the Wood—when we squeezed out our shillings apiece to sit three or four times in a season in the one-shilling gallery—where you felt all the time that you ought not to have brought me—and more strongly I felt obligation to you for having brought me—and the pleasure was the better for a little shame—and when the curtain drew up, what cared we for our place in the house, or what mattered it where we were sitting, when our thoughts were with Rosalind in Arden, or with Viola at the Court of Illyria? You used to say that the gallery was the best place of all for enjoying a play socially—that the relish of such exhibitions must be in proportion to the infrequency of going—that the company we met there, not being in general readers of plays, were obliged to attend the more, and did attend, to what was going on, on the stage—because a word lost would have been a chasm, which it was impossible for them to fill up. With such reflections we consoled our pride then—and I appeal to you whether, as a woman, I met generally with less attention and accommodation than I have done since in more expensive situations in the house? The getting in, indeed, and the crowding up those inconvenient staircases, was bad enough,—but there was still a law of civility to woman recognized to quite as great an extent as we ever found in the other passages—and how a little difficulty overcome heightened the snug seat, and the play, afterwards! Now we can only pay our money, and walk in. You cannot see, you say, in the galleries now. I am sure we saw, and heard too, well enough then—but sight, and all, I think, is gone with our poverty.

"There was pleasure in eating strawberries, before they became quite common—in the first dish of peas, while they were yet dear—to have them for a nice supper, a treat. What treat can we have now? If we were to treat ourselves now—that is, to have dainties a little above our means, it would be selfish and wicked. It is the very little more that we allow ourselves beyond what the actual poor can get at, that makes what I call a treat—when two people living together, as we have done, now and then indulge themselves in a cheap luxury, which both like; while each apologizes, and is willing to take both halves of the blame to his single share. I see no harm in people making much of themselves in that sense of the word. It may give them a hint how to make much of others. But now—what I mean by the word—we never *do* make much of ourselves. None but the poor can do it. I do not mean the veriest poor of all, but persons as we were, just above poverty.

"I know what you were going to say, that it is mighty pleasant at the end of the year to make all meet,—and much ado we used to have every Thirty-first Night of December to account for our exceedings—many a long face did you make over your puzzled accounts, and in contriving to make it out how we had spent so much—or that we had not spent so much—or that it was impossible we should spend so much next year—and still we found our slender capital decreasing —but then, betwixt ways, and projects, and compromises of one sort or another, and talk of curtailing this charge, and doing without that for the future—and the hopes that youth brings, and laughing spirits (in which you were never poor till now), we pocketed up our loss, and in conclusion, with 'lusty brimmers' (as you used to quote it out of *hearty, cheerful Mr. Cotton,* as you called him), we used to welcome in the 'coming guest.' Now we have no reckoning at all at the end of the old year—no flattering promises about the new year doing better for us."

Bridget is so sparing of her speech on most occasions, that when she gets into a rhetorical vein, I am careful how I interrupt it. I could not help, however, smiling at the phantom of wealth which her dear imagination had conjured up out of a clear income of poor———hundred pounds a year. "It is true we were happier when we were poorer, but we were also younger, my cousin. I am afraid we must put up with the excess, for if we were to shake the superflux into the sea, we should not much mend ourselves. That we had much to struggle with, as we grew up together, we have reason to be most thankful. It strengthened and knit our compact closer. We could never have been what we have been to each other, if we had always had the sufficiency which you now complain of. The resisting power—those natural dilations of the youthful spirit, which circumstances cannot straiten— with us are long since passed away. Competence to age is supplementary youth, a sorry supplement indeed, but I fear the best that is to be had. We must ride, where we formerly walked: live better, and lie softer—and shall be wise to do so —than we had means to do in those good old days you speak of. Yet could those days return—could you and I once more walk our thirty miles a day—could Bannister and Mrs. Bland again be young, and you and I be young to see them— could the good old one-shilling gallery days return—they are dreams, my cousin, now—but could you and I at this moment, instead of this quiet argument, by our well-carpeted fireside, sitting on this luxurious sofa—be once more struggling up those inconvenient staircases, pushed about, and squeezed, and elbowed by the poorest rabble of poor gallery scramblers—could I once more hear those anxious shrieks of yours—and the delicious *Thank God, we are safe,* which always followed when the topmost stair, conquered, let in the first light of the whole cheerful theatre down beneath us— I know not the fathom line that ever touched a descent so deep as I would be willing to bury more wealth in than Crœsus had, or the great Jew R[othschild] is supposed to have, to purchase it. And now do just look at that merry little Chinese waiter holding an umbrella, big enough for a bed-tester, over the head of that pretty insipid half-Madonna-ish chit of a lady in that very blue summer-house.

The rooms at 4 Inner Temple Lane were the scene of the famous "Wednesday Evenings," when Lamb and his sister kept open house. Not only did many of the more prominent writers of the time, such as Wordsworth, Southey, Hazlitt and Leigh Hunt attend these gatherings, but there came also a number of less worthy associates in whose company Lamb sometimes fell from his better self. After there had been eating, drinking, smoking and talking, the evenings usually ended with Lamb "very smoky and drinky." The temptation to take more wine than was good for him was very strong, for wine unloosed his stammering tongue and enabled him to talk freely, eloquently and gloriously, in fact. The spirit of these gatherings is well shown in the following note of invitation sent to Manning a short time before he left for China.

LETTER TO MANNING

[Undated, 1805 (?)]

Dear Manning,—Certainly you could not have called at all hours from two till ten, for we have been only out of an evening Monday and Tuesday in this week. But if you think you have, your thought shall go for the deed. We did pray for you on Wednesday night. Oysters unusually luscious; pearls of extraordinary magnitude found in them. I have made bracelets of them; given them in clusters to ladies. Last night we went out in despite, because you were not come at your hour.

This night we shall be at home; so shall we certainly, both, on Sunday, Monday, Tuesday, and Wednesday. Take your choice, mind I don't say of one: but choose which evening you will not come, and come the other four. Doors open at five o'clock. Shells forced about nine. Every gentleman smokes or not as he pleases.   C. L.

Lamb was the type of man who lived most happily and contentedly among the activity and variety of city life. After any one of his trips away, he returned to thorough satisfaction and content among the sights and sounds of what he called "Enchanting London." His feeling for the city and its life is given strongly enough in the two letters that follow:

LETTER TO WORDSWORTH

Jan. 30th, 1801.

I ought before this to have replied to your very kind invitation into Cumberland. With you and your sister I could gang anywhere; but I am afraid whether I shall ever be able to afford so desperate a journey. Separate from the pleasure of your company, I don't much care if I never see a mountain in my life. I have passed all my days in London, until I have formed as many and intense local attachments as any of you mountaineers can have done with dead Nature. The lighted shops of the Strand and Fleet Street; the innumerable trades, tradesmen, and customers, coaches, waggons, playhouses; all the bustle and wickedness round about

Covent Garden; the very women of the Town; the watch-men, drunken scenes, rattles; life awake, if you awake, at all hours of the night; the impossibility of being dull in Fleet Street; the crowds, the very dirt and mud, the sun shining upon houses and pavements, the print-shops, the old book-stalls, parsons cheapening books, coffee-houses, steams of soups from kitchens, the pantomimes—London it-self a pantomime and a masquerade—all these things work themselves into my mind, and feed me, without a power of satiating me. The wonder of these sights impels me into night-walks about her crowded streets, and I often shed tears in the motley Strand from fulness of joy at so much life. All these emotions must be strange to you; so are your rural emotions to me. But consider, what must I have been doing all my life, not to have lent great portions of my heart with usury to such scenes?

My attachments are all local, purely local. I have no passion (or have had none since I was in love, and then it was the spurious engendering of poetry and books,) for groves and valleys. The rooms where I was born, the furni-ture which has been before my eyes all my life, a book-case which has followed me about like a faithful dog, (only ex-ceeding him in knowledge,) wherever I have moved, old chairs, old tables, streets, squares, where I have sunned my-self, my old school,—these are my mistresses. Have I not enough, without your mountains? I do not envy you. I should pity you, did I not know that the mind will make friends of any thing. Your sun, and moon, and skies, and hills, and lakes, affect me no more, or scarcely come to me in more venerable characters, than as a gilded room with tapestry and tapers, where I might live with handsome visible objects. I consider the clouds above me but as a roof beautifully painted, but unable to satisfy the mind: and at last, like the pictures of the apartment of a connoisseur, unable to afford him any longer a pleasure. So fading upon me, from disuse, have been the beauties of Nature, as they have been confinedly called; so ever fresh, and green, and warm are all the inventions of men, and assemblies of men in this great city. I should certainly have laughed with dear Joanna.

Give my kindest love, and my sister's, to D. and yourself; and a kiss from me to little Barbara Lewthwaite. Thank you for liking my play.   C. L.

LETTER TO MANNING

London, September 24, 1802.

My dear Manning—Since the date of my last letter I have been a traveller. A strong desire seized me of visiting remote regions. My first impulse was to go and see Paris. It was a trivial objection to my aspiring mind, that I did not understand a word of the language, since I certainly intend some time in my life to see Paris, and equally certainly intend never to learn the language; therefore that could be no objection. However, I am very glad I did not go, because you had left Paris (I see) before I could have set out. I believe, Stoddart promising to go with me another year, prevented that plan. My next scheme (for to my restless, ambitious mind London was become a bed of thorns) was to visit the far-famed peak in Derbyshire, where the Devil sits, they say, without breeches. *This* my purer mind rejected as indelicate. And my final resolve was, a tour to the Lakes. I set out with Mary to Keswick, without giving Coleridge any notice, for my time, being precious, did not admit of it. He received us with all the hospitality in the world, and gave up his time to show us all the wonders of the country. He dwells upon a small hill by the side of Keswick, in a comfortable house, quite enveloped on all sides by a net of mountains: great floundering bears and monsters they seemed, all couchant and asleep. We got in in the evening, travelling in a post-chaise from Penrith, in the midst of a gorgeous sunshine, which transmuted all the mountains into colours, purple, etc. etc. We thought we had got into fairyland. But that went off (as it never came again; while we stayed we had no more fine sunsets), and we entered Coleridge's comfortable study just in the dusk, when the mountains were all dark with clouds upon their heads. Such an impression I never received from objects of sight before, nor do I suppose I can ever again. Glorious creatures, fine old fellows, Skiddaw, etc. I never shall forget ye, how ye lay about that night, like an intrenchment; gone to bed, as it seemed for the night, but promising that ye were to be seen in the morning. Coleridge had got a blazing fire in his study; which is a large antique, ill-shaped room, with an old-fashioned organ, never played upon, big enough for a church, shelves of scattered folios, an Æolian harp, and an old sofa, half bed, etc. And all looking out upon the last fading view of Skiddaw, and his broad-breasted brethren: what a night! Here we stayed three full weeks, in which time I visited Wordsworth's cottage, where we stayed a day or two with the Clarksons (good people, and most hospitable, at whose house we tarried one day and night), and saw Lloyd. The Wordsworths were gone to Calais. They have since been in London, and past much time with us: he is now gone into Yorkshire to be married. So we have seen Keswick, Grasmere, Ambleside, Ulswater (where the Clarksons live), and a place at the other end of Ulswater; I forget the name; to which we travelled on a very sultry day, over the middle of Helvellyn. We have clambered up to the top of Skiddaw, and I have waded up the bed of Lodore. In fine, I have satisfied myself that there is such a thing as that which tourists call *romantic*, which I very much suspected before: they make such a spluttering about it, and toss their splendid epithets around them, till they give as dim a light as at four o'clock next morning the lamps do after an illumination. Mary was excessively tired when she got about half-way up Skiddaw, but we came to a cold rill (than which nothing can be imagined more cold, running over cold stones), and with the reinforcement of a draught of cold water she surmounted it most manfully. Oh, its fine black head, and the bleak air atop of it, with a prospect of mountains all about and about, making you giddy; and then Scotland afar off, and the border countries so famous in song and ballad! It was a day that will stand out like a mountain, I am sure, in my life.

But I am returned (I have now been come home near three weeks; I was a month out), and you cannot conceive the degradation I felt at first, from being accustomed to wander free as air among mountains, and bathe in rivers without being controlled by any one, to come home and *work*. I felt very *little*. I had been dreaming I was a very great man. But that is going off, and I find I shall conform in time to that state of life to which it has pleased God to call me. Besides, after all, Fleet Street and the Strand are better places to live in for good and all than amidst Skiddaw. Still I turn back to those great places where I wandered about, participating in their greatness. After all, I could not *live* in Skiddaw. I could spend a year, two, three years among them, but I must have a prospect of seeing Fleet Street at the end of that time, or I should mope and pine away, I know. Still, Skiddaw is a fine creature.

My habits are changing, I think, *i. e.* from drunk to sober.

Whether I shall be happier or not remains to be proved. I shall certainly be more happy in a morning; but whether I shall not sacrifice the fat, and the marrow, and the kidneys, *i. e.* the night, glorious care-drowning night, that heals all our wrongs, pours wine into our mortifications, changes the scene from indifferent and flat to bright and brilliant! O Manning, if I should have formed a diabolical resolution, by the time you come to England, of not admitting any spirituous liquors into my house, will you be my guest on such shameworthy terms? Is life, with such limitations, worth trying? The truth is, that my liquors bring a nest of friendly harpies about my house, who consume me. This is a pitiful tale to be read at St. Gothard, but it is just now nearest my heart. Fenwick is a ruined man. He is hiding himself from his creditors, and has sent his wife and children into the country. Fell, my other drunken companion (that has been: *nam hic cæstus artemque repono*), is turned editor of a Naval Chronicle. Godwin, with a pitiful artificial wife, continues a steady friend, though the same facility does not remain of visiting him often. That . . . has detached Marshall from his house; Marshall, the man who went to sleep when the "Ancient Mariner" was reading; the old, steady, unalterable friend of the Professor. Holcroft is not yet come to town. I expect to see him, and will deliver your message. Things come crowding in to say, and no room for 'em. Some things are too little to be told,—*i. e.* to have a preference; some are too big and circumstantial. Thanks for yours, which was most delicious. Would I had been with you, benighted, etc.! I fear my head is turned with wandering. I shall never be the same acquiescent being. Farewell. Write again quickly, for I shall not like to hazard a letter, not knowing where the fates have carried you. Farewell, my dear fellow.   C. LAMB.

Several of Lamb's most delightful essays grew out of his interest in what was going on about him in the city. They were eminently "things seen" compositions. His tender heart went out toward the little chimney-sweepers, boys condemned to a life of hardship and danger. He also noticed the very beggars along the street and if one of them disappeared he felt that something was gone from the city.

THE PRAISE OF CHIMNEY-SWEEPERS

I like to meet a sweep—understand me—not a grown sweeper—old chimney-sweepers are by no means attractive —but one of those tender novices, blooming through their first nigritude, the maternal washings not quite effaced from the cheek—such as come forth with the dawn, or somewhat earlier, with their little professional notes sounding like the *peep-peep* of a young sparrow; or liker to the matin lark should I pronounce them, in their aërial ascents not seldom anticipating the sun-rise?

I have a kindly yearning towards these dim specks—poor blots—innocent blacknesses—

I reverence these young Africans of our own growth— these almost clergy imps, who sport their cloth without assumption; and from their little pulpits (the tops of chimneys), in the nipping air of a December morning, preach a lesson of patience to mankind.

When a child, what a mysterious pleasure it was to witness their operation! to see a chit no bigger than one's self enter, one knew not by what process, into what seemed the *fauces Averni*—to pursue him in imagination, as he went sounding on through so many dark stifling caverns, horrid shades! to shudder with the idea that "now, surely he must be lost for ever!"—to revive at hearing his feeble shout of discovered daylight—and then (O fulness of delight!) run-

ning out of doors, to come just in time to see the sable
phenomenon emerge in safety, the brandished weapon of his
art victorious like some flag waved over a conquered citadel!
I seem to remember having been told, that a bad sweep was
once left in a stack with his brush, to indicate which way the
wind blew. It was an awful spectacle, certainly; not much
unlike the old stage direction in Macbeth, where the "Apparition of a child crowned, with a tree in his hand,
rises."

Reader, if thou meetest one of these small gentry in thy
early rambles, it is good to give him a penny,—it is better
to give him two-pence. If it be starving weather, and to the
proper troubles of his hard occupation, a pair of kibed heels
(no unusual accompaniment) be superadded, the demand on
thy humanity will surely rise to a tester.

There is a composition, the groundwork of which I have
understood to be the sweet wood yclept sassafras. This wood
boiled down to a kind of tea, and tempered with an infusion of milk and sugar, hath to some tastes a delicacy
beyond the China luxury. I know not how thy palate may
relish it; for myself, with every deference to the judicious
Mr. Read, who hath time out of mind kept open a shop
(the only one he avers in London) for the vending of this
"wholesome and pleasant beverage," on the south side of
Fleet-street, as thou approachest Bridge-street—*the only
Salopian house;*—I have never yet adventured to dip my
own particular lip in a basin of his commended ingredients
—a cautious premonition to the olfactories constantly whispering to me, that my stomach must infallibly, with all
due courtesy, decline it. Yet I have seen palates, otherwise
not uninstructed in dietetical elegancies, sup it up with
avidity.

I know not by what particular conformation of the organ

it happens, but I have always found that this composition is surprisingly gratifying to the palate of a young chimney-sweeper—whether the oily particles (sassafras is slightly oleaginous) do attenuate and soften the fuliginous concretions, which are sometimes found (in dissections) to adhere to the roof of the mouth in these unfledged practitioners; or whether Nature, sensible that she had mingled too much of bitter wood in the lot of these raw victims, caused to grow out of the earth her sassafras for a sweet lenitive—but so it is, that no possible taste or odour to the senses of a young chimney-sweeper can convey a delicate excitement comparable to this mixture. Being penniless, they will yet hang their black heads over the ascending steam, to gratify one sense if possible, seemingly no less pleased than those domestic animals—cats—when they purr over a new-found sprig of valerian. There is something more in these sympathies than philosophy can inculcate.

Now albeit Mr. Read boasteth, not without reason, that his is the *only Salopian house*; yet be it known to thee, Reader—if thou are one who keepest what are called good hours, thou art haply ignorant of the fact—he hath a race of industrious imitators, who from stalls, and under open sky, dispense the same savoury mess to humbler customers, at that dead time of the dawn, when (as extremes meet) the rake, reeling home from his midnight cups, and the hard-handed artisan leaving his bed to resume the premature labours of the day, jostle, not unfrequently to the manifest disconcerting of the former, for the honours of the pavement. It is the time when, in summer, between the expired and the not yet relumined kitchen-fires, the kennels of our fair metropolis give forth their least satisfactory odours. The rake, who wisheth to dissipate his o'ernight vapours in more grateful coffee, curses the ungenial fume, as he passeth;

but the artisan stops to taste, and blesses the fragrant breakfast.

This is *Saloop*—the precocious herb-woman's darling—the delight of the early gardener, who transports his smoking cabbages by break of day from Hammersmith to Covent Garden's famed piazzas—the delight, and oh! I fear, too often the envy, of the unpennied sweep. Him shouldst thou haply encounter, with his dim visage pendent over the grateful steam, regale him with a sumptuous basin (it will cost thee but three-halfpennies) and a slice of delicate bread and butter (an added halfpenny)—so may thy culinary fires, eased of the o'ercharged secretions from thy worse-placed hospitalities, curl up a lighter volume to the welkin—so may the descending soot never taint thy costly well-ingredienced soups—nor the odious cry, quick-reaching from street to street, of the *fired chimney*, invite the rattling engines from ten adjacent parishes, to disturb for a casual scintillation thy peace and pocket!

I am by nature extremely susceptible of street affronts; the jeers and taunts of the populace; the low-bred triumph they display over the casual trip, or splashed stocking, of a gentleman. Yet can I endure the jocularity of a young sweep with something more than forgiveness.—In the last winter but one, pacing along Cheapside with my accustomed precipitation when I walk westward, a treacherous slide brought me upon my back in an instant. I scrambled up with pain and shame enough—yet outwardly trying to face it down, as if nothing had happened—when the roguish grin of one of these young wits encountered me. There he stood, pointing me out with his dusky finger to the mob, and to a poor woman (I suppose his mother) in particular, till the tears for the exquisiteness of the fun (so he thought) worked themselves out the corners of his poor red eyes, red from many a previous weeping, and soot-inflamed, yet twinkling through all with such a joy, snatched out of desolation, that Hogarth——but Hogarth has got him already (how could he miss him?) in the March to Finchley, grinning at the pie-man—there he stood, as he stands in the picture, irremovable, as if the jest was to last for ever—with such a maximum of glee, and minimum of mischief, in his mirth—for the grin of a genuine sweep hath absolutely no malice in it—that I could have been content, if the honour of a gentleman might endure it, to have remained his butt and his mockery till midnight.

I am by theory obdurate to the seductiveness of what are called a fine set of teeth. Every pair of rosy lips (the ladies must pardon me) is a casket presumably holding such jewels; but, methinks, they should take leave to "air" them as frugally as possible. The fine lady, or fine gentleman, who show me their teeth, show me bones. Yet must I confess, that from the mouth of a true sweep a display (even to ostentation) of those white and shiny ossifications, strikes me as an agreeable anomaly in manners, and an allowable piece of foppery. It is, as when

A sable cloud
Turns forth her silver lining on the night.

It is like some remnant of gentry not quite extinct; a badge of better days; a hint of nobility:—and, doubtless, under the obscuring darkness and double night of their forlorn disguisement, oftentimes lurketh good blood and gentle conditions, derived from lost ancestry, and a lapsed pedigree. The premature apprenticements of these tender victims give but too much encouragement, I fear, to clandestine and almost infantile abductions; the seeds of civility and true courtesy, so often discernible in these young grafts (not otherwise to be accounted for) plainly hint at some forced adoptions; many noble Rachels mourning for their children, even in our days, countenance the fact; the tales of fairy-spiriting may shadow a lamentable verity, and the recovery of the young Montagu be but a solitary instance of good fortune out of many irreparable and hopeless *defiliations*.

In one of the state-beds at Arundel Castle, a few years since—under a ducal canopy—(that seat of the Howards is an object of curiosity to visitors, chiefly for its beds, in which the late duke was especially a connoisseur)—encircled with curtains of delicatest crimson, with starry coronets inwoven—folded between a pair of sheets whiter and softer than the lap where Venus lulled Ascanius—was discovered by chance, after all methods of search had failed, at noonday, fast asleep, a lost chimney-sweeper. The little creature, having somehow confounded his passage among the intricacies of those lordly chimneys, by some unknown aperture had alighted upon this magnificent chamber; and, tired with his tedious explorations, was unable to resist the delicious invitement to repose, which he there saw exhibited; so, creeping between the sheets very quietly, laid his black head upon the pillow, and slept like a young Howard.

Such is the account given to the visitors at the Castle.—But I cannot help seeming to perceive a confirmation of what I had just hinted at in this story. O high instinct was at work in the case, or I am mistaken. Is it probable that a poor child of that description, with whatever weariness he might be visited, would have ventured, under such a penalty as he would be taught to expect, to uncover the sheets of a Duke's bed, and deliberately to lay himself down between them, when the rug, or the carpet, presented an obvious couch, still far above his pretensions—is this probable, I would ask, if the great power of nature, which I contend for, had not been manifested within him, prompting to the adventure? Doubtless this young nobleman (for such my mind misgives me that he must be) was allured by some memory, not amounting to full consciousness, of his condition in infancy, when he was used to be lapped by his mother, or his nurse, in just such sheets as he there found, into which he was now but creeping back as into his proper *incunabula*, and resting-place.—By no other theory than by this sentiment of a pre-existent state (as I may call it), can I explain a deed so venturous, and, indeed, upon any other system, so indecorous, in this tender, but unseasonable, sleeper.

My pleasant friend Jem White was so impressed with a belief of metamorphoses like this frequently taking place, that in some sort to reverse the wrongs of fortune in these poor changelings, he instituted an annual feast of chimney-sweepers, at which it was his pleasure to officiate as host and waiter. It was a solemn supper held in Smithfield, upon the yearly return of the fair of St. Bartholomew. Cards were issued a week before to the master-sweeps in and about the metropolis, confining the invitation to their younger fry. Now and then an elderly stripling would get in among us, and be good-naturedly winked at; but our main body were infantry. One unfortunate wight, indeed, who, relying upon his dusky suit, had intruded himself into our party, but by tokens was providentially discovered in time to be no chimney-sweeper, (all is not soot which looks so,) was quoited out of the presence with universal indignation, as not having on the wedding garment; but in general the greatest harmony prevailed. The place chosen was a convenient spot among the pens, at the north side of the fair, not so far distant as to be impervious to the agreeable hubbub of that vanity; but remote enough not to be obvious

to the interruption of every gaping spectator in it. The
guests assembled about seven. In those little temporary parlours three tables were spread with napery, not so fine as
substantial, and at every board a comely hostess presided
with her pan of hissing sausages. The nostrils of the young
rogues dilated at the savour. James White, as head waiter,
had charge of the first table; and myself, with our trusty
companion Bigod, ordinarily ministered to the other two.
There was clambering and jostling, you may be sure, who
should get at the first table,—for Rochester in his maddest
days could not have done the humours of the scene with
more spirit than my friend. After some general expression
of thanks for the honour the company had done him, his
inaugural ceremony was to clasp the greasy waist of old dame
Ursula (the fattest of the three), that stood frying and
fretting, half-blessing, half-cursing "the gentleman," and
imprint upon her chaste lips a tender salute, whereat the
universal host would set up a shout that tore the concave,
while hundreds of grinning teeth startled the night with
their brightness. O it was a pleasure to see the sable younkers
lick in the unctuous meat, with *his* more unctuous sayings—
how he would fit the *tit-bits* to the puny mouths, reserving
the lengthier links for the seniors—how he would intercept
a morsel even in the jaws of some young desperado, declaring it "must to the pan again to be browned, for it was
not fit for a gentleman's eating"—how he would recommend
this slice of white bread, or that piece of kissing-crust, to a
tender juvenile, advising them all to have a care of cracking
their teeth, which were their best patrimony,—how gen-
teelly he would deal about the small ale, as if it were wine,
naming the brewer, and protesting, if it were not good, he
should lose their custom; with a special recommendation to
wipe the lip before drinking. Then we had our toasts—"the

King"—"the Cloth,"—which, whether they understood or not, was equally diverting and flattering;—and for a crowning sentiment, which never failed, "May the Brush supersede the Laurel!" All these, and fifty other fancies, which were rather felt than comprehended by his guests, would he utter, standing upon tables, and prefacing every sentiment with a "Gentlemen, give me the leave to propose so and so," which was a prodigious comfort to those young orphans; every now and then stuffing into his mouth (for it did not do to be squeamish on these occasions) indiscriminate pieces of those reeking sausages, which pleased them mightily, and was the savouriest part, you may believe, of the entertainment.

> Golden lads and lasses must,
> As chimney-sweepers, come to dust—

James White is extinct, and with him these suppers have long ceased. He carried away with him half the fun of the world when he died—of my world at least. His old clients look for him among the pens; and, missing him, reproach the altered feast of St. Bartholomew, and the glory of Smithfield departed for ever.

A COMPLAINT OF THE DECAY OF BEGGARS IN THE METROPOLIS

The all-sweeping besom of societarian reformation—your only modern Alcides' club to rid the time of its abuses—is uplift with many-handed sway to extirpate the last fluttering tatters of the bugbear MENDICITY from the metropolis. Scrips, wallets, bags—staves, dogs, and crutches—the whole mendicant fraternity, with all their baggage, are fast posting out of the purlieus of this eleventh persecution. From the crowded crossing, from the corners of streets and turnings of alleys, the parting Genius of Beggary is "with sighing sent."

I do not approve of this wholesale going to work, this impertinent crusado, or *bellum ad exterminationem*, proclaimed against a species. Much good might be sucked from these Beggars.

They were the oldest and the honourablest form of pauperism. Their appeals were to our common nature; less revolting to an ingenuous mind than to be a suppliant to the particular humours or caprice of any fellow-creature, or set of fellow-creatures, parochial or societarian. Theirs were the only rates uninvidious in the levy, ungrudged in the assessment.

There was a dignity springing from the very depth of their desolation; as to be naked is to be so much nearer to the being a man, than to go in livery.

The greatest spirits have felt this in their reverses; and when Dionysius from king turned schoolmaster, do we feel anything towards him but contempt? Could Vandyke have made a picture of him, swaying a ferula for a sceptre, which would have affected our minds with the same heroic pity, the same compassionate admiration, with which we regard his Belisarius begging for an *obolus*? Would the moral have been more graceful, more pathetic?

The Blind Beggar in the legend—the father of pretty Bessy—whose story doggerel rhymes and ale-house signs cannot so degrade or attenuate but that some sparks of a lustrous spirit will shine through the disguisements—this noble Earl of Cornwall (as indeed he was) and memorable sport of fortune, fleeing from the unjust sentence of his liege lord, stript of all, and seated on the flowering green of Bethnal, with his more fresh and springing daughter by his side, illumining his rags and his beggary—would the child and parent have cut a better figure doing the honours of a counter, or expiating their fallen condition upon the three-foot eminence of some sempstering shop-board?

In tale or history your Beggar is ever the just antipode to your King. The poets and romancical writers (as dear Margaret Newcastle would call them), when they would most sharply and feelingly paint a reverse of fortune, never stop till they have brought down their hero in good earnest to rags and the wallet. The depth of the descent illustrates the height he falls from. There is no medium which can be presented to the imagination without offence. There is no breaking the fall. Lear, thrown from his palace, must divest him of his garments, till he answer "mere nature;" and Cresseid, fallen from a prince's love, must extend her pale arms, pale with other whiteness than of beauty, supplicating lazar arms with bell and clap-dish.

The Lucian wits knew this very well; and, with a converse policy, when they would express scorn of greatness without the pity, they show us an Alexander in the shades cobbling shoes, or a Semiramis getting up foul linen.

How would it sound in song, that a great monarch had declined his affections upon the daughter of a baker! yet do we feel the imagination at all violated when we read the "true ballad," where King Cophetua woos the beggar maid?

Pauperism, pauper, poor man, are expressions of pity, but pity alloyed with contempt. No one properly contemns a Beggar. Poverty is a comparative thing, and each degree of it is mocked by its "neighbour grice." Its poor rents and comings-in are soon summed up and told. Its pretences to property are almost ludicrous. Its pitiful attempts to save excite a smile. Every scornful companion can weigh his trifle-bigger purse against it. Poor man reproaches poor man in the streets with impolitic mention of his condition, his own being a shade better, while the rich pass by and jeer at both. No rascally comparative insults a Beggar, or thinks of weighing purses with him. He is not in the scale of comparison. He is not under the measure of property. He confessedly hath none, any more than a dog or a sheep. No one twitteth him with ostentation above his means. No one accuses him of pride, or upbraideth him with mock humility. None jostle with him for the wall, or pick quarrels for precedency. No wealthy neighbour seeketh to eject him from his tenement. No man sues him. No man goes to law with him. If I were not the independent gentleman that I am, rather than I would be a retainer to the great, a led captain, or a poor relation, I would choose, out of the delicacy and true greatness of my mind, to be a Beggar.

Rags, which are the reproach of poverty, are the Beggar's robes, and graceful *insignia* of his profession, his tenure, his full dress, the suit in which he is expected to show himself in public. He is never out of the fashion, or limpeth awkwardly behind it. He is not required to put on court mourning. He weareth all colours, fearing none. His costume hath undergone less change than the Quaker's. He is the only man in the universe who is not obliged to study appearances. The ups and downs of the world concern him no longer. He alone continueth in one stay. The price of stock or land affecteth him not. The fluctuations of agricultural or commercial prosperity touch him not, or at worst but change his customers. He is not expected to become bail or surety for any one. No man troubleth him with questioning his religion or politics. He is the only free man in the universe.

The Mendicants of this great city were so many of her sights, her lions. I can no more spare them than I could the Cries of London. No corner of a street is complete without them. They are as indispensable as the Ballad Singer; and in their picturesque attire as ornamental as the signs of old London. They were the standing morals, emblems, mementoes, dial-mottoes, the spital sermons, the books for children, the salutary checks and pauses to the high and rushing tide of greasy citizenry—

> ————Look
> Upon that poor and broken bankrupt there.

Above all, those old blind Tobits that used to line the wall of Lincoln's Inn Garden, before modern fastidiousness had expelled them, casting up their ruined orbs to catch a ray of pity, and (if possible) of light, with their faithful Dog Guide at their feet,—whither are they fled? or into what corners, blind as themselves, have they been driven, out of the wholesome air and sun-warmth? immersed between four walls, in what withering poor-house do they endure the penalty of double darkness, where the chink of the dropt halfpenny no more consoles their forlorn bereavement, far from the sound of the cheerful and hope-stirring tread of the passenger? Where hang their useless staves? and who will farm their dogs?—Have the overseers of St. L—caused them to be shot? or were they tied up in sacks and dropt into the Thames, at the suggestion of B—, the mild rector of——?

Well fare the soul of unfastidious Vincent Bourne, most classical, and, at the same time, most English of the Latinists! —who has treated of this human and quadrupedal alliance, this dog and man friendship, in the sweetest of his poems, the *Epitaphium in Canem,* or *Dog's Epitaph.* Reader, peruse it; and say, if customary sights, which could call up such gentle poetry as this, were of a nature to do more harm or good to the moral sense of the passengers through the daily thoroughfares of a vast and busy metropolis.

Pauperis hic Iri requiesco Lyciscus, herilis,
Dum vixi, tutela vigil columenque senectæ,
Dux cæco fidus: nec, me ducente, solebat,
Prætenso hinc atque hinc baculo, per iniqua locorum
Incertam explorare viam; sed fila secutus,
Quæ dubios regerent passûs, vestigia tuta
Fixit inoffenso gressu; gelidumque sedile
In nudo nactus saxo, quâ prætereuntium
Unda frequens confluxit, ibi miserisque tenebras
Lamentis, noctemque oculis ploravit obortam.
Ploravit nec frustra; obolum dedit alter et alter,
Queis corda et mentem indiderat natura benignam.
Ad latus interea jacui sopitus herile,
Vel mediis vigil in somnis; ad herilia jussa
Auresque atque animum arrectus; seu frustula amicè
Porrexit sociasque dapes, seu longa diei
Tædia perpessus, reditum sub nocte parabat.
    Hi mores, hæc vita fuit, dum fata sinebant,
Dum neque languebam morbis, nec inerte senectâ
Quæ tandem obrepsit, veterique satellite cæcum
Orbavit dominum; prisci sed gratia facti
Ne tota intereat, longos deleta per annos,
Exiguum hunc Irus tumulum de cespite fecit,
Etsi inopis, non ingratæ, munuscula dextræ;
Carmine signavitque brevi, dominumque canemque,
Quod memoret, fidumque canem dominumque benignum.

Poor Irus' faithful wolf-dog here I lie,
That wont to tend my old blind master's steps,
His guide and guard; nor, while my service lasted,
Had he occasion for that staff, with which
He now goes picking out his path in fear
Over the highways and crossings; but would plant,
Safe in the conduct of my friendly string,
A firm foot forward still, till he had reach'd
His poor seat on some stone, nigh where the tide
Of passers-by in thickest confluence flow'd:
To whom with loud and passionate laments
From morn to eve his dark estate he wail'd.
Nor wail'd to all in vain: some here and there,
The well-disposed and good, their pennies gave.
I meantime at his feet obsequious slept;
Not all-asleep in sleep, but heart and ear

Prick'd up at his least motion; to receive
At his kind hand my customary crumbs,
And common portion in his feast of scraps;
Or when night warn'd us homeward, tired and spent
With our long day and tedious beggary.
　　These were my manners, this my way of life,
Till age and slow disease me overtook,
And sever'd from my sightless master's side.
But lest the grace of so good deeds should die,
Through tract of years in mute oblivion lost,
This slender tomb of turf hath Irus reared,
Cheap monument of no ungrudging hand,
And with short verse inscribed it, to attest,
In long and lasting union to attest,
The virtues of the Beggar and his Dog.

These dim eyes have in vain explored for some months past a well-known figure, or part of the figure, of a man, who used to glide his comely upper half over the pavements of London, wheeling along with most ingenious celerity upon a machine of wood; a spectacle to natives, to foreigners, and to children. He was of a robust make, with a florid sailor-like complexion, and his head was bare to the storm and sunshine. He was a natural curiosity, a speculation to the scientific, a prodigy to the simple. The infant would stare at the mighty man brought down to his own level. The common cripple would despise his own pusillanimity, viewing the hale stoutness, and hearty heart, of this half-limbed giant. Few but must have noticed him; for the accident which brought him low, took place during the riots of 1780, and he has been a groundling so long. He seemed earth-born, an Antæus, and to suck in fresh vigour from the soil which he neighboured. He was a grand fragment; as good as an Elgin marble. The nature, which should have recruited his reft legs and thighs, was not lost, but only retired into his upper parts, and he was half a Hercules. I heard a tremendous voice thundering and growling, as before an earthquake, and casting down my eyes, it was this mandrake reviling a steed that had started at his portentous appearance. He seemed to want but his just stature to have rent the offending quadruped in shivers. He was as the man-part of a Centaur, from which the horse-half had been cloven in some dire Lapithan controversy. He moved on, as if he could have made shift with yet half of the body-portion which was left him. The *os sublime* was not wanting; and he threw out yet a jolly countenance upon the heavens. Forty-and-two years had he driven this out-of-door trade, and now that his hair is grizzled in the service, but his good spirits no way impaired, because he is not content to exchange his free air and exercise for the restraints of a poor-house, he is expiating his contumacy in one of those houses (ironically christened) of Correction.

Was a daily spectacle like this to be deemed a nuisance, which called for legal interference to remove? or not rather a salutary and a touching object to the passers-by in a great city? Among her shows, her museums, and supplies for ever-gaping curiosity (and what else but an accumulation of sights—endless sights—*is* a great city; or for what else is it desirable?) was there not room for one *Lusus* (not *Naturæ,* indeed, but) *Accidentium?* What if in forty-and-two-years going about, the man had scraped together enough to give a portion to his child (as the rumour ran) of a few hundreds —whom had he injured?—whom had he imposed upon? The contributors had enjoyed their *sight* for their pennies. What if after being exposed all day to the heats, the rains, and the frosts of heaven—shuffling his ungainly trunk along in an elaborate and painful motion—he was enabled to retire at night to enjoy himself at a club of his fellow cripples over a dish of hot meat and vegetables, as the charge was gravely brought against him by a clergyman deposing before a House of Commons' Committee—was *this*, or was his truly paternal consideration, which (if a fact) deserved a statue rather than a whipping-post, and is inconsistent, at least, with the exaggeration of nocturnal orgies which he has been slandered with—a reason that he should be deprived of his chosen, harmless, nay, edifying, way of life, and be committed in hoary age for a sturdy vagabond?—

There was a Yorick once, whom it would not have shamed to have sate down at the cripples' feast, and to have thrown in his benediction, ay, and his mite too, for a companionable symbol. "Age, thou hast lost thy breed."—

Half of these stories about the prodigious fortunes made by begging are (I verily believe) misers' calumnies. One was much talked of in the public papers some time since, and the usual charitable inferences deduced. A clerk in the Bank was surprised with the announcement of a five-hundred-pound legacy left him by a person whose name he was a stranger to. It seems that in his daily morning walks from Peckham (or some village thereabouts) where he lived, to his office, it has been his practice for the last twenty years to drop his halfpenny duly into the hat of some blind Bartimeus, that sate begging alms by the wayside in the Borough. The good old beggar recognised his daily benefactor by the voice only; and, when he died, left all the amassings of his alms (that had been half a century perhaps in the accumulating) to his old Bank friend. Was this a story to purse up people's hearts, and pennies, against giving an alms to the blind?—or not rather a beautiful moral of well-directed charity on the one part, and noble gratitude upon the other?

I sometimes wish I had been that Bank clerk.

I seem to remember a poor old grateful kind of creature, blinking, and looking up with his no eyes in the sun—

Is it possible I could have steeled my purse against him? Perhaps I had no small change.

Reader, do not be frightened at the hard words imposition, imposture—*give, and ask no questions*. Cast thy bread upon the waters. Some have unawares (like this Bank clerk) entertained angels.

Shut not thy purse-strings always against painted distress. Act a charity sometimes. When a poor creature (outwardly and visibly such) comes before thee, do not stay to inquire whether the "seven small children," in whose name he implores thy assistance, have a veritable existence. Rake not into the bowels of unwelcome truth, to save a halfpenny. It is good to believe him. If he be not all that he pretendeth, *give,* and under a personate father of a family, think (if thou pleasest) that thou hast relieved an indigent bachelor. When they come with their counterfeit looks and mumping tones, think them players. You pay your money to see a comedian feign these things, which, concerning these poor people, thou canst not certainly tell whether they are feigned or not.

Lamb especially liked the theater. His living in the city gave him an opportunity to gratify his taste for playgoing. The essays *On Some of the Old Actors* could never have been written if he had not been all his life an enthusiastic attendant on plays.

ON SOME OF THE OLD ACTORS

The casual sight of an old Play Bill, which I picked up the other day—I know not by what chance it was preserved so long—tempts me to call to mind a few of the Players, who make the principal figure in it. It presents the cast of parts in the Twelfth-Night, at the old Drury-lane Theatre two-

and-thirty years ago. There is something very touching in these old remembrances. They make us think how we *once* used to read a Play Bill—not, as now peradventure, singling out a favourite performer, and casting a negligent eye over the rest; but spelling out every name, down to the very mutes and servants of the scene; when it was a matter of no small moment to us whether Whitfield, or Packer, took the part of Fabian; when Benson, and Burton, and Phillimore—names of small account—had an importance, beyond what we can be content to attribute now to the time's best actors.—"Orsino, by Mr. Barrymore."—What a full Shakspearian sound it carries! how fresh to memory arise the image and the manner of the gentle actor!

Those who have only seen Mrs. Jordan within the last ten or fifteen years, can have no adequate notion of her performance of such parts as Ophelia; Helena, in All's Well that Ends Well; and Viola, in this play. Her voice had latterly acquired a coarseness, which suited well enough with her Nells and Hoydens, but in those days it sank, with her steady, melting eye, into the heart. Her joyous parts—in which her memory now chiefly lives—in her youth were outdone by her plaintive ones. There is no giving an account how she delivered the disguised story of her love for Orsino. It was no set speech, that she had foreseen, so as to weave it into an harmonious period, line necessarily following line, to make up the music—yet I have heard it so spoken, or rather *read*, not without its grace and beauty—but, when she had declared her sister's history to be a "blank," and that she "never told her love," there was a pause, as if the story had ended—and then the image of the "worm in the bud" came up as a new suggestion—and the heightened image of "Patience" still followed after that as by some growing (and not mechanical) process, thought springing up after thought,

I would almost say, as they were watered by her tears. So in those fine lines

> Write loyal cantons of contemned love—
> Halloo your name to the reverberate hills—

there was no preparation made in the foregoing image for that which was to follow. She used no rhetoric in her passion; or it was nature's own rhetoric, most legitimate then, when it seemed altogether without rule or law.

Mrs. Powel (now Mrs. Renard), then in the pride of her beauty, made an admirable Olivia. She was particularly excellent in her unbending scenes in conversation with the Clown. I have seen some Olivias—and those very sensible actresses too—who in these interlocutions have seemed to set their wits at the jester, and to vie conceits with him in downright emulation. But she used him for her sport, like what he was, to trifle a leisure sentence or two with, and then to be dismissed, and she to be the Great Lady still. She touched the imperious fantastic humour of the character with nicety. Her fine spacious person filled the scene.

The part of Malvolio has, in my judgment, been so often misunderstood, and the *general merits* of the actor, who then played it, so unduly appreciated, that I shall hope for pardon, if I am a little prolix upon these points.

Of all the actors who flourished in my time—a melancholy phrase if taken aright, Reader—Bensley had most of the swell of soul, was greatest in the delivery of heroic conceptions, the emotions consequent upon the presentment of a great idea to the fancy. He had the true poetical enthusiasm —the rarest faculty among players. None that I remember possessed even a portion of that fine madness which he threw out in Hotspur's famous rant about glory, or the transports of the Venetian incendiary at the vision of the fired city. His voice had the dissonance, and at times the inspiriting effect of the trumpet. His gait was uncouth and stiff, but no way embarrassed by affectation; and the thorough-bred gentleman was uppermost in every movement. He seized the moment of passion with the greatest truth; like a faithful clock, never striking before the time; never anticipating or leading you to anticipate. He was totally destitute of trick and artifice. He seemed come upon the stage to do the poet's message simply, and he did it with as genuine fidelity as the nuncios in Homer deliver the errands of the gods. He let the passion or the sentiment do its own work without prop or bolstering. He would have scored to mountebank it; and betrayed none of that *cleverness* which is the bane of serious acting. For this reason, his Iago was the only endurable one which I remember to have seen. No spectator from his action could divine more of his artifice than Othello was supposed to do. His confessions in soliloquy alone put you in possession of the mystery. There were no by-intimations to make the audience fancy their own discernment so much greater than that of the Moor—who commonly stands like a great helpless mark set up for mine Ancient, and a quantity of barren spectators, to shoot their bolts at. The Iago of Bensley did not go to work so grossly. There was a triumphant tone about the character, natural to a general consciousness of power; but none of that petty vanity which chuckles and cannot contain itself upon any little successful stroke of its knavery—as is common with your small villains, and green probationers in mischief. It did not clap or crow before its time. It was not a man setting his wits at a child, and winking all the while at other children, who are mightily pleased at being let into the secret; but a consummate villain entrapping a noble nature into toils against which no discernment was available, where the manner was as fathomless as the purpose seemed dark, and without motive. The part of Malvolio, in the Twelfth Night, was performed by Bensley with a richness and a dignity, of which (to judge from some recent castings of that character) the very tradition must be worn out from the stage. No manager in those days would have dreamed of giving it to Mr. Baddely, or Mr. Parsons; when Bensley was occasionally absent from the theatre, John Kemble, thought it no derogation to succeed to the part. Malvolio is not essentially ludicrous. He becomes comic but by accident. He is cold, austere, repelling; but dignified, consistent, and, for what appears, rather of an over-stretched morality. Maria describes him as a sort of Puritan; and he might have worn his gold chain with honour in one or our old roundhead families, in the service of a Lambert, or a Lady Fairfax. But his morality and his manners are misplaced in Illyria. He is opposed to the proper *levities* of the piece, and falls in the unequal contest. Still his pride, or his gravity (call it which you will), is inherent, and native to the man, not mock or affected, which latter only are the fit objects to excite laughter. His quality is at the best unlovely, but neither buffoon nor contemptible. His bearing is lofty, a little above his station, but probably not much above his deserts. We see no reason why he should not have been brave, honourable, accomplished. His careless committal of the ring to the ground (which he was commissioned to restore to Cesario), bespeaks a generosity of birth and feeling. His dialect on all occasions is that of a gentleman, and a man of education. We must not confound him with the eternal old, low steward of comedy. He is master of the household to a great Princess; a dignity probably conferred upon him for other respects than age or length of service. Olivia, at the first indication of his supposed madness, declares that she "would not have him mis-

carry for half of her dowry." Does this look as if the
character was meant to appear little or insignificant? Once,
indeed, she accuses him to his face—of what?—of being
"sick of self-love,"—but with a gentleness and considerate-
ness which could not have been, if she had not thought that
this particular infirmity shaded some virtues. His rebuke to
the knight and his sottish revellers, is sensible and spirited;
and when we take into consideration the unprotected condition of his mistress, and the strict regard with which her state
of real or dissembled mourning would draw the eyes of the
world upon her house-affairs, Malvolio might feel the honour
of the family in some sort in his keeping; as it appears not
that Olivia had any more brothers, or kinsmen, to look to
it—for Sir Toby had dropped all such nice respects at the
buttery-hatch. That Malvolio was meant to be represented
as possessing estimable qualities, the expression of the Duke,
in his anxiety to have him reconciled, almost infers: "Pursue
him, and entreat him to a peace." Even in his abused state
of chains and darkness, a sort of greatness seems never to
desert him. He argues highly and well with the supposed Sir
Topas, and philosophizes gallantly upon his straw. There
must have been some shadow of worth about the man; he
must have been something more than a mere vapour—a
thing of straw, or Jack in office—before Fabian and Maria
could have ventured sending him upon a courting-errand
to Olivia. There was some consonancy (as he would say) in
the undertaking, or the jest would have been too bold even
for that house of misrule.

Bensley, accordingly, threw over the part an air of Spanish loftiness. He looked, spake, and moved like an old
Castilian. He was starch, spruce, opinionated, but his super-
structure of pride seemed bottomed upon a sense of worth.
There was something in it beyond the coxcomb. It was big

and swelling, but you could not be sure that it was hollow.
You might wish to see it taken down, but you felt that it
was upon an elevation. He was magnificent from the outset;
but when the decent sobrieties of the character began to
give way, and the poison of self-love, in his conceit of the
Countess's affection, gradually to work, you would have
thought that the hero of La Mancha in person stood before
you. How he went smiling to himself! with what ineffable
carelessness would he twirl his gold chain! what a dream it
was! you were infected with the illusion, and did not wish
that it should be removed! you had no room for laughter!
if an unseasonable reflection of morality obtruded itself, it
was a deep sense of the pitiable infirmity of man's nature,
that can lay him open to such frenzies—but in truth you
rather admired than pitied the lunacy while it lasted—you
felt that an hour of such mistake was worth an age with
the eyes open. Who would not wish to live but for a day in
the conceit of such a lady's love as Olivia? Why, the Duke
would have given his principality but for a quarter of a
minute, sleeping or waking, to have been so deluded. The
man seemed to tread upon air, to taste manna, to walk with
his head in the clouds, to mate Hyperion. O! shake not the
castles of his pride—endure yet for a season, bright moments
of confidence—"stand still, yet watches of the element,"
that Malvolio may be still in fancy fair Olivia's lord!—but
fate and retribution say no—I hear the michievous titter of
Maria—the witty taunts of Sir Toby—the still more insup-
portable triumph of the foolish knight—the counterfeit Sir
Topas is unmasked—and "thus the whirligig of time," as the
true clown hath it, "brings in his revenges." I confess that I
never saw the catastrophe of this character, while Bensley
played it, without a kind of tragic interest. There was good
foolery too. Few now remember Dodd. What an Aguecheek

the stage lost in him! Lovegrove, who came nearest to the old actors, revived the character some few seasons ago, and made it sufficiently grotesque; but Dodd was *it,* as it came out of nature's hands. It might be said to remain *in puris naturalibus.* In expressing slowness of apprehension, this actor surpassed all others. You could see the first dawn of an idea stealing slowly over his countenance, climbing up by little and little, with a painful process, till it cleared up at last to the fulness of a twilight conception—its highest meridian. He seemed to keep back his intellect, as some have had the power to retard their pulsation. The balloon takes less time in filling than it took to cover the expansion of his broad moony face over all its quarters with expression. A glimmer of understanding would appear in a corner of his eye, and for lack of fuel go out again. A part of his forehead would catch a little intelligence, and be a long time in communicating it to the remainder.

I am ill at dates, but I think it is now better than five-and-twenty years ago, that walking in the gardens of Gray's Inn—they were then far finer than they are now—the accursed Verulam Buildings had not encroached upon all the east side of them, cutting out delicate green crankles, and shouldering away one or two of the stately alcoves of the terrace—the survivor stands gaping and relationless as if it remembered its brother—they are still the best gardens of any of the Inns of Court, my beloved Temple not forgotten—have the gravest character, their aspect being altogether reverend and law-breathing—Bacon has left the impress of his foot upon their gravel walks—taking my afternoon solace on a summer day upon the aforesaid terrace, a comely sad personage came towards me, whom, from his grave air and deportment, I judged to be one of the old Benchers of the Inn. He had a serious, thoughtful forehead, and seemed to be in meditations of mortality. As I have an instinctive awe of old Benchers, I was passing him with that sort of sub-indicative token of respect which one is apt to demonstrate towards a venerable stranger, and which rather denotes an inclination to greet him, than any positive motion of the body to that effect—a species of humility and will-worship which I observe, nine times out of ten, rather puzzles than pleases the person it is offered to—when the face turning full upon me strangely identified itself with that of Dodd. Upon close inspection I was not mistaken. But could this sad thoughtful countenance be the same vacant face of folly which I had hailed so often under circumstances of gaiety; which I had never seen without a smile, or recognised but as the usher of mirth; that looked out so formally flat in Foppington, so frothily pert in Tattle, so impotently busy in Backbite; so blankly divested of all meaning, or resolutely expressive of none, in Acres, in Fribble, and a thousand agreeable impertinences? Was this the face—full of thought and carefulness—that had so often divested itself at will of every trace of either to give me diversion, to clear my cloudy face for two or three hours at least of its furrows! Was this the face—manly, sober, intelligent— which I had so often despised, made mocks at, made merry with! The remembrance of the freedoms which I had taken with it came upon me with a reproach of insult. I could have asked it pardon. I thought it looked upon me with a sense of injury. There is something strange as well as sad in seeing actors—your pleasant fellows particularly—subjected to and suffering the common lot;—their fortunes, their casualties, their deaths, seem to belong to the scene, their actions to be amenable to poetic justice only. We can hardly connect them with more awful responsibilities. The death of this fine actor took place shortly after this meeting. He had quitted the stage some months; and, as I learned afterwards, had been in the habit of resorting daily to these gardens almost to the day of his decease. In these serious walks, probably, he was divesting himself of many scenic and some real vanities —weaning himself from the frivolities of the lesser and the greater theatre—doing gentle penance for a life of no very reprehensible fooleries,—taking off by degrees the buffoon mask which he might feel he had worn too long—and rehearsing for a more solemn cast of part. Dying, he "put on the weeds of Dominic.

If few can remember Dodd, many yet living will not easily forget the pleasant creature, who in those days enacted the part of the Clown to Dodd's Sir Andrew.—Richard, or rather Dicky, Suett—for so in his life-time he delighted to be called, and time hath ratified the appellation—lieth buried on the north side of the cemetery of Holy Paul, to whose service his nonage and tender years were dedicated. There are who do yet remember him at that period—his pipe clear and harmonious. He would often speak of his chorister days, when he was "cherub Dicky."

What clipped his wings, or made it expedient that he should exchange the holy for the profane state; whether he had lost his good voice (his best recommendation to that office), like Sir John, "with hallooing and singing of anthems;" or whether he was adjudged to lack something, even in those early years, of the gravity indispensable to an occupation which professeth to "commerce with the skies," —I could never rightly learn; but we find him, after the probation of a twelvemonth or so, reverting to a secular condition, and become one of us.

I think he was not altogether of that timber out of which cathedral seats and sounding-boards are hewed. But if a glad heart—kind and therefore glad—be any part of sanctity, then might the robe of Motley, with which he invested himself with so much humility after his deprivation, and which he wore so long with so much blameless satisfaction to himself and to the public, be accepted for a surplice—his white stole, and *albe*.

The first fruits of his secularization was an engagement upon the boards of Old Drury, at which theatre he commenced, as I have been told, with adopting the manner of Parsons in old men's characters. At the period in which most of us knew him, he was no more an imitator than he was in any true sense himself imitable.

He was the Robin Goodfellow of the stage. He came in to trouble all things with a welcome perplexity, himself no whit troubled for the matter. He was known, like Puck, by his note—*Ha! Ha! Ha!*—sometimes deepening to *Ho! Ho! Ho!* with an irresistible accession, derived perhaps remotely from his ecclesiastical education, foreign to his prototype of *O La!* Thousands of hearts yet respond to the chuckling *O La!* of Dicky Suett, brought back to their remembrance by the faithful transcript of his friend Mathew's mimicry. The "force of nature could no further go." He drolled upon the stock of these two syllables richer than the cuckoo.

Care, that troubles all the world, was forgotten in his composition. Had he had but two grains (nay, half a grain) of it, he could never have supported himself upon those two spider's strings, which served him (in the latter part of his unmixed existence) as legs. A doubt or a scruple must have made him totter, a sigh have puffed him down; the weight of a frown had staggered him, a wrinkle made him lose his balance. But on he went, scrambling upon those airy stilts of his, with Robin Goodfellow, "thorough brake, thorough briar," reckless of a scratched face or a torn doublet.

Shakspeare foresaw him, when he framed his fools and jesters. They have all the true Suett stamp, a loose and shambling gait, a slippery tongue, this last the ready mid-wife to a without-pain-delivered jest; in words, light as air, venting truths deep as the centre; with idlest rhymes tagging conceit when busiest, singing with Lear in the tempest, or Sir Toby at the buttery-hatch.

Jack Bannister and he had the fortune to be more of personal favourites with the town than any actors before or after. The difference, I take it, was this:—Jack was more *beloved* for his sweet, good-natured, moral pretensions. Dicky was more *liked* for his sweet, good-natured, no pretensions at all. Your whole conscience stirred with Bannister's performance of Walter in the Children in the Wood— but Dicky seemed like a thing, as Shakspeare says of Love, too young to know what conscience is. He put us into Vesta's days. Evil fled before him—not as from Jack, as from an antagonist,—but because it could not touch him, any more than a cannon-ball a fly. He was delivered from the burthen of that death; and, when Death came himself, not in meta-phor, to fetch Dicky, it is recorded of him by Robert Palmer, who kindly watched his exit, that he received the last stroke, neither varying his accustomed tranquillity, nor tune, with the simple exclamation, worthy to have been recorded in his epitaph—*O La! O La! Bobby!*

The elder Palmer (of stage-trading celebrity) commonly played Sir Toby in those days; but there is a solidity of wit in the jests of that half-Falstaff which he did not quite fill out. He was as much too showy as Moody (who sometimes took the part) was dry and sottish. In sock or buskin there was an air of swaggering gentility about Jack Palmer. He was a *gentleman* with a slight infusion of *the footman*. His brother Bob (of recenter memory), who was his shadow in everything while he lived, and dwindled into less than a shadow afterwards—was a *gentleman* with a little stronger infusion of the *latter ingredient;* that was all. It is amazing how a little of the more or less makes a difference in these things. When you saw Bobby in the Duke's Servant, you said, what a pity such a pretty fellow was only a servant! When you saw Jack figuring in Captain Absolute, you thought you could trace his promotion to some lady of quality who fancied the handsome fellow in his topknot, and had bought him a commission. Therefore Jack in Dick Amlet was insuperable.

Jack had two voices,—both plausible, hypocritical, and insinuating; but his secondary or supplemental voice still more decisively histrionic than his common one. It was reserved for the spectator; and the *dramatis personæ* were supposed to know nothing at all about it. The *lies* of Young Wilding, and the *sentiments* in Joseph Surface, were thus marked out in a sort of italics to the audience. This secret correspondence with the company before the curtain (which is the bane and death of tragedy) has an extremely happy effect in some kinds of comedy, in the more highly artificial comedy of Congreve or of Sheridan especially, where the absolute sense of reality (so indispensable to scenes of interest) is not required, or would rather interfere to diminish your pleasure. The fact is, you do not believe in such characters as Surface—the villain of artificial comedy—even while you read or see them. If you did, they would shock and not divert you. When Ben, in Love for Love, returns from sea, the following exquisite dialogue occurs at his first meeting with his father:—

Sir Sampson. Thou hast been many a weary league, Ben, since I saw thee.
Ben. Ey, ey, been. Been far enough, an that be all.—Well, father, and how do all at home? how does brother Dick and brother Val?

Sir Sampson. Dick! body o' me, Dick has been dead these two years. I writ you word when you were at Leghorn.

Ben. Mess, that's true; Marry, I had forgot. Dick's dead, as you say—Well, and how?—I have a many questions to ask you.

Here is an instance of insensibility which in real life would be revolting, or rather in real life could not have co-existed with the warm-heated temperament of the character. But when you read it in the spirit with which such playful selections and specious combinations rather than strict *metaphrases* of nature should be taken, or when you saw Bannister play it, it neither did, nor does, wound the moral sense at all. For what is Ben—the pleasant sailor which Bannister gives us—but a piece of satire—a creation of Congreve's fancy—a dreamy combination of all the accidents of a sailor's character—his contempt of money—his credulity to women—with that necessary estrangement from home which it is just within the verge of credibility to suppose *might* produce such an hallucination as is here described. We never think the worst of Ben for it, or feel it as a stain upon his character. But when an actor comes, and instead of the delightful phantom—the creature dear to half-belief—which Bannister exhibited—displays before our eyes a downright concretion of a Wapping sailor—a jolly warm-hearted Jack Tar—and nothing else—when instead of investing it with a delicious confusedness of the head, and a veering undirected goodness of purpose—he gives to it a downright daylight understanding, and a full consciousness of its actions; thrusting forward the sensibilities of the character with a pretence as if it stood upon nothing else, and was to be judged by them alone—we feel the discord of the thing; the scene is disturbed; a real man has got in among the *dramatis personæ,* and puts them out. We want the sailor turned out. We feel that his true place is not behind the curtain but in the first or second gallery.

IV

PREFERENCES AND PREJUDICES

Few writers have had so true a knowledge of their own capacities and limitations as did Charles Lamb. The Preface that he wrote for the volume of *Last Essays of Elia* shows his power to understand himself and to criticize and appraise his own work. Lamb's fondness for mystification leads him to represent this Preface as by "a friend of the late Elia."

PREFACE

BY A FRIEND OF THE LATE ELIA

This poor gentleman, who for some months past had been in a declining way, hath at length paid his final tribute to nature.

To say truth, it is time he were gone. The humour of the thing, if there was ever much in it, was pretty well exhausted; and a two years and a half existence has been a tolerable duration for a phantom.

I am now at liberty to confess, that much which I have heard objected to my late friend's writings was well-founded. Crude they are, I grant you—a sort of unlicked, incondite things—villanously pranked in an affected array of antique modes and phrases. They had not been *his*, if they had been other than such; and better it is, that a writer should be natural in a self-pleasing quaintness, than to affect a naturalness (so called) that should be strange to him. Egotistical they have been pronounced by some who did not know, that what he tells us, as of himself, was often true only (historically) of another; as in a former Essay (to save many instances) where under the *first person* (his favourite figure) he shadows forth the forlorn estate of a country-boy placed at a London school, far from his friends and connections—in direct opposition to his own early history. If it be egotism to imply and twine with his own identity the griefs and affections of another—making himself many, or reducing many unto himself—then is the skilful novelist, who all along brings in his hero, or heroine, speaking of themselves, the greatest egotist of all; who yet has never, therefore, been accused of that narrowness. And how shall the intenser dramatist escape being faulty, who doubtless, under cover of passion uttered by another, oftentimes gives blameless vent to his most inward feelings, and expresses his own story modestly?

My late friend was in many respects a singular character. Those who did not like him, hated him; and some, who once liked him, afterwards became his bitterest haters. The truth is, he gave himself too little concern what he uttered, and in whose presence. He observed neither time nor place, and would e'en out with what came uppermost. With the severe religionist he would pass for a free-thinker; while the other faction set him down for a bigot, or persuaded themselves that he belied his sentiments. Few understood him; and I am not certain that at all times he quite understood himself. He too much affected that dangerous figure—irony. He sowed doubtful speeches, and reaped plain, unequivocal hatred. He would interrupt the gravest discussion with some light jest; and yet, perhaps, not quite irrelevant in ears that could understand it. Your long and much talkers hated him. The informal habit of his mind, joined to an inveterate impediment of speech, forbade him to be an orator;

and he seemed determined that no one else should play that part when he was present. He was *petit* and ordinary in his person and appearance. I have seen him sometimes in what is called good company, but where he has been a stranger, sit silent, and be suspected for an odd fellow; till some unlucky occasion provoking it, he would stutter out some senseless pun (not altogether senseless perhaps, if rightly taken), which has stamped his character for the evening. It was hit or miss with him; but nine times out of ten he contrived by this device to send away a whole company of his enemies. His conceptions rose kindlier than his utterance, and his happiest *impromptus* had the appearance of effort. He has been accused of trying to be witty, when in truth he was but struggling to give his poor thoughts articulation. He chose his companions for some individuality of character which they manifested.—Hence, not many persons of science, and few professed *literati*, were of his councils. They were, for the most part, persons of an uncertain fortune; and, as to such people commonly nothing is more obnoxious than a gentleman of settled (though moderate) income, he passed with most of them for a great miser. To my knowledge this was a mistake. His *intimados*, to confess a truth, were in the world's eye a ragged regiment. He found them floating on the surface of society; and the colour, or something else, in the weed pleased him. The burrs stuck to him— but they were good and loving burrs for all that. He never greatly cared for the society of what are called good people. If any of these were scandalised (and offences were sure to arise), he could not help it. When he has been remonstrated with for not making more concessions to the feelings of good people, he would retort by asking, what one point did these good people ever concede to him? He was temperate in his meals and diversions, but always kept a little on this side of abstemiousness. Only in the use of the Indian weed he might be thought a little excessive. He took it, he would say, as a solvent of speech. Marry—as the friendly vapour ascended, how his prattle would curl up sometimes with it! the ligaments which tongue-tied him were loosened, and the stammerer proceeded a statist.

I do not know whether I ought to bemoan or rejoice that my old friend is departed. His jests were beginning to grow obsolete, and his stories to be found out. He felt the approaches of age; and while he pretended to cling to life, you saw how slender were the ties left to bind him. Discoursing with him latterly on this subject, he expressed himself with a pettishness, which I thought unworthy of him. In our walks about his suburban retreat (as he called it) at Shacklewell, some children belonging to a school of industry had met us, and bowed and curtseyed, as he thought, in an especial manner to *him*. "They take me for a visiting governor," he muttered earnestly. He had a horror, which he carried to a foible, of looking like anything important and parochial. He thought that he approached nearer to that stamp daily. He had a general aversion from being treated like a grave or respectable character, and kept a wary eye upon the advances of age that should so entitle him. He herded always, while it was possible, with people younger than himself. He did not conform to the march of time, but was dragged along in the procession. His manners lagged behind his years. He was too much of the boy-man. The *toga virilis* never sate gracefully on his shoulders. The impressions of infancy had burnt into him, and he resented the impertinence of manhood. These were weaknesses; but such as they were, they are a key to explicate some of his writings.

Lamb has indulged in another bit of self-analysis in the earlier part of the essay *The Old and the New Schoolmaster*. The remainder is suggestive of his ideal of education and his opinion of a certain type of schoolmaster.

THE OLD AND THE NEW SCHOOLMASTER

My reading has been lamentably desultory and immethodical. Odd, out of the way, old English plays, and treatises, have supplied me with most of my notions, and ways of feeling. In everything that relates to *science*, I am a whole Encyclopædia behind the rest of the world. I should have scarcely cut a figure among the franklins, or country gentlemen, in King John's days. I know less geography than a schoolboy of six weeks' standing. To me a map of old Ortelius is as authentic as Arrowsmith. I do not know whereabout Africa merges into Asia; whether Ethiopia lie in one or other of those great divisions; nor can form the remotest conjecture of the position of New South Wales, or Van Diemen's Land. Yet do I hold a correspondence with a very dear friend in the first-named of these two Terræ Incognitæ. I have no astronomy. I do not know where to look for the Bear, or Charles's Wain; the place of any star; or the name of any of them at sight. I guess at Venus only by her brightness—and if the sun on some portentous morn were to make his first appearance in the West, I verily believe, that, while all the world were gasping in apprehension about me, I alone should stand unterrified, from sheer incuriosity and want of observation. Of history and chronology I possess some vague points, such as one cannot help picking up in the course of miscellaneous study; but I never deliberately sat down to a chronicle, even of my own country. I have most dim apprehensions of the four great monarchies; and sometimes the

Assyrian, sometimes the Persian, floats as *first* in my fancy. I make the widest conjectures concerning Egypt, and her shepherd kings. My friend M[anning], with great painstaking, got me to think I understood the first proposition in Euclid, but gave me over in despair at the second. I am entirely unacquainted with the modern languages; and, like a better man than myself, have "small Latin and less Greek." I am a stranger to the shapes and texture of the commonest trees, herbs, flowers—not from the circumstance of my being town-born—for I should have brought the same inobservant spirit into the world with me, had I first seen it "on Devon's leafy shores,"—and am no less at a loss among purely town objects, tools, engines, mechanic processes.—Not that I affect ignorance—but my head has not many mansions, nor spacious; and I have been obliged to fill it with such cabinet curiosities as it can hold without aching. I sometimes wonder how I have passed my probation with so little discredit in the world, as I have done, upon so meagre a stock. But the fact is, a man may do very well with a very little knowledge, and scarce be found out, in mixed company; everybody is so much more ready to produce his own, than to call for a display of your acquisitions. But in a *tête-à-tête* there is no shuffling. The truth will out. There is nothing which I dread so much, as the being left alone for a quarter of an hour with a sensible, well-informed man, that does not know me. I lately got into a dilemma of this sort.—

In one of my daily jaunts between Bishopsgate and Shacklewell, the coach stopped to take up a staid-looking gentleman, about the wrong side of thirty, who was giving his parting directions (while the steps were adjusting), in a tone of mild authority, to a tall youth, who seemed to be neither his clerk, his son, nor his servant, but something partaking of all three. The youth was dismissed, and we drove on. As we were the sole passengers, he naturally enough addressed his conversation to me; and we discussed the merits of the fare; the civility and punctuality of the driver; the circumstance of an opposition coach having been lately set up, with the probabilities of its success—to all which I was enabled to return pretty satisfactory answers, having been drilled into this kind of etiquette by some years' daily practice of riding to and fro in the stage aforesaid—when he suddenly alarmed me by a startling question, whether I had seen the show of prize cattle that morning in Smithfield? Now, as I had not seen it, and do not greatly care for such sort of exhibitions, I was obliged to return a cold negative. He seemed a little mortified, as well as astonished, at my declaration, as (it appeared) he was just come fresh from the sight, and doubtless had hoped to compare notes on the subject. However, he assured me that I had lost a fine treat, as it far exceeded the show of last year. We were now approaching Norton Folgate, when the sight of some shop-goods *ticketed* freshened him up into a dissertation upon the cheapness of cottons this spring. I was now a little in heart, as the nature of my morning avocations had brought me into some sort of familiarity with the raw material; and I was surprised to find how eloquent I was becoming on the state of the India market—when, presently, he dashed my incipient vanity to the earth at once, by inquiring whether I had ever made any calculation as to the value of the rental of all the retail shops in London. Had he asked of me what song the Sirens sang, or what name Achilles assumed when he hid himself among women, I might, with Sir Thomas Browne, have hazarded a "wide solution." My companion saw my embarrassment, and, the almshouses beyond Shoreditch just coming in view, with great good nature and dexterity shifted his conversation to the subject of public charities; which led to the comparative merits of provision for the poor in past and present times, with observations on the old monastic institutions, and charitable orders;—but, finding me rather dimly impressed with some glimmering notions from old poetic associations, than strongly fortified with any speculations reducible to calculation on the subject, he gave the matter up; and, the country beginning to open more and more upon us, as we approached the turnpike at Kingsland (the destined termination of his journey), he put a home thrust upon me, in the most unfortunate position he could have chosen, by advancing some queries relative to the North Pole Expedition. While I was muttering out something about the Panorama of those strange regions (which I had actually seen), by way of parrying the question, the coach stopping relieved me from any further apprehensions. My companion getting out, left me in the comfortable possession of my ignorance; and I heard him, as he went off, putting questions to an outside passenger, who had alighted with him, regarding an epidemic disorder that had been rife about Dalston, and which, my friend assured him, had gone through five or six schools in that neighbourhood. The truth now flashed upon me, that my companion was a schoolmaster; and that the youth, whom he had parted from at our first acquaintance, must have been one of the bigger boys, or the usher.—He was evidently a kind-hearted man, who did not seem so much desirous of provoking discussion by the questions which he put, as of obtaining information at any rate. It did not appear that he took any interest, either, in such kind of inquiries, for their own sake; but that he was in some way bound to seek for knowledge. A greenish-coloured coat, which he had on, forbade me to surmise that he was a clergyman. The adventure gave birth to some reflections on the difference between persons of his profession in past and present times.

Rest to the souls of those fine old Pedagogues; the breed, long since extinct, of the Lilys, and the Linacres: who believing that all learning was contained in the languages which they taught, and despising every other acquirement as superficial and useless, came to their task as to a sport! Passing from infancy to age, they dreamed away all their days as in a grammar-school. Revolving in a perpetual cycle of declensions, conjugations, syntaxes, and prosodies; renewing constantly the occupations which had charmed their studious childhood; rehearsing continually the part of the past; life must have slipped from them at last like one day. They were always in their first garden, reaping harvests of their golden time, among their *Flori-* and their *Spici-legia;* in Arcadia still, but kings; the ferule of their sway not much harsher, but of like dignity with that mild sceptre attributed to king Basileus, the Greek and Latin, their stately Pamela and their Philoclea; with the occasional duncery of some untoward tyro, serving for a refreshing interlude of a Mopsa, or a clown Damœtas!

With what a savour doth the Preface to Colet's, or (as it is sometimes called) Paul's Accidence, set forth! "To exhort every man to the learning of grammar, that intendeth to attain the understanding of the tongues, wherein is contained a great treasury of wisdom and knowledge, it would seem but vain and lost labour; for so much as it is known, that nothing can surely be ended, whose beginning is either feeble or faulty; and no building be perfect whereas the foundation and groundwork is ready to fall, and unable to uphold the burden of the frame." How well doth this stately preamble (comparable to those which Milton commendeth as "having been the usage to prefix to some solemn law, then first promulgated by Solon or Lycurgus") correspond with and illustrate that pious zeal for conformity, expressed in a succeeding clause, which would fence about grammar-rules with the severity of faith-articles!—"as for the diversity of grammars, it is well profitably taken away by the king's majesties wisdom, who foreseeing the inconvenience, and favourably providing the remedie, caused one kind of grammar by sundry learned men to be diligently drawn, and so to be set out, only everywhere to be taught for the use of learners, and for the hurt in changing of schoolmaisters." What a *gusto* in that which follows: "wherein it is profitable that he (the pupil) can orderly decline his noun and his verb." *His* noun!

The fine dream is fading away fast; and the least concern of a teacher in the present day is to inculcate grammar-rules.

The modern schoolmaster is expected to know a little of everything, because his pupil is required not to be entirely ignorant of anything. He must be superficially, if I may so say, omniscient. He is to know something of pneumatics; of chemistry; of whatever is curious, or proper to excite the attention of the youthful mind; an insight into mechanics is desirable, with a touch of statistics; the quality of soils, etc., botany, the constitution of his country, *cum multis aliis.* You may get a notion of some part of his expected duties by consulting the famous Tractate on Education addressed to Mr. Hartlib.

All these things—these, or the desire of them—he is expected to instil, not by set lessons from professors, which he may charge in the bill, but at school intervals, as he walks the streets, or saunters through green fields (those natural instructors), with his pupils. The least part of what is expected from him is to be done in school-hours. He must insinuate knowledge at the *mollia tempora fandi.* He must seize every occasion—the season of the year—the time of the day—a passing cloud—a rainbow—a waggon of hay—a regiment of soldiers going by—to inculcate something useful. He can receive no pleasure from a casual glimpse of Nature, but must catch at it as an object of instruction. He must interpret beauty into the picturesque. He cannot relish a beggar-man, or a gipsy, for thinking of the suitable improvement. Nothing comes to him, not spoiled by the sophisticating medium of moral uses. The Universe—that Great Book, as it has been called—is to him indeed, to all intents and purposes, a book, out of which he is doomed to read tedious homilies to distasting schoolboys.—Vacations themselves are none to him, he is only rather worse off than before; for commonly he has some intrusive upper-boy fastened upon him at such times; some cadet of a great family; some neglected lump of nobility, or gentry; that he must drag after him to the play, to the Panorama, to Mr. Bartley's Orrery, to the Panopticon, or into the country, to a friend's house, or his favourite watering-place. Wherever he goes, this uneasy shadow attends him. A boy is at his board, and in his path, and in all his movements. He is boy-rid, sick of perpetual boy.

Boys are capital fellows in their own way, among their mates; but they are unwholesome companions for grown people. The restraint is felt no less on the one side than on the other.—Even a child, that "plaything for an hour," tires *always*. The noises of children, playing their own fancies —as I now hearken to them by fits, sporting on the green before my window, while I am engaged in these grave speculations at my neat suburban retreat at Shacklewell—by distance made more sweet—inexpressibly take from the labour of my task. It is like writing to music. They seem to modulate my periods. They ought at least to do so—for in the voice of that tender age there is a kind of poetry, far unlike the harsh prose-accents of man's conversation.—I should not spoil their sport, and diminish my own sympathy for them, by mingling in their pastime.

I would not be domesticated all my days with a person of very superior capacity to my own—not, if I know myself at all, from any considerations of jealousy or self-comparison, for the occasional communion with such minds has constituted the fortune and felicity of my life—but the habit of too constant intercourse with spirits above you, instead of raising you, keeps you down. Too frequent doses of original thinking from others restrain what lesser portion of that faculty you may possess of your own. You get entangled in another man's mind, even as you lose yourself in another man's grounds. You are walking with a tall varlet, whose strides out-pace yours to lassitude. The constant operation of such potent agency would reduce me, I am convinced, to imbecility. You may derive thoughts from others; your way of thinking, the mould in which your thoughts are cast, must be your own. Intellect may be imparted, but not each man's intellectual frame.—

As little as I should wish to be always thus dragged upward, as little (or rather still less) is it desirable to be stunted downwards by your associates. The trumpet does not more stun you by its loudness, than a whisper teases you by its provoking inaudibility.

Why are we never quite at our ease in the presence of a schoolmaster?—because we are conscious that he is not quite at his ease in ours. He is awkward, and out of place in the society of his equals. He comes like Gulliver from among his little people, and he cannot fit the stature of his understanding to yours. He cannot meet you on the square. He wants a point given him, like an indifferent whist-player. He is so used to teaching, that he wants to be teaching *you*. One of these professors, upon my complaining that these little sketches of mine were anything but methodical, and that I was unable to make them otherwise, kindly offered to instruct me in the method by which young gentlemen in *his* seminary were taught to compose English themes. The jests of a schoolmaster are coarse, or thin. They do not *tell* out of school. He is under the restraint of a formal and didactive hypocrisy in company, as a clergyman is under a moral one. He can no more let his intellect loose in society than the other can his inclinations. He is forlorn among his coevals; his juniors cannot be his friends.

"I take blame to myself," said a sensible man of this profession, writing to a friend respecting a youth who had quitted his school abruptly, "that your nephew was not more attached to me. But persons in my situation are more to be pitied than can well be imagined. We are surrounded by young, and, consequently, ardently affectionate hearts, but *we* can never hope to share an atom of their affections. The relation of master and scholar forbids this. *How pleasing this must be to you, how I envy your feelings!* my friends will sometimes say to me, when they see young men whom I have educated, return after some years absence from school, their eyes shining with pleasure, while they shake hands with their old master, bringing a present of game to me, or a toy to my wife, and thanking me in the warmest terms for my care of their education. A holiday is begged for the boys; the house is a scene of happiness; I, only, am sad at heart.—This fine-spirited and warm-hearted youth, who fancies he repays his master with gratitude for the care of his boyish years—this young man—in the eight long years I watched over him with a parent's anxiety, never could repay me with one look of genuine feeling. He was proud, when I praised; he was submissive, when I reproved him; but he did never *love* me—and what he now mistakes for gratitude and kindness for me, is but the pleasant sensation which all persons feel at revisiting the scenes of their boyish hopes and fears; and the seeing on equal terms the man they were accustomed to look up to with reverence. My wife too," this interesting correspondent goes on to say, "my once darling Anna, is the wife of a schoolmaster.—When I married her—knowing that the wife of a schoolmaster ought to be a busy notable creature, and fearing that my gentle Anna would ill supply the loss of my dear bustling mother, just then dead, who never sat still, was in every part of the house in a moment, and whom I was obliged sometimes to threaten to fasten down in a chair, to save her from fatiguing herself to death—I expressed my fears that I was bringing her into a way of life unsuitable to her; and she, who loved me tenderly, promised for my sake to exert herself to perform the duties of her new situation. She promised, and she has kept her word. What wonders will not woman's love perform?—My house is managed with a propriety and decorum unknown in other schools; my boys are well fed, look healthy, and have every proper accommodation; and all this performed with a careful economy, that never descends to meanness. But I have lost my gentle *helpless* Anna! When we sit down to enjoy an hour of repose after the fatigue of the day, I am compelled to listen to what have been her useful (and they are really useful) employments through the day, and what she proposes for her to-morrow's task. Her heart and her features are changed by the duties of her situation. To the boys, she never appears other than the *master's wife*, and she looks up to me as the *boys' master;* to whom all show of love and affection would be highly improper, and unbecoming the dignity of her situation and mine. Yet *this* my gratitude forbids me to hint to her. For my sake she submitted to be this altered creature, and can I reproach her for it?"— For the communication of this letter I am indebted to my cousin Bridget.

The essay *Imperfect Sympathies* had its scope revealed in its original title, *Jews, Quakers, Scotchmen and Other Imperfect Sympathies*. In it Lamb has been frank enough to confess that he was like most mortals in being a curious compound of whimsical likes and dislikes.

IMPERFECT SYMPATHIES

I am of a constitution so general, that it consorts and sympathiseth with all things; I have no antipathy, or rather idiosyncrasy in anything. Those national repugnancies do not touch me, nor do I behold with prejudice the French, Italian, Spaniard, or Dutch.—*Religio Medici.*

That the author of the Religio Medici mounted upon the airy stilts of abstraction, conversant about notional and conjectural essences; in whose categories of Being the possible took the upper hand of the actual; should have overlooked the impertinent individualities of such poor concretions as mankind, is not much to be admired. It is rather to be wondered at, that in the genus of animals he should have condescended to distinguish that species at all. For myself—earth-bound and fettered to the scene of my activities,—

Standing on earth, not rapt above the sky,

I confess that I do feel the differences of mankind, national or individual, to an unhealthy excess. I can look with no indifferent eye upon things or persons. Whatever is, is to me a matter of taste or distaste; or when once it becomes indifferent it begins to be disrelishing. I am, in plainer words, a bundle of prejudices—made up of likings and dislikings—the veriest thrall to sympathies, apathies, antipathies. In a certain sense, I hope it may be said of me that I am a lover of my species. I can feel for all indifferently, but I cannot feel towards all equally. The more purely-English word that expresses sympathy, will better explain my meaning. I can be a friend to a worthy man, who upon another account cannot be my mate or *fellow*. I cannot *like* all people alike.

I have been trying all my life to like Scotchmen, and am obliged to desist from the experiment in despair. They cannot like me—and in truth, I never knew one of that nation who attempted to do it. There is something more plain and ingenuous in their mode of proceeding. We know one another at first sight. There is an order of imperfect intellects (under which mine must be content to rank) which in its constitution is essentially anti-Caledonian. The owners of the sort of of faculties I allude to have minds rather suggestive than comprehensive. They have no pretences to much clearness or precision in their ideas, or in their manner of expressing them. Their intellectual wardrobe (to confess fairly) has few whole pieces in it. They are content with fragments and scattered pieces of Truth. She presents no full front to them—a feature or side-face at the most. Hints and glimpses, germs and crude essays at a system, is the utmost they pretend to. They beat up a little game peradventure—and leave it to knottier heads, more robust constitutions, to run it down. The light that lights them is not steady and polar, but mutable and shifting: waxing, and again waning. Their conversation is accordingly. They will throw out a random word in or out of season, and be content to let it pass for what it is worth. They cannot speak always as if they were upon their oath—but must be understood, speaking or writing, with some abatement. They seldom wait to mature a proposition, but e'en bring it to market in the green ear. They delight to impart their defective discoveries as they arise, without waiting for their full development. They are no systematizers, and would but err more by attempting it. Their minds, as I said before, are suggestive merely. The brain of a true Caledonian (if I am not mistaken) is constituted upon quite a different plan. His Minerva is born in panoply. You are never admitted to see his ideas in their growth—if, indeed, they do grow, and are not rather put together upon principles of clock-work. You never catch his mind in an undress. He never hints or suggests anything, but unlades his stock of ideas in perfect order and completeness. He brings his total wealth into company, and gravely unpacks it. His riches are always about him. He never stoops to catch a glittering something in your presence, to share it with you, before he quite knows whether it be true touch or not. You cannot cry *halves* to anything that he finds. He does not find, but bring. You never witness his first apprehension of a thing. His understanding is always at its meridian—you never see the first dawn, the early streaks.—He has no falterings of self-suspicion. Surmises, guesses, misgivings, half-intuitions, semi-consciousnesses, partial illuminations, dim instincts, embryo conceptions, have no place in his brain or vocabulary. The twilight of dubiety never falls upon him. Is he orthodox—he has no doubts. Is he an infidel—he has none either. Between the affirmative and the negative there is no border-land with him. You cannot hover with him upon the confines of truth, or wander in the maze of a probable argument. He always keeps the path. You cannot make excursions with him—for he sets you right. His taste never fluctuates. His morality never abates. He cannot compromise, or understand middle actions. There can be but a right and a wrong. His conversation is as a book. His affirmations have the sanctity of an oath. You must speak upon the square with him. He stops a metaphor like a suspected person in an enemy's country. "A healthy book!"—said one of his countrymen to me, who had ventured to give that application to John Buncle,—"Did I catch rightly what you said? I have heard of a man in health, and of a healthy state of body, but I do not see how that epithet can be properly applied to a book." Above all, you must beware of indirect expressions before a Caledonian. Clap an extinguisher upon your irony, if you are unhappily blest with a vein of it. Remember you are upon your oath. I have a print of a graceful female after Leonardo da Vinci, which I was showing off to Mr. ———. After he had examined it minutely, I ventured to ask him how he liked MY BEAUTY (a foolish name it goes by among my friends)—when he very gravely assured me, that "he had considerable respect for my character and talents" (so he was pleased to say), "but had not given much thought about the degree of my personal pretensions." The misconception staggered me, but did not seem much to disconcert him.—Persons of this nation are particularly fond of affirming a truth—which nobody doubts. They do not so properly affirm, as annunciate it. They do indeed appear to have such a love of truth (as if, like virtue, it were valuable for itself) that all truth becomes equally valuable, whether the proposition that contains it be new or old, disputed, or such as is impossible to become a subject of disputation. I was present not long since at a party of North Britons, where a son of Burns was expected; and happened to drop a silly expression (in my South British way), that I wished it were the father instead of the son—when four of them started up at once to inform me that "that was impossible, because he was dead." An impracticable wish, it seems, was more than they could conceive. Swift has hit off this part of their character, namely their love of truth, in his biting way, but with an illiberality that necessarily confines the passage to the margin. The tediousness of these people is certainly provoking. I wonder if they ever tire one another!

—In my early life I had a passionate fondness for the poetry of Burns. I have sometimes foolishly hoped to ingratiate myself with his countrymen by expressing it. But I have always found that a true Scot resents your admiration of his compatriot, even more than he would your contempt of him. The latter he imputes to your "imperfect acquaintance with many of the words which he uses;" and the same objection makes it a presumption in you to suppose that you can admire him.—Thomson they seem to have forgotten. Smollett they have neither forgotten nor forgiven, for his delineation of Rory and his companion, upon their first introduction to our metropolis.—Speak of Smollett as a great genius, and they will retort upon you Hume's History compared with *his* Continuation of it. What if the historian had continued Humphrey Clinker?

I have, in the abstract, no disrespect for Jews. They are a piece of stubborn antiquity, compared with which Stonehenge is in its nonage. They date beyond the pyramids. But I should not care to be in habits of familiar intercourse with any of that nation. I confess that I have not the nerves to enter their synagogues. Old prejudices cling about me. I cannot shake off the story of Hugh of Lincoln. Centuries of injury, contempt, and hate, on the one side,—of cloaked revenge, dissimulation, and hate, on the other, between our and their fathers, must and ought to affect the blood of the children. I cannot believe it can run clear and kindly yet; or that a few fine words, such as candour, liberality, the light of a nineteenth century, can close up the breaches of so deadly a disunion. A Hebrew is nowhere congenial to me. He is least distasteful on 'Change—for the mercantile spirit levels all distinctions, as all are beauties in the dark. I boldly confess that I do not relish the approximation of Jew and Christian, which has become so fashionable. The reciprocal endearments have, to me, something hypocritical and unnatural in them. I do not like to see the Church and Synagogue kissing and congeeing in awkward postures of an affected civility. If *they* are converted, why do they not come over to us altogether? Why keep up a form of separation, when the life of it is fled? If they can sit with us at table, why do they keck at our cookery? I do not understand these half convertites. Jews christianizing—Christians judaizing—puzzles me. I like fish or flesh. A moderate Jew is a more confounding piece of anomaly than a wet Quaker. The spirit of the synagogue is essentially *separative*. B[raham] would have been more in keeping if he had abided by the faith of his forefathers. There is a fine scorn in his face, which nature meant to be of——Christians. The Hebrew spirit is strong in him, in spite of his proselytism. He cannot conquer the Shibboleth. How it breaks out when he sings, "The Children of Israel passed through the Red Sea!" The auditors, for the moment, are as Egyptians to him, and he rides over our necks in triumph. There is no mistaking him, B—— has a strong expression of sense in his countenance, and it is confirmed by his singing. The foundation of his vocal excellence is sense. He sings with understanding, as Kemble delivered dialogue. He would sing the Commandments, and give an appropriate character to each prohibition. His nation, in general, have not over-sensible countenances. How should they?—but you seldom see a silly expression among them.—Gain, and the pursuit of gain, sharpens a man's visage. I never heard of an idiot being born among them.—Some admire the Jewish female-physiognomy. I admire it—but with trembling. Jael had those full dark inscrutable eyes.

In the Negro countenance you will often meet with strong traits of benignity. I have felt yearnings of tenderness towards some of these faces—or rather masks—that have looked out kindly upon one in casual encounters in the streets and highways. I love what Fuller beautifully calls—these "images of God cut in ebony." But I should not like to associate with them, to share my meals and my good nights with them—because they are black.

I love Quaker ways, and Quaker worship. I venerate the Quaker principles. It does me good for the rest of the day when I meet any of their people in my path. When I am ruffled or disturbed by any occurrence, the sight, or quiet voice of a Quaker, acts upon me as a ventilator, lightening the air, and taking off a load from the bosom. But I cannot like the Quakers (as Desdemona would say) "to live with them." I am all over sophisticated—with humours, fancies, craving hourly sympathy. I must have books, pictures, the-atres, chit-chat, scandal, jokes, ambiguities, and a thousand whim-whams, which their simpler taste can do without. I should starve at their primitive banquet. My appetites are too high for the salads which (according to Evelyn) Eve dressed for the angel; my gusto too excited

To sit a guest with Daniel at his pulse.

The indirect answers which Quakers are often found to return to a question put to them may be explained, I think, without the vulgar assumption, that they are more given to evasion and equivocating than other people. They naturally look to their words more carefully, and are more cautious of committing themselves. They have a peculiar character to keep up on this head. They stand in a manner upon their veracity. A Quaker is by law exempted from taking an oath. The custom of resorting to an oath in extreme cases, sanctified as it is by all religious antiquity, is apt (it must be confessed) to introduce into the laxer sort of minds the notion of two kinds of truth—the one applicable to the solemn affairs of justice, and the other to the common proceedings of daily intercourse. As truth bound upon the conscience by an oath can be but truth, so in the common affirmations of the shop and the market-place a latitude is expected and conceded upon questions wanting this solemn covenant. Something less than truth satisfies. It is common to hear a person say, "You do not expect me to speak as if I were upon my oath." Hence a great deal of incorrectness and inadvertency, short of falsehood, creeps into ordinary conversation; and a kind of secondary or laic-truth is tolerated, where clergy-truth—oath-truth, by the nature of the circumstances, is not required. A Quaker knows none of this distinction. His simple affirmation being received upon the most sacred occasions, without any further test, stamps a value upon the words which he is to use upon the most indifferent topics of life. He looks to them, naturally, with more severity. You can have of him no more than his word. He knows, if he is caught tripping in a casual expression, he forfeits, for himself at least, his claim to the invidious exemption. He knows that his syllables are weighed—and how far a consciousness of this particular watchfulness, exerted against a person, has a tendency to produce indirect answers, and a diverting of the question by honest means, might be illustrated, and the practice justified, by a more sacred example than is proper to be adduced upon this occasion. The admirable presence of mind, which is notorious in Quakers upon all contingencies, might be traced to this imposed self-watchfulness—if it did not seem rather an humble and secular scion of that old stock of religious constancy, which never bent or faltered, in the Primitive Friends, or gave way to the winds of persecution, to the violence of judge or accuser, under trials and racking examinations. "You will never be the wiser, if I sit here answering your questions till midnight," said one of those upright Justicers to Penn, who had been putting law-cases with a puzzling subtlety. "Thereafter as the answers may be," retorted the Quaker. The astonishing composure of this people is sometimes ludicrously displayed in lighter instances.—I was travelling in a stage-coach with three male Quakers, buttoned up in the straitest nonconformity of their sect. We stopped to bait at Andover, where a meal, partly tea apparatus, partly supper, was set before us. My friends confined themselves to the tea-table. I in my way took supper. When the landlady brought in the bill, the eldest of my companions discovered that she had charged for both meals. This was resisted. Mine hostess was very clamorous and positive. Some mild arguments were used on the part of the Quakers, for which the heated mind of the good lady seemed by no means a fit recipient. The guard came in with his usual peremptory notice. The Quakers pulled out their money and formally tendered it—so much for tea—I, in humble imitation, tendering mine—for the supper which I had taken. She would not relax in her demand. So they all three quietly put up their silver, as did myself, and marched out of the room, the eldest and gravest going first, with myself closing up the rear, who thought I could not do better than follow the examples of such grave and warrantable personages. We got in. The steps went up. The coach drove off. The murmurs of mine hostess, not very indistinctly or ambiguously pronounced, became after a time inaudible—and now my conscience, which the whimsical scene had for a while suspended, beginning to give some twitches, I waited, in the hope that some justification would be offered by these serious persons for the seeming injustice of their conduct. To my great surprise not a syllable was dropped on the subject. They sat as mute as at a meeting. At length the eldest of them broke silence, by inquiring of his next neighbour, "Hast thee heard how indigos go at the India House?" and the question operated as a soporific on my moral feeling as far as Exeter.

One of Lamb's best known eccentricities among his friends was an indifference toward music, or at least, toward certain kinds of music and a certain sort of musical appreciation. In the essay entitled *A Chapter on Ears* he expatiates on this topic.

A CHAPTER ON EARS

I have no ear.—

Mistake me not, Reader—nor imagine that I am by nature destitute of those exterior twin appendages, hanging ornaments, and (architecturally speaking) handsome volutes to the human capital. Better my mother had never borne me.— I am, I think, rather delicately than copiously provided with those conduits; and I feel no disposition to envy the mule for his plenty, or the mole for her exactness, in those ingenious labyrinthine inlets—those indispensable side-intelligencers.

Neither have I incurred, or done anything to incur, with Defoe, that hideous disfigurement, which constrained him to draw upon assurance—to feel "quite unabashed," and at ease upon that article. I was never, I thank my stars in the pillory; nor, if I read them aright, is it within the compass of my destiny, that I ever should be.

When therefore I say that I have no ear, you will understand me to mean—*for music*. To say that this heart never melted at the concourse of sweet sounds, would be a foul self-libel.—"*Water parted from the sea*" never fails to move it strangely. So does "*In infancy.*" But they were used to be sung at her harpsichord (the old-fashioned instrument in vogue in those days) by a gentlewoman—the gentlest, sure, that ever merited the appellation—the sweetest—why should I hesitate to name Mrs. S——, once the blooming Fanny Weatheral of the Temple—who had power to thrill the soul of Elia, small imp as he was, even in his long coats; and to make him glow, tremble, and blush with a passion, that not faintly indicated the day-spring of that absorbing sentiment which was afterwards destined to overwhelm and subdue his nature quite, for Alice W[interto]n.

I even think that *sentimentally* I am disposed to harmony. But *organically* I am incapable of a tune. I have been practising *"God save the King"* all my life; whistling and humming of it over to myself in solitary corners; and am not yet arrived, they tell me, within many quavers of it. Yet hath the loyalty of Elia never been impeached.

I am not without suspicion, that I have an undeveloped faculty of music within me. For thrumming, in my wild way, on my friend A[yrton]'s piano, the other morning, while he was engaged in an adjoining parlour,—on his return he was pleased to say, *"he thought it could not be the maid!"* On his first surprise at hearing the keys touched in somewhat an airy and masterful way, not dreaming of me, his suspicions had lighted on *Jenny*. But a grace, snatched from a superior refinement, soon convinced him that some being— technically perhaps deficient, but higher informed from a principle common to all the fine arts—had swayed the keys to a mood which Jenny, with all her (less cultivated) enthusiasm, could never have elicited from them. I mention this as a proof of my friend's penetration, and not with any view of disparaging Jenny.

Scientifically I could never be made to understand (yet have I taken some pains) what a note in music is; or how one note should differ from another. Much less in voices can I distinguish a soprano from a tenor. Only sometimes the thorough-bass I contrive to guess at, from its being super-eminently harsh and disagreeable. I tremble, however, for my misapplication of the simplest terms of *that* which I disclaim. While I profess my ignorance, I scarce know what to *say* I am ignorant of. I hate, perhaps, by misnomers. *Sostenuto* and *adagio* stand in the like relation of obscurity to me; and *Sol, Fa, Mi, Re,* is as conjuring as *Baralipton.*

It is hard to stand alone in an age like this,—(constituted to the quick and critical perception of all harmonious combinations, I verily believe, beyond all proceeding ages, since Jubal stumbled upon the gamut)—to remain, as it were, singly unimpressible to the magic influences of an art, which is said to have such an especial stroke at soothing, elevating, and refining the passions.—Yet, rather than break the candid current of my confessions, I must avow to you that I have received a great deal more pain than pleasure from this so cried up faculty.

I am constitutionally susceptible of noises. A carpenter's hammer, in a warm summer noon, will fret me into more than midsummer madness. But those unconnected, unset sounds, are nothing to the measured malice of music. The ear is passive to those single strokes; willingly enduring stripes, while it hath no task to con. To music it cannot be passive. It will strive—mine at least will—'spite of its inaptitude, to thrid the maze; like an unskilled eye painfully poring upon hieroglyphics. I have sat through an Italian Opera, till, for sheer pain, and inexplicable anguish, I have rushed out into the noisiest places of the crowded streets, to solace myself with sounds, which I was not obliged to follow, and get rid of the distracting torment of endless, fruitless, barren attention! I take refuge in the unpretending assemblage of

honest common-life sounds;—and the purgatory of the En-
raged Musician becomes my paradise.

I have sat at an oratorio (that profanation of the purposes
of the cheerful playhouse) watching the faces of the auditory
in the pit (what a contrast to Hogarth's Laughing Audience!) immoveable, or affecting some faint emotion—till (as
some have said, that our occupations in the next world will
be but a shadow of what delighted us in this) I have imagined myself in some cold Theatre in Hades, where some of
the *forms* of the earthly one should be kept up, with none of
the *enjoyment;* or like that

> ————Party in a parlour
> All silent, and all DAMNED.

Above all, those insufferable concertos, and pieces of music,
as they are called, do plague and embitter my apprehension.
—Words are something; but to be exposed to an endless
battery of mere sounds; to be long a dying; to lie stretched
upon a rack of roses; to keep up languor by unintermitted
effort; to pile honey upon sugar, and sugar upon honey, to
an interminable tedious sweetness; to fill up sound with
feeling, and strain ideas to keep pace with it; to gaze on
empty frames, and be forced to make the pictures for yourself; to read a book, *all stops,* and be obliged to supply the
verbal matter; to invent extempore tragedies to answer to
the vague gestures of an inexplicable rambling mime—these
are faint shadows of what I have undergone from a series
of the ablest-executed pieces of this empty *instrumental
music.*

I deny not, that in the opening of a concert, I have experienced something vastly lulling and agreeable:—afterwards
followeth the languor and the oppression.—Like that disappointing book in Patmos; or, like the comings on of mel-

ancholy, described by Burton, doth music make her first insinuating approaches:—"Most pleasant it is to such as are melancholy given, to walk alone in some solitary grove, betwixt wood and water, by some brook side, and to meditate upon some delightsome and pleasant subject, which shall affect him most, *amabilis, insania,* and *mentis gratissimus error.* A most incomparable delight to build castles in the air, to go smiling to themselves, acting an infinite variety of parts, which they suppose, and strongly imagine, they act, or that they see done.—So delightsome these toys at first, they could spend whole days and nights without sleep, even whole years in such contemplations, and fantastical meditations, which are like so many dreams, and will hardly be drawn from them—winding and unwinding themselves as so many clocks, and still pleasing their humours, until at the last the SCENE TURNS UPON A SUDDEN, and they being now habitated to such meditations and solitary places, can endure no company, can think of nothing but harsh and distasteful subjects. Fear, sorrow, suspicion, *subrusticus pudor,* discontent, cares, and weariness of life, surprise them on a sudden, and they can think of nothing else; continually suspecting, no sooner are their eyes open, but this infernal plague of melancholy seizeth on them, and terrifies their souls, representing some dismal object to their minds; which now, by no means, no labour, no persuasions they can avoid, they cannot be rid of, they cannot resist."

Something like this *"scene-turning"* I have experienced at the evening parties, at the house of my good Catholic friend Nov[ello]; who, by the aid of a capital organ, himself the most finished of players, converts his drawing-room into a chapel, his week days into Sundays, and these latter into minor heavens.

When my friend commences upon one of these solemn

anthems, which peradventure struck upon my heedless ear, rambling in the side aisles of the dim Abbey, some five and thirty years since, waking a new sense, and putting a soul of old religion into my young apprehension—(whether it be *that*, in which the Psalmist, weary of the persecutions of bad men, wisheth to himself dove's wings—or *that other*, which, with a like measure of sobriety and pathos, inquireth by what means the young man shall best cleanse his mind)— a holy calm pervadeth me.—I am for the time.

> ——rapt above earth,
> And possess joys not promised at my birth.

But when this master of the spell, not content to have laid a soul prostrate, goes on, in his power, to inflict more bliss than lies in her capacity to receive—impatient to overcome her "earthly" with his "heavenly,"—still pouring in, for pro- tracted hours, fresh waves and fresh from the sea of sound, or from that inexhausted *German* ocean, above which, in triumphant progress, dolphin-seated, ride those Arions *Haydn* and *Mozart*, with their attendant Tritons, *Bach, Beethoven*, and a countless tribe, whom to attempt to reckon up would but plunge me again in the deeps,—I stagger under the weight of harmony, reeling to and fro at my wits' end;— clouds, as of frankincense, oppress me—priests, altars, cen- sers, dazzle before me—the genius of *his* religion hath me in her toils—a shadowy triple tiara invests the brow of my friend, late so naked, so ingenuous—he is Pope,—and by him sits, like as in the anomaly of dreams, a she-Pope too,— tri-coronated like himself!—I am converted, and yet a Pro- testant;—at once *malleus hereticorum*, and myself grand heresiarch: or three heresies centre in my person:—I am Marcion, Ebio, and Cerinthus—Gog and Magog—what not? —till the coming of the friendly supper-tray dissipates the figment, and a draught of true Lutheran beer (in which chiefly my friend shows himself no bigot) at once reconciles me to the rationalities of a purer faith; and restores to me the genuine unterrifying aspects of my pleasant-countenanced host and hostess.

Lamb appreciated very keenly the pleasures of eating, and was altogether unashamed of this characteristic. He displayed it in many occasions in his letters, and he celebrated roast pig in particular yet more gloriously in the essay *A Dissertation upon Roast Pig*. The three entertaining letters that follow reveal certain of Lamb's "hobbies in the eating way."

LETTER TO MANNING

16, Mitre Court Buildings,
Saturday, 24th Feb. 1805.

Dear Manning,—I have been very unwell since I saw you: a sad depression of spirits, a most unaccountable nervousness; from which I have been partially relieved by an odd accident. You knew Dick Hopkins, the swearing scullion of Caius? This fellow, by industry and agility, has thrust himself into the important situations (no sinecures, believe me) of cook to Trinity Hall and Caius College: and the generous creature has contrived, with the greatest delicacy imaginable, to send me a present of Cambridge brawn. What makes it the more extraordinary is, that the man never saw me in his life that I know of. I suppose he has *heard* of me. I did not immediately recognise the donor; but one of Richard's cards, which had accidently fallen into the straw, detected him in a moment. Dick, you know, was always remarkable for flourishing. His card imports, that "orders (to wit, for brawn) from any part of England, Scotland, or

Ireland, will be duly executed," &c. At first, I thought of declining the present; but Richard knew my blind side when he pitched upon brawn. 'Tis of all my hobbies the supreme in the eating way. He might have sent sops from the pan, skimmings, crumpets, chips, hog's lard, the tender brown judiciously scalped from a fillet of veal (dexterously replaced by a salamander), the tops of asparagus, fugitive livers, runaway gizzards of fowls, the eyes of martyred pigs, tender effusions of laxative woodcocks, the red spawn of lobsters, leverets' ears, and such pretty filchings common to cooks; but these had been ordinary presents, the every-day courtesies of dish-washers to their sweethearts. Brawn was a noble thought. It is not every common gullet-fancier that can properly esteem it. It is like a picture of one of the choice old Italian masters. Its gusto is of that hidden sort. As Wordsworth sings of a modest poet,—"you must love him, ere to you he will seem worthy of your love;" so brawn, you must taste it ere to you it will seem to have any taste at all. But 'tis nuts to the adept: those that will send out their tongue and feelers to find it out. It will be wooed, and not unsought be won. Now, ham-essence, lobsters, turtle, such popular minions, absolutely *court you,* lay themselves out to strike you at first smack, like one of David's pictures (they call him *Darveed*) compared with the plain russet-coated wealth of a Titian or a Correggio, as I illustrated above. Such are the obvious glaring heathen virtues of a corporation dinner, compared with the reserved collegiate worth of brawn. Do me the favour to leave off the business which you may be at present upon, and go immediately to the kitchens of Trinity and Caius, and make my most respectful compliments to Mr. Richard Hopkins, and assure him that his brawn is most excellent; and that I am moreover obliged to him for his innuendo about salt water and bran, which choose to pay him the civility of asking him to dinner while you stay in Cambridge, or in whatever other way you choose to stay in Cambridge, or in whatever other way you may best like to show your gratitude to *my friend*. Richard Hopkins, considered in many points of view, is a very extraordinary character. Adieu. I hope to see you to supper in London soon, where we will taste Richard's brawn, and drink his health in a cheerful but moderate cup. We have not many such men in any rank of life as Mr. R. Hopkins. Crisp, the barber, of St. Mary's, was just such another. I wonder *he* never sent me any little token, some chestnuts, or a puff, or two pound of hair: just to remember him by. Gifts are like nails. *Præsens ut absens!* that is, your *present* makes amends for your absence.

Yours,　　　　C. Lamb.

LETTER TO COLERIDGE

March 9th, 1822.

Dear Coleridge,—It gives me great satisfaction to hear that the pig turned out so well: they are interesting creatures at a certain age. What a pity such buds should blow out into the maturity of rank bacon! You had all some of the crackling and brain sauce. Did you remember to rub it with butter, and gently dredge it a little, just before the crisis? Did the eyes come away kindly with no Œdipean avulsion? Was the crackling the colour of the ripe pomegranate? Had you no compliment of boiled neck of mutton before it, to blunt the edge of delicate desire? Did you flesh maiden teeth in it? Not that *I* sent the pig, or can form the remotest guess what part Owen could play in the business. I never knew him give any thing away in my life. He would not begin with strangers. I suspect the pig, after all, was meant for me; but at the unlucky juncture of time being absent, the present somehow went round to Highgate. To confess an honest truth, a pig is one of those things which I could never think of sending away. Teal, widgeon, snipes, barn-door fowls, ducks, geese—your tame villatic things—Welsh mutton, collars of brawn, sturgeon, fresh or pickled, your potted char, Swiss cheeses, French pies, early grapes, musca-dines, I impart as freely unto my friends as to myself. They are but sex-extended; but pardon me if I stop somewhere. Where the fine feeling of benevolence giveth a higher smack than the sensual rarity, there my friends (or any good man) may command me; but pigs are pigs, and I myself therein am nearest to myself. Nay, I should think it an affront, an undervaluing done to Nature who bestowed such a boon upon me, if in a churlish mood I parted with the precious gift. One of the bitterest pangs of remorse I ever felt was when a child—when my kind old aunt had strained her pocket-strings to bestow a sixpenny whole plum-cake upon me. In my way home through the Borough I met a venerable old man, not a mendicant, but thereabouts; a look-beggar, not a verbal petitionist; and in the coxcombry of taught charity I gave away the cake to him. I walked on a little in all the pride of an Evangelical peacock, when of a sudden my old aunt's kindness crossed me; the sum it was to her; the pleasure she had a right to expect that I—not the old imposter—should take in eating her cake; the ingratitude by which, under the colour of a Christian virtue, I had frus-trated her cherished purpose. I sobbed, wept, and took it to heart grievously, that I think I never suffered the like; and I was right. It was a piece of unfeeling hypocrisy, and it proved a lesson to me ever after. The cake has long been masticated, consigned to the dung-hill with the ashes of that unseasonable pauper.

But when Providence, who is better to us all than our aunts, gives me a pig, remembering my temptation and my fall, I shall endeavour to act towards it more in the spirit of the donor's purpose.

Yours (short of pig) to command in everything,

C. L.

LETTER TO CHAMBERS

1 Sept. 1817.

With regard to a John Dory, which you desire to be particularly informed about,—I honour the fish, but it is rather on account of Quin who patronised it, and whose taste (of a *dead* man) I had as lieve go by as any body's, Apicius and Heliogabalus excepted—this latter started nightingales' brains and peacocks' tongues as a garnish. Else, in *itself*, and trusting to my own poor single judgment, it hath not the moist, mellow, oleaginous, gliding, smooth descent from the tongue to the palate, thence to the stomach, etc., as your Brighton turbot hath, which I take to be the most friendly and familiar flavour of any that swims—most genial and at home to the palate.

Nor has it, on the other hand, that fine falling-off flakiness, that obsequious peeling off (as it were like a sea onion) which endears your cod's-head and shoulders to some appetites, that manly firmness, combined with a sort of womanish coming-in-pieces, which the same cod's-head and shoulders hath—where the *whole* is easily separable, pliant to a knife or spoon, but each *individual flake* presents a pleasing resistance to the opposed tooth—you understand me; these delicate subjects are necessarily obscure.

But it has a third flavour of its own, totally distinct from cod or turbot, which it must be owned may to some not injudicious palates render it acceptable; but to my unpractised tooth it presented rather a crude river-fish-flavour, like your pike or carp, and perhaps, like them, should have been tamed and corrected by some laborious and well-chosen sauce. Still I always suspect a fish which requires so much of artificial settings-off. Your choicest relishes (like native loveliness) need not the foreign aid of ornament, but are, when unadorned (that is, with nothing but a little plain anchovy and a squeeze of lemon)—are then adorned the most. However, I shall go to Brighton again, next summer, and shall have an opportunity of correcting my judgment, if it is not sufficiently informed. I can only say that when Nature was pleased to make the John Dory so notoriously deficient in outward graces (as, to be sure, he is the very rhinoceros of fishes, the ugliest dog that swims, except perhaps the sea satyr, which I never saw, but which they say is terrible)— when she formed him with so few external advantages, she might have bestowed a more elaborate finish on his parts internal, and have given him a relish, a sapor, to recommend him, as she made Pope a poet to make up for making him crooked.

I am sorry to find that you have got a knack of saying things which are not sure to show your wit. If I had no wit, but what I must show at the expense of my virtue or my modesty, I had as lieve be as stupid as . . . at the tea warehouse. Depend upon it, my dear Chambers, that an ounce of integrity at our death-bed will stand us in more avail than all the wit of Congreve or . . . . For instance, you tell me a fine story about Truss, and his playing at Leamington, which I know to be false, because I have advice from Derby that he was whipt through the town on that very day you say he appeared in some character or other for robbing an old woman at church of a seal ring. And Dr. Parr has been two months dead. So it won't do to scatter these random

stories about among people that know anything. Besides, your
forte is not invention. It is *judgment,* particularly shown in
your choice of dishes. We seem in that instance born under
one star. I like you for liking hare. I esteem you for disrelishing minced veal. Liking is too cold a word: I love you
for your noble attachment to the fat, unctuous juices of
deer's flesh and the green unspeakable of turtle. I honour you
for your endeavours to esteem and approve of my favourite,
which I ventured to recommend to you as substitute for
hare, bullock's heart, and I am not offended that you cannot
taste it with *my* palate. A true son of Epicurus should reserve one taste peculiar to himself. For a long time I kept the
secret about the exceeding deliciousness of the marrow of
boiled knuckle of veal, till my tongue weakly ran out in
its praises, and now it is prostitute and common. But I have
made one discovery which I will not impart till my dying
scene is over—perhaps it will be my last mouthful in this
world: delicious thought, enough to sweeten (or rather make

s a v o u r y) the   hour of death. It
is a little square   bit a b o u t this
size, in or near   the knuckle-bone
of a fried joint of   . . . fat I can't
call it, nor lean   n e i t h e r alto-

gether, it is that beautiful compound which Nature must
have made in Paradise, Park Venison, before she separated
the two substances, the dry and the oleaginous, to punish
sinful mankind: Adam ate them entire and inseparable, and
this little taste of Eden in the knuckle-bone of a fried . . .
seems the only relique of a Paradisaical state. When I die, an
exact description of its topography shall be left in a cupboard
with a key, inscribed on which these words, "C. Lamb, dying,
imparts this to C. Chambers, as the only worthy depository
of such a secret." You'll drop a tear. . . .

Lamb greatly enjoyed playing whist with his friends. In *Mrs. Battle's Opinions on Whist*, he seems to have used an imaginary person as a lay-figure on which to drape his own attitude toward the pastime, as well as some philosophizing upon why people enjoy such games.

MRS. BATTLE'S OPINIONS ON WHIST

"A clear fire, a clean hearth, and the rigour of the game." This was the celebrated *wish* of old Sarah Battle (now with God), who, next to her devotions, loved a good game at whist. She was none of your lukewarm gamesters, your half-and-half players, who have no objection to take a hand, if you want one to make up a rubber; who affirm that they have no pleasure in winning; that they like to win one game, and lose another; that they can while away an hour very agreeably at a card-table, but are indifferent whether they play or no; and will desire an adversary, who has slipped a wrong card, to take it up and play another. These insufferable triflers are the curse of a table. One of these flies will spoil a whole pot. Of such it may be said that they do not play at cards, but only play at playing at them.

Sarah Battle was none of that breed. She detested them, as I do, from her heart and soul; and would not, save upon a striking emergency, willingly seat herself at the same table with them. She loved a thorough-paced partner, a determined enemy. She took, and gave, no concessions. She hated favours. She never made a revoke, nor ever passed it over in her adversary without exacting the utmost forfeiture. She fought a good fight; cut and thrust. She held not her good sword (her cards) "like a dancer." She sate bolt upright; and neither showed you her cards, nor desired to see yours. All people have their blind side—their superstitions; and I have heard her declare, under the rose, that Hearts was her favourite suit.

I never in my life—and I knew Sarah Battle many of the best years of it—saw her take out her snuff-box when it was her turn to play; or snuff a candle in the middle of a game; or ring for a servant, till it was fairly over. She never introduced, or connived at, miscellaneous conversation during its process. As she emphatically observed, cards were cards; and if I ever saw unmingled distaste in her fine last-century countenance, it was at the airs of a young gentleman of a literary turn, who had been with difficulty persuaded to take a hand; and who, in his excess of candour, declared, that he thought there was no harm in unbending the mind now and then, after serious studies, in recreations of that kind! She could not bear to have her noble occupation, to which she wound up her faculties, considered in that light. It was her business, her duty, the thing she came into the world to do,—and she did it. She unbent her mind afterwards—over a book.

Pope was her favourite author: his Rape of the Lock her favourite work. She once did me the favour to play over with me (with the cards) his celebrated game of Ombre in that poem; and to explain to me how far it agreed with, and in what points it would be found to differ from, tradille. Her illustrations were apposite and poignant; and I had the pleasure of sending the substance of them to Mr. Bowles; but suppose they came too late to be inserted among his ingenious notes upon that author.

Quadrille, she has often told me, was her first love; but whist had engaged her maturer esteem. The former, she said, was showy and specious, and likely to allure young persons. The uncertainty and quick shifting of partners—a thing which the constancy of whist abhors; the dazzling supremacy and regal investiture of Spadille—absurd, as she justly observed, in the pure aristocracy of whist, where his crown and garter give him no proper power above his brother-nobility of the Aces;—the giddy vanity, so taking to the inexperienced, of playing alone;—above all, the overpowering attractions of a *Sans Prendre Vole*,—to the triumph of which there is certainly nothing parallel or approaching, in the contingencies of whist;—all these, she would say, make quadrille a game of captivation to the young and enthusiastic. But whist was the *solider* game: that was her word. It was a long meal; not, like quadrille, a feast of snatches. One or two rubbers might coextend in duration with an evening. They gave time to form rooted friendships, to cultivate steady enmities. She despised the chance-started, capricious, and ever-fluctuating alliances of the other. The skirmishes of quadrille, she would say, reminded her of the petty ephemeral embroilments of the little Italian states, depicted by Machiavel: perpetually changing postures and connexions; bitter foes today, sugared darlings to-morrow; kissing and scratching in a breath;—but the wars of whist comparable to the long, steady, deep-rooted, rational antipathies of the great French and English nations.

A grave simplicity was what she chiefly admired in her favourite game. There was nothing silly in it, like the nob in cribbage—nothing superfluous. No *flushes*—that most irrational of all pleas that a reasonable being can set up:—that any one should claim four by virtue of holding cards of the same mark and colour, without reference to the playing of the game, or the individual worth or pretensions of the cards themselves! She held this to be a solecism; as pitiful an ambition at cards as alliteration is in authorship. She despised superficiality, and looked deeper than the colours of things.—Suits were soldiers, she would say, and must have a uniformity of array to distinguish them: but what should we say to a foolish squire, who should claim a merit from dressing up his tenantry in red jackets, that never were to be marshalled—never to take the field?—She even wished that whist were more simple than it is; and, in my mind, would have stripped it of some appendages, which, in the state of human frailty, may be venially, and even commendably, allowed of. She saw no reason for the deciding of the trump by the turn of the card. Why not one suit always trumps?— Why two colours, when the mark of the suits would have sufficiently distinguished them without it?

"But the eye, my dear Madam, is agreeably refreshed with the variety. Man is not a creature of pure reason—he must have his senses delightfully appealed to. We see it in Roman Catholic countries, where the music and the paintings draw in many to worship, whom your quaker spirit of unsensual-ising would have kept out.—You, yourself, have a pretty collection of paintings—but confess to me, whether, walking in your gallery at Sandham, among those clear Vandykes, or among the Paul Potters in the ante-room, you ever felt your bosom glow with an elegant delight, at all comparable to *that* you have it in your power to experience most eve-nings over a well-arranged assortment of the court-cards? —the pretty antic habits, like heralds in a procession—the gay triumph-assuring scarlets—the contrasting deadly-kill-ing sables—the 'hoary majesty of spades'—Pam in all his glory!—

"All these might be dispensed with; and with their naked names upon the drab pasteboard, the game might go on very well, pictureless; but the *beauty* of cards would be extin-guished for ever. Stripped of all that is imaginative in them, they must degenerate into mere gambling.—Imagine a dull deal board, or drum head, to spread them on, instead of that nice verdant carpet (next to nature's), fittest arena for those courtly combatants to play their gallant jousts and turneys in!—Exchange those delicately-turned ivory markers—(work of Chinese artist, unconscious of their symbol,—or as profanely slighting their true application as the arrantest Ephesian journeyman that turned out those little shrines for the goddess)—exchange them for little bits of leather (our ancestors' money), or chalk and a slate!"—

The old lady, with a smile, confessed the soundness of my logic; and to her approbation of my arguments on her favourite topic that evening I have always fancied myself indebted for the legacy of a curious cribbage-board, made of the finest Sienna marble, which her maternal uncle (old Walter Plumer, whom I have elsewhere celebrated) brought with him from Florence;—this, and a trifle of five hundred pounds, came to me at her death.

The former bequest (which I do not least value) I have kept with religious care; though she herself, to confess a truth, was never greatly taken with cribbage. It was an essentially vulgar game, I have heard her say,—disputing with her uncle, who was very partial to it. She could never heartily bring her mouth to pronounce *"Go,"* or *"That's a go."* She called it an ungrammatical game. The pegging teased her. I once knew her to forfeit a rubber (a five-dollar stake), because she would not take advantage of the turn-up knave, which would have given it her, but which she must have claimed by the disgraceful tenure of declaring *"two for his heels."* There is something extremely genteel in this sort of self-denial. Sarah Battle was a gentlewoman born.

Piquet she held the best game at the cards for two persons, though she would ridicule the pedantry of the terms—such as pique—repique—the capot—they savoured (she thought) of affectation. But games for two, or even three, she never greatly cared for. She loved the quadrate, or square. She would argue thus:—Cards are warfare: the ends are gain, with glory. But cards are war, in disguise of a sport: when single adversaries encounter, the ends proposed are too palpable. By themselves, it is too close a fight; with spectators, it is not much bettered. No looker on can be interested, except for a bet, and then it is a mere affair of money; he cares not for your luck *sympathetically*, or for your play.— Three are still worse; a mere naked war of every man against every man, as in cribbage, without league or alliance; or a rotation of petty and contradictory interests, a succession of heartless leagues, and not much more hearty infractions of them, as in tradrille.—But in square games (*she meant whist*), all that is possible to be attained in card-playing is accomplished. There are the incentives of profit with honour, common to every species—though the *latter* can be but very imperfectly enjoyed in those other games, where the spectator is only feebly a participator. But the parties in whist are spectators and principals too. They are a theatre to themselves, and a looker-on is not wanted. He is rather worse than nothing, and an impertinence. Whist abhors neutrality, or interests beyond its sphere. You glory in some surprising stroke of skill or fortune, not because a cold—or even an interested—bystander witnesses it, but because your *partner* sympathises in the contingency. You win for two. You triumph for two. Two are exalted. Two again are mortified; which divides their disgrace, as the conjunction doubles (by taking off the invidiousness) your glories. Two losing to two are better reconciled, than one to one in that close butchery. The hostile feeling is weakened by multiplying the channels. War becomes a civil game.—By such reasonings as these the old lady was accustomed to defend her favourite pastime.

No inducement could ever prevail upon her to play at any game, where chance entered into the composition, *for noth-*

ing. Chance, she would argue—and here again, admire the subtlety of her conclusion!—chance is nothing, but where something else depends upon it. It is obvious that cannot be *glory.* What rational cause of exultation could it give to a man to turn up size ace a hundred times together by himself? or before spectators, where no stake was depending?—Make a lottery of a hundred thousand tickets with but one fortunate number—and what possible principle of our nature, except stupid wonderment, could it gratify to gain that number as many times successively, without a prize? Therefore she disliked the mixture of chance in backgammon, where it was not played for money. She called it foolish, and those people idiots, who were taken with a lucky hit under such circumstances. Games of pure skill were as little to her fancy. Played for a stake, they were a mere system of overreaching. Played for glory, they were a mere setting of one man's wit,—his memory, or combination-faculty rather—against another's; like a mock-engagement at a review, bloodless and profitless.—She could not conceive a *game* wanting the sprightly infusion of chance, the handsome excuses of good fortune. Two people playing at chess in a corner of a room, whilst whist was stirring in the centre, would inspire her with insufferable horror and ennui. Those well-cut similitudes of Castles and Knights, the *imagery* of the board, she would argue (and I think in this case justly), were entirely misplaced and senseless. Those hardhead contests can in no instance ally with the fancy. They reject form and colour. A pencil and dry slate (she used to say) were the proper arena for such combatants.

To those puny objectors against cards, as nurturing the bad passions, she would retort, that man is a gaming animal. He must be always trying to get the better in something or other:—that this passion can scarcely be more safely expended than upon a game at cards: that cards are a temporary illusion; in truth, a mere drama; for we do but *play* at being mightily concerned, where a few idle shillings are at stake, yet, during the illusion, we *are* as mightily concerned as those whose stake is crowns and kingdoms. They are a sort of dream-fighting; much ado, great battling, and little bloodshed; mighty means for disproportioned ends; quite as diverting, and a great deal more innoxious, than many of those more serious *games* of life, which men play, without esteeming them to be such.—

With great deference to the old lady's judgment on these matters, I think I have experienced some moments in my life when playing at cards *for nothing* has even been agreeable. When I am in sickness, or not in the best spirits, I sometimes call for the cards, and play a game at piquet *for love* with my cousin Bridget—Bridget Elia.

I grant there is something sneaking in it; but with a toothache, or a sprained ankle,—when you are subdued and humble,—you are glad to put up with an inferior spring of action.

There is such a thing in nature, I am convinced, as *sick whist*.

I grant it is not the highest style of man—I deprecate the manes of Sarah Battle—she lives not, alas! to whom I should apologise.—

At such times, those *terms* which my old friend objected to, come in as something admissible.—I love to get a tierce or a quatorze, though they mean nothing. I am subdued to an inferior interest. Those shadows of winning amuse me.

That last game I had with my sweet cousin (I capotted her)—(dare I tell thee, how foolish I am?)—I wished it might have lasted for ever, though we gained nothing, and lost nothing, though it was a mere shade of play: I would be content to go on in that idle folly for ever. The pipkin should be ever boiling, that was to prepare the gentle lenitive to my foot, which Bridget was doomed to apply after the game was over: and, as I do not much relish appliances, there it should ever bubble. Bridget and I should be ever playing.

Lamb's fondness for books, especially for those to which might be applied the phrase "quaint and curious volumes of forgotten lore," has been shown incidentally in the essays and letters that have been given before in this book. His friend Crabb Robinson once indicated the character of Lamb's library, acquired mostly from the second-hand bookstalls of London, by remarking, "He has the finest collection of shabby books I ever saw; such a number of first rate books in very bad condition is, I think, nowhere to be found." But Lamb's library included books that he had personally read and loved, books that were in truth his "midnight darlings." In *Detached Thoughts on Books and Reading* is the essence of his experience as a reader and book-lover. Of this essay, Mr. John Macy, the American critic, has said with entire truth, "I recommend as the best possible short guide to literature, Lamb's essay, *Detached Thoughts on Books and Reading,* for it has more of the true spirit of reading packed into it than is to be found in many a thick volume of literary criticism."

DETACHED THOUGHTS ON BOOKS AND READING

To mind the inside of a book is to entertain one's self with the forced product of another man's brain. Now I think a man of quality and breeding may be much amused with the natural sprouts of his own.— *Lord Foppington, in The Relapse.*

An ingenious acquaintance of my own was so much struck with this bright sally of his Lordship, that he has left off reading altogether, to the great improvement of his originality. At the hazard of losing some credit on this head, I must confess that I dedicate no inconsiderable portion of my time to other people's thoughts. I dream away my life in others' speculations. I love to lose myself in other men's minds. When I am not walking, I am reading; I cannot sit and think. Books think for me.

I have no repugnances. Shaftesbury is not too genteel for me, nor Jonathan Wild too low. I can read anything which I call *a book*. There are things in that shape which I cannot allow for such.

In this catalogue of *books which are no books—biblia a-biblia*—I reckon Court Calendars, Directories, Pocket Books, Draught Boards bound and lettered on the back, Scientific Treatises, Almanacks, Statutes at Large; the works of Hume, Gibbon, Robertson, Beattie, Soame Jenyns, and generally, all those volumes which "no gentleman's library should be without;" the Histories of Flavius Josephus (that learned Jew), and Paley's Moral Philosophy. With these exceptions, I can read almost anything. I bless my stars for a taste so catholic, so unexcluding.

I confess that it moves my spleen to see these *things in books' clothing* perched upon shelves, like false saints, usurpers of true shrines, intruders into the sanctuary, thrusting out the legitimate occupants. To reach down a well-bound semblance of a volume, and hope it some kind-hearted play-book, then, opening what "seem its leaves," to come bolt upon a withering Population Essay. To expect a Steele or a Farquhar, and find—Adam Smith. To view a well-arranged assortment of blockheaded Encyclopædias (Anglicanas or Metropolitanas) set out in an array of Russia, or Morocco, when a tithe of that good leather would comfortably reclothe my shivering folios; would renovate Paracelsus himself, and enable old Raymund Lully to look like himself again in the world. I never see these impostors, but I long to strip them, to warm my ragged veterans in their spoils.

To be strong-backed and neat-bound is the desideratum of a volume. Magnificence comes after. This, when it can be afforded, is not to be lavished upon all kinds of books indiscriminately. I would not dress a set of Magazines, for instance, in full suit. The dishabille, or half-binding (with Russia back ever) is *our* costume. A Shakspeare, or a Milton (unless the first editions), it were mere foppery to trick out in gay apparel. The possession of them confers no distinction. The exterior of them (the things themselves being so common), strange to say, raises no sweet emotions, no tickling sense of property in the owner. Thomson's Seasons, again, looks best (I maintain it) a little torn and dog's-eared. How beautiful to a genuine lover of reading are the sullied leaves, and worn-out appearance, nay, the very odour (beyond Russia), if we would not forget kind feelings in fastidiousness, of an old "Circulating Library" Tom Jones, or Vicar of Wakefield! How they speak of the thousand thumbs that have turned over their pages with delight!—of the lone sempstress, whom they may have cheered (milliner, or harder-working mantua-maker) after her long day's needle-toil, running far into midnight, when she has snatched an hour, ill spared from sleep, to steep her cares, as in some Lethean cup, in spelling out their enchanting contents! Who would have them a whit less soiled? What better condition could we desire to see them in?

In some respects the better a book is, the less it demands from binding. Fielding, Smollett, Sterne, and all that class of perpetually self-reproductive volumes—Great Nature's Stereotypes—we see them individually perish with less regret, because we know the copies of them to be "eterne."

But where a book is at once both good and rare—where the individual is almost the species, and when *that* perishes,

> We know not where is that Promethean torch
> That can its light relumine;—

such a book, for instance, as the Life of the Duke of Newcastle, by his Duchess—no casket is rich enough, no casing sufficiently durable, to honour and keep safe such a jewel.

Not only rare volumes of this description, which seem hopeless ever to be reprinted; but old editions of writers, such as Sir Philip Sydney, Bishop Taylor, Milton in his prose works, Fuller—of whom we *have* reprints, yet the books themselves, though they go about, and are talked of here and there, we knew have not endenizened themselves (nor possibly ever will) in the national heart, so as to become stock books—it is good to possess these in durable and costly covers. I do not care for a First Folio of Shakspeare. I rather prefer the common editions of Rowe and Tonson, without notes, and with *plates,* which, being so execrably bad, serve as maps or modest remembrancers, to the text; and without pretending to any supposable emulation with it, are so much better than the Shakspeare gallery *engravings,* which *did.* I have a community of feeling with my countrymen about his Plays, and I like those editions of him best which have been oftenest tumbled about and handled.—On the contrary, I cannot read Beaumont and Fletcher but in Folio. The Octavo editions are painful to look at. I have no sympathy with them. If they were as much read as the current editions of the other poet, I should prefer them in that shape to the older one. I do not know a more heartless sight than the reprint of the Anatomy of Melancholy. What need was there of unearthing the bones of that fantastic old great man, **to expose** them in a winding-sheet of the newest fashion **to** modern censure? what hapless stationer could dream of Burton ever becoming popular?—The wretched Malone could not do worse, when he bribed the sexton of Stratford church to let him whitewash the painted effigy of old Shakspeare, which stood there, in rude but lively fashion depicted, to the very colour of the cheek, the eye, the eyebrow, hair, the very dress he used to wear—the only authentic testimony we had, however imperfect, of these curious parts and parcels of him. They covered him over with a coat of white paint. By ——, if I had been a justice of peace for Warwickshire, I would have clapped both commentator and sexton fast in the stocks, for a pair of meddling sacrilegious varlets.

I think I see them at their work—these sapient trouble-tombs.

Shall I be thought fastastical if I confess that the names of some of our poets sound sweeter, and have a finer relish to the ear—to mine, at least—than that of Milton or of Shakspeare? It may be, that the latter are more staled and rung upon in common discourse. The sweetest names, and which carry a perfume in the mention, are, Kit Marlowe, Drayton, Drummond of Hawthornden, and Cowley.

Much depends upon *when* and *where* you read a book. In the five or six impatient minutes, before the dinner is quite ready, who would think of taking up the Fairy Queen for a stop-gap, or a volume of Bishop Andrewes' sermons?

Milton almost requires a solemn service of music to be played before you enter upon him. But he brings his music, to which, who listens, had need bring docile thoughts, and purged ears.

Winter evenings—the world shut out—with less of ceremony the gentle Shakspeare enters. At such a season, the Tempest, or his own Winter's Tale—

These two poets you cannot avoid reading aloud—to yourself, or (as it chances) to some single person listening. More than one—and it degenerates into an audience.

Books of quick interest, that hurry on for incidents, are for the eye to glide over only. It will not do to read them out. I could never listen to even the better kind of modern novels without extreme irksomeness.

A newspaper, read out, is intolerable. In some of the Bank offices it is the custom (to save so much individual time) for one of the clerks—who is the best scholar—to commence upon the *Times* or the *Chronicle* and recite its entire contents aloud *pro bono publico*. With every advantage of lungs and elocution, the effect is singularly vapid. In barbers' shops and public-houses a fellow will get up, and spell out a paragraph, which he communicates as some discovery. Another follows with *his* selection. So the entire journal transpires at length by piecemeal. Seldom-readers are slow readers, and, without this expedient, no one in the company would probably ever travel through the contents of a whole paper.

Newspapers always excite curiosity. No one ever lays one down without a feeling of disappointment.

What an eternal time that gentleman in black, at Nando's, keeps the paper! I am sick of hearing the waiter bawling out incessantly, "The *Chronicle* is in hand, Sir."

Coming into an inn at night—having ordered your supper—what can be more delightful than to find lying in the window-seat, left there time out of mind by the carelessness of some former guest—two or three numbers of the old Town and Country Magazine, with its amusing *tête-à-tête* pictures—"The Royal Lover and Lady G——;" "The Melting Platonic and the old Beau,"—and such-like antiquated scandal? Would you exchange it—at that time, and in that place —for a better book?

Poor Tobin, who latterly fell behind, did not regret it so

much for the weightier kinds of reading—the Paradise Lost,
or Comus, he could have *read* to him—but he missed the
pleasure of skimming over with his own eye a magazine, or
a light pamphlet.

I should not care to be caught in the serious avenue of
some cathedral alone, and reading *Candide*.

I do not remember a more whimsical surprise than having
been once detected—by a familiar damsel—reclined at my
ease upon the grass, on Primrose Hill (her Cythera) reading
—*Pamela*. There was nothing in the book to make a man
seriously ashamed at the exposure; but as she seated herself
down by me, and seemed determined to read in company, I
could have wished it had been—any other book. We read on
very sociably for a few pages; and, not finding the author
much to her taste, she got up, and—went away. Gentle
casuist, I leave it to thee to conjecture, whether the blush (for
there was one between us) was the property of the nymph
or the swain in this dilemma. From me you shall never get
the secret.

I am not much a friend to out-of-doors reading. I cannot
settle my spirits to it. I knew a Unitarian minister, who was
generally to be seen upon Snow-Hill (as yet Skinner's Street
was not), between the hours of ten and eleven in the morning, studying a volume of Lardner. I own this to have been a
strain of abstraction beyond my reach. I used to admire how
he sidled along, keeping clear of secular contacts. An illiterate
encounter with a porter's knot, or a bread basket, would have
quickly put to flight all the theology I am master of, and
have left me worse than indifferent to the five points.

There is a class of street readers, whom I can never contemplate without affection—the poor gentry, who, not having wherewithal to buy or hire a book, filch a little learning
at the open stalls—the owner, with his hard eye, casting

envious looks at them all the while, and thinking when they will have done. Venturing tenderly, page after page, expecting every moment when he shall interpose his interdict, and yet unable to deny themselves the gratification, they "snatch a fearful joy." Martin B[urney], in this way, by daily fragments, got through two volumes of Clarissa, when the stall-keeper damped his laudable ambition, by asking him (it was in his younger days) whether he meant to purchase the work. M. declares, that under no circumstances of his life did he ever peruse a book with half the satisfaction which he took in those uneasy snatches. A quaint poetess of our day has moralised upon this subject in two very touching but homely stanzas:—

> I saw a boy with eager eye
> Open a book upon a stall,
> And read, as he'd devour it all;
> Which, when the stall-man did espy,
> Soon to the boy I heard him call
> "You, Sir, you never buy a book,
> Therefore in one you shall not look."
> The boy pass'd slowly on, and with a sigh
> He wish'd he never had been taught to read,
> Then of the old churl's books he should have had no need.
>
> Of sufferings the poor have many,
> Which never can the rich annoy.
> I soon perceived another boy,
> Who look'd as if he had not any
> Food, for that day at least—enjoy
> The sight of cold meat in a tavern larder.
> This boy's case, then thought I, is surely harder,
> Thus hungry, longing, thus without a penny,
> Beholding choice of dainty-dressèd meat:
> No wonder if he wish he ne'er had learn'd to eat.

V

LAMB AMONG HIS FRIENDS

Lamb naturally drew around him friends. He had, indeed, as someone has remarked, an unusual genius for friendship. Sometimes he complained, as in the letter below to Mrs. Wordsworth, about the interference of so many friends, but on the whole Lamb would have been very unhappy if he had been deprived of them. He was the type who could be on friendly terms with all sorts and conditions of men, and the "fine vagaries," as he called it, of these friendships are surprising. In A. P. Russell's essay on Lamb in "Characteristics" is a catalogue of these worthies and unworthies, which will serve as an introduction to those who appear in the extracts from Lamb's correspondence, as well as to others who do not make an epistolary appearance in this book.

"And here a word or two about Lamb's friends—mostly an odd set of intellectual worthies. Coleridge—deep in metaphysical subtleties, or up in the empyrean; scholarly George Dyer—simple-hearted as my uncle Toby—always conjecturing and always absent-minded—at one time emptying the contents of his snuff-box into the teapot, at another walking straight into the river at noonday; Barton—the healthful friend, and good Quaker poet; Hazlitt—passionate and untamable—with a face as pale as marble, yet pointed at as the 'pimpled Hazlitt'—who never tasted anything but water, yet was held up as an habitual gin-drinker; Crabb Robinson—with the most hospitable of intellects—who had seen everything and everybody, and was always entertaining; Talfourd—full of law and literature, and ever ready with his reason or his rhetoric; Rickman—bounding, as a roe, and as fresh as the morning; Rough—a chronic and incurable borrower, to whom some of Lamb's most amusing letters were written; Manning—the most wonderful of all,

Lamb said; Barry Cornwall—who wrote sea songs, yet was rarely if ever on the tossing element—whose poetry, it was said, is a record of the extravagances of one who was habitually cautious, the eloquence of one who was habitually reserved; Godwin—who write against matrimony and was twice married, and while scouting all commonplace duties, was a good husband and a kind father; Lloyd—an insane poet, who took lodgings at a working brazier's shop to distract his mind from melancholy and postpone his madness; Southey—a bookworm and book-maker—who loved books so well that some of his last hours were spent caressing them; DeQuincey—who had made himself famous by confessing to the sin of opium; Hammond—an incomprehensible character, who journalized his food, his sleep, his dreams—who had a conviction that he was to have been, and ought to have been the greatest of men, but was conscious of the fact that he was not—and who said, the chief philosophical value of his papers consisted in the fact that they recorded something of a mind that was very near taking a station far above all that had hitherto appeared in the world; Blake—artist, genius, mystic, madman—of whom it was said, he possessed the highest and most exalted powers of the mind, but not the lower—who could fly but could not walk—who had genius and inspiration, without the prosaic balance wheel of common sense —who all his life was a victim of poverty and privation, but who, in his old age, put his hands on the head of a little girl, and said, 'May God make this world to you, my child, as beautiful as it has been to me;' and Wordsworth—who heard and saw in abounding nature what nobody saw or heard but himself without his assistance—who loved himself chiefly, and disparaged Burns, and even Shakespeare; and Hood—'so grave, and sad, and silent'—one of Lamb's youngest friends; and Cottle, the kind old bookseller; and Munden, his favorite comedian; and Liston; and Charles Kemble; and Morgan; and Jem White, 'the drollest of fellows,' the author of the *Falstaff Letters;* and the passionate Thelwell; and Clarkson, the destroyer of the slave trade; and Basil Montagu, the constant opponent of the judicial infliction of death; and scholarly Barnes, the editor of the *Times* newspaper; and the turbulent, ambitious Haydon; and the frank-hearted Captain Burney, who voyaged round the world with Captain Cook; and stalwart Allan Cunningham; and Cary, 'pleasantest of clergymen,' who 'rendered the adamantine poetry of Dante into English'; and the Reverend Edward Irving; and easy-going, delightful Leigh Hunt; and ever so many more, only a little more obscure—all of whom were visitors, friends, associates, favorites, or pets, of Lamb—walking with him in London streets—talking with him in quiet upper rooms, all about books and authors, plays and players, pictures and artists—any thing about which any one of them was interested."

LETTER TO MRS. WORDSWORTH

East-India House, 18th Feb., 1818.

My dear Mrs. Wordsworth,—I have repeatedly taken pen in hand to answer your kind letter. My sister should more properly have done it, but she having failed, I consider myself answerable for her debts. I am now trying to do it in the midst of commercial noises, and with a quill which seems more ready to glide into arithmetical figures and names of gourds, cassia, cardamoms, aloes, ginger, or tea, than into kindly responses and friendly recollections. The reason why I cannot write letters at home, is, that I am never alone. Plato's—(I write to W. W. now)—Plato's double-animal parted never longed more to be reciprocally re-united in the system of its first creation than I sometimes do to be but for a moment single and separate. Except my morning's walk to the office, which is like treading on sands of gold for that reason, I am never so. I cannot walk home from office but some officials friend offers his unwelcome courtesies to accompany me. All the morning I am pestered. I could sit and gravely cast up sums in great books, or compare sum with sum, and write "paid" against this, and "unpaid" against t'other, and yet reserve in some corner of my mind "some

darling thoughts all my own,"—faint memory of some passage in a book, or the tone of an absent friend's voice—a
snatch of Miss Burrell's singing, or a gleam of Fanny Kelly's
divine plain face. The two operations might be going on at
the same time without thwarting, as the sun's two motions,
(earth's I mean,) or as I sometimes turn round till I am
giddy, in my back parlour, while my sister is walking longi-
tudinally in the front; or as the shoulder of veal twists
round with the spit, while the smoke wreaths up the chimney. But there are a set of amateurs of the Belles Lettres—
the gay science—who come to me as a sort of rendezvous,
putting questions of criticism, of British Institutions, Lalla
Rookhs, &c.—what Coleridge said at the lecture last night—
who have the form of reading men, but, for any possible
use reading can be to them, but to talk of, might as well
have been Ante-Cadmeans born, or have lain sucking out
the sense of an Egyptian hieroglyph as long as the pyramids
will last, before they should find it. These pests worrit me at
business, and in all its intervals, perplexing my accounts,
poisoning my little salutary warming-time at the fire, puzzling my paragraphs if I take a newspaper, cramming in
between my own free thoughts and a column of figures,
which had come to an amicable compromise but for them.
Their noise ended, one of them, as I said, accompanies me
home, lest I should be solitary for a moment; he at length
takes his welcome leave at the door; up I go, mutton on table,
hungry as hunter, hope to forget my cares, and bury them in
the agreeable abstraction of mastication; knock at the door,
in comes Mr. Hazlitt, or Mr. Martin Burney, or Morgan,
Demi-gorgon, or my brother, or somebody, to prevent my
eating alone—a process absolutely necessary to my poor
wretched digestion. O the pleasure of eating alone!—eating
my dinner alone! let me think of it. But in they come, and

make it absolutely necessary that I should open a bottle of orange; for my meat turns into stone when any one dines with me, if I have not wine. Wine can mollify stones; then *that* wine turns into acidity, acerbity, misanthropy, a hatred of my interrupters—(God bless 'em! I love some of 'em dearly), and with the hatred, a still greater aversion to their going away. Bad is the dead sea they bring upon me, choking and deadening, but worse is the deader dry sand they leave me on, if they go before bed-time. Come never, I would say to these spoilers of my dinner; but if you come, never go! The fact is, this interruption does not happen very often; but every time it comes by surprise, that present bane of my life, orange wine, with all its dreary stifling consequences, follows. Evening company I should always like had I any mornings, but I am saturated with human faces (*divine* forsooth!) and voices all the golden morning; and five evenings in a week would be as much as I should covet to be in company; but I assure you that is a wonderful week in which I can get two, or one to myself. I am never C. L., but always C. L. & Co.

He who thought it not good for man to be alone, preserve me from the more prodigious monstrosity of being never by myself! I forget bed-time, but even there these sociable frogs clamber up to annoy me. Once a week, generally some singular evening that, being alone, I go to bed at the hour I ought always to be a-bed; just close to my bedroom window is the club-room of a public-house, where a set of singers, I take them to be chorus singers of the two theatres, (it must be *both of them*,) begin their orgies. They are a set of fellows (as I conceive) who, being limited by their talents to the burthen of the song at the play-houses, in revenge have got the common popular airs by Bishop, or some cheap composer, arranged for choruses; that is, to be sung all in chorus. At least I never can catch any of the text of the plain song, nothing but the Babylonish choral howl at the tail on't. "That fury being quenched"—the howl I mean—a burden succeeds of shouts and clapping, and knocking of the table. At length overtasked nature drops under it, and escapes for a few hours into the society of the sweet silent creature of dreams, which go away with mocks and mows at cockcrow. And then I think of the words Christabel's father used (bless me, I have dipt in the wrong ink!) to say every morning by way of variety when he awoke:

> Every knell, the Baron saith,

or something like it. All I mean by this senseless interrupted tale, is, that by my central situation I am a little over-companied. Not that I have any animosity against the good creatures that are so anxious to drive away the harpy solitude from me. I like 'em, and cards, and a cheerful glass; but I mean merely to give you an idea, between office confinement and after-office society, how little time I can call my own. I mean only to draw a picture, not to make an inference. I would not that I know of have it otherwise. I only wish sometimes I could exchange some of my faces and voices for the faces and voices which a late visitation brought most welcome, and carried away, leaving regret, but more pleasure, even a kind of gratitude, at being so often favoured with that kind northern visitation. My London faces and noises don't hear me—I mean no disrespect, or I should explain myself, that instead of their return 220 times a year, and the return of W. W., &c., seven times in 104 weeks, some more equal distribution might be found. I have scarce room to put in Mary's kind love, and my poor name,

C. LAMB.

This to be read last.

W. H. goes on lecturing against W. W. and making copious use of quotations from said W. W. to give a zest to said lectures. S. T. C. is lecturing with success. I have not heard either him or H., but I dined with S. T. C. at Gilman's a Sunday or two since, and he was well and in good spirits. I mean to hear some of the course; but lectures are not much to my taste, whatever the lecturer may be. If *read*, they are dismal flat, and you can't think why you are brought together to hear a man read his works, which you could read so much better at leisure yourself. If delivered extempore, I am always in pain, lest the gift of utterance should suddenly fail the orator in the middle, as it did me at the dinner given in honour of me at the London Tavern. "Gentlemen," said I, and there I stopped; the rest my feelings were under the necessity of supplying. Mrs. Wordsworth *will* go on, kindly haunting us with visions of seeing the lakes once more, which never can be realised. Between us there is a great gulf, not of inexplicable moral antipathies and distances, I hope, as there seemed to be between me and that gentleman concerned in the Stamp Office, that I so strangely recoiled from at Haydon's. I think I had an instinct that he was the head of an office. I hate all such people—accountants' deputy accountants. The dear abstract notion of the East India Company, as long as she is unseen, is pretty, rather poetical; but as she makes herself manifest by the persons of such beasts, I loathe and detest her as the scarlet what-do-you-call-her of Babylon, I thought, after abridging us of all our red-letter days, they had done their worst; but I was deceived in the length to which heads of offices, those true liberty-haters, can go. They are the tyrants; not Ferdinand, nor Nero. By a decree passed this week, they have abridged us of the immemorially-observed custom of going at one o'clock of a Saturday, the little shadow of a holiday left us. Dear W. W., be thankful for liberty.

The origin of the life-long friendship between Lamb and Coleridge has already been described. Despite Coleridge's irresponsible habits, which alienated most people from him, Lamb remained a sympathetic friend. Shortly after Coleridge's death, Lamb wrote: "His great and dear spirit haunts me. I cannot think a thought, I cannot make a criticism on men or books, without an ineffectual turning and reference to him. He was the proof and touchstone of all my cogitations. Never saw I his likeness, nor probably the world can see again." Yet Lamb did not refrain from having a degree of fun in his letters and essays with some of Coleridge's weaknesses, particularly his borrowing books and then forgetting to return them. In the letter below we find Lamb protesting to Coleridge himself about a case of this unauthorized borrowing, and in the latter part of the essay *The Two Races of Men,* Coleridge, the irresponsible borrower and enricher of books, is again presented.

LETTER TO COLERIDGE

[Undated. Probably in 1820.]

Dear Coleridge,—Why will you make your visits which should give pleasure, matter of regret to your friends? You never come but you take away some folio, that is part of my existence. With a great deal of difficulty I was made to comprehend the extent of my loss. My maid, Becky, brought me a dirty bit of paper, which contained her description of some book which Mr. Coleridge had taken away. It was "Luster's Tables," which, for some time, I could not make out. "What! has he carried away any of the *tables,* Becky?" "No, it wasn't any tables, but it was a book that he called Luster's Tables." I was obliged to search personally among my shelves, and a huge fissure suddenly disclosed to me the true nature of the damage I had sustained. That book, Coleridge, you should not have taken away, for it is not mine; it is the property of a friend, who does not know its value, nor indeed have I been very sedulous in explaining to him the estimate of it; but was rather contented in giving a sort of corroboration to a hint that he let fall, as to its being suspected to be not genuine, so that in all probability it would have fallen to me as a deodand; not but I am as sure it is Luther's as I am sure that Jack Bunyan wrote the *Pilgrim's Progress*; but it was not for me to pronounce upon the validity of testimony that had been disputed by learneder clerks than I; so I quietly let it occupy the place it had usurped upon my shelves, and should never have thought of issuing an ejectment against it; for why should I be so bigoted as to allow rites of hospitality to none but my own books, children, &c.?—a species of egotism I abhor from my heart. No; let 'em all snug together, Hebrews and Proselytes of the gate; no selfish partiality of mine shall make distinction between them, I charge no warehouse room for my friend's commodities; they are welcome to come and stay as long as they like, without paying rent. I have several such strangers that I treat with more than Arabian courtesy. There's a copy of More's fine poem, which is none of mine, but I cherish it as my own. I am none of those churlish landlords that advertise the goods to be taken away in ten days' time, or then to be sold to pay expenses. So you see I had no right to lend you that book. I may lend you my own books, because it is at my own hazard; but it is not honest to hazard a friend's property; I always make that distinction. I hope you will bring it with you, or send it by Hartley; or he can bring that, and you the *Polemical Discourses,* and come and eat some atoning mutton with us one of these days shortly. We are engaged two or three Sundays deep, but always dine at home on week-days at half-past four. So come all four—men and books I mean. My third shelf (northern compartment) from the top has two devilish gaps, where you have knocked out its two eye-teeth.

Your wronged friend,

C. LAMB.

THE TWO RACES OF MEN

The human species, according to the best theory I can form of it, is composed of two distinct races, *the men who borrow*, and *the men who lend*. To these two original diversities may be reduced all those impertinent classifications of Gothic and Celtic tribes, white men, black men, red men. All the dwellers upon earth, "Parthians, and Medes, and Elamites," flock hither and do naturally fall in with one or other of these primary distinctions. The infinite superiority of the former, which I chose to designate as the *great race*, is discernible in their figure, port, and a certain instinctive sovereignty. The latter are born degraded. "He shall serve his brethren." There is something in the air of one of this cast, lean and suspicious; contrasting with the open, trusting, generous manners of the other.

Observe who have been the greatest borrowers of all ages—Alcibiades—Falstaff—Sir Richard Steele—our late incomparable Brinsley—what a family likeness in all four!

What a careless, even deportment hath your borrower! what rosy gills! what a beautiful reliance on Providence doth he manifest,—taking no more thought than lilies! What contempt for money,—accounting it (yours and mine especially) no better than dross! What a liberal confounding of those pedantic distinctions of *meum* and *tuum*! or rather, what a noble simplification of language (beyond Tooke), resolving these supposed opposites into one clear, intelligible pronoun adjective!—What near approaches does he make to the primitive *community,*—to the extent of one half of the principle at least!

He is the true taxer who "calleth all the world up to be taxed;" and the distance is as vast between him and *one of us,* as subsisted between the Augustan Majesty and the poorest obolary Jew that paid its tribute-pittance at Jerusalem!—His exactions, too, have such a cheerful, voluntary air! So far removed from your sour parochial or state-gatherers,—those ink-horn varlets, who carry their want of welcome in their faces! He cometh to you with a smile, and troubleth you with no receipt; confining himself to no set season. Every day is his Candlemas, or his feast of Holy Michael. He applieth the *lene tormentum* of a pleasant look to your purse,—which to that gentle warmth expands her silken leaves, as naturally as the cloak of the traveller, for which sun and wind contended! He is the true Propontic which never ebbeth! The sea which taketh handsomely at each man's hand. In vain the victim, whom he delighteth to honour, struggles with destiny; he is in the net. Lend therefore cheerfully, O man ordained to lend—that thou lose not in the end, with thy worldly penny, the reversion promised. Combine not preposterously in thine own person the penalties of Lazarus and of Dives!—but, when thou seest the proper authority coming, meet it smilingly, as it were half-way. Come, a handsome sacrifice! See how light *he* makes of it! Strain not courtesies with a noble enemy.

Reflections like the foregoing were forced upon my mind by the death of my old friend, Ralph Bigod, Esq., who parted this life on Wednesday evening; dying, as he had lived, without much trouble. He boasted himself a descendant from mighty ancestors of that name, who heretofore held ducal dignities in this realm. In his actions and sentiments he belied not the stock to which he pretended. Early in life he found himself invested with ample revenues; which, with that noble disinterestedness which I have noticed as inherent in men of the *great race*, he took almost immediate measures entirely to dissipate and bring to nothing: for there is something revolting in the idea of a king holding a private purse; and the thoughts of Bigod were all regal. Thus furnished, by the very act of disfurnishment; getting rid of the cumbersome luggage of riches, more apt (as one sings)

> To slacken virtue, and abate her edge,
> Than prompt her to do aught may merit praise,

he set forth, like some Alexander, upon his great enterprise, "borrowing and to borrow!"

In his periegesis, or triumphant progress throughout this island, it has been calculated that he laid a tythe part of the inhabitants under contribution. I reject this estimate as greatly exaggerated:—but having had the honour of accompanying my friend, divers times, in his perambulations about this vast city, I own I was greatly struck at first with the prodigious number of faces we met, who claimed a sort of respectful acquaintance with us. He was one day so obliging as to explain the phenomenon. It seems, these were his tributaries; feeders of his exchequer; gentlemen, his good friends (as he was pleased to express himself), to whom he had occasionally been beholden for a loan. Their multitudes did no way disconcert him. He rather took a pride in numbering them; and, with Comus, seemed pleased to be "stocked with so fair a herd."

With such sources, it was a wonder how he contrived to keep his treasury always empty. He did it by force of an aphorism, which he had often in his mouth, that "money kept longer than three days stinks." So he made use of it while it was fresh. A good part he drank away (for he was an excellent toss-pot), some he gave away, the rest he threw away, literally tossing and hurling it violently from him— as boys do burrs, or as if it had been infectious,—into ponds, or ditches, or deep holes, inscrutable cavities of the earth;— or he would bury it (where he would never seek it again) by a river's side under some bank, which (he would facetiously observe) paid no interest—but out away from him it must go peremptorily, as Hagar's offspring into the wilderness, while it was sweet. He never missed it. The streams were perennial which fed his fisc. When new supplies became necessary, the first person that had the felicity to fall in with him, friend or stranger, was sure to contribute to the deficiency. For Bigod had an *undeniable* way with him. He had a cheerful, open exterior, a quick jovial eye, a bald forehead, just touched with grey (*cana fides*). He anticipated no excuse, and found none. And, waiving for a while my theory as to the *great race,* I would put it to the most untheorising reader, who may at times have disposable coin in his pocket, whether it is not more repugnant to the kindliness of his nature to refuse such a one as I am describing, than to say *no* to a poor petitionary rogue (your bastard borrower), who, by his mumping visnomy, tells you that he expects nothing better; and, therefore, whose preconceived notions and expectations you do in reality so much less shock in the refusal.

When I think of this man; his fiery glow of heart; his swell of feeling; how magnificent, how *ideal* he was; how great at the midnight hour; and when I compare with him the companions with whom I have associated since, I grudge the saving of a few idle ducats, and think that I am fallen into the society of *lenders,* and *little* men.

To one like Elia, whose treasures are rather cased in leather covers than closed in iron coffers, there is a class of alienators more formidable than that which I have touched upon; I mean your *borrowers of books*—those multitudes of collections, spoilers of the symmetry of shelves, and creators of odd volumes. There is Comberbatch, matchless in his depredations!

That foul gap in the bottom shelf facing you, like a great eye-tooth knocked out—(you are now with me in my little back study in Bloomsbury, Reader!)—with the huge Switzerlike tomes on each side (like the Guildhall giants, in their reformed posture, guardant of nothing) once held the tallest of my folios, *Opera Bonaventuræ*, choice and massy divinity, to which its two supporters (school divinity also, but of a lesser calibre,—Bellarmine, and Holy Thomas), showed but as dwarfs,—itself an Ascapart!—*that* Comberbatch abstracted upon the faith of a theory he holds, which is more easy, I confess, for me to suffer by than to refute, namely, that "the title to property in a book (my Bonaventure, for instance) is in exact ratio to the claimant's powers of understanding and appreciating the same." Should he go on acting upon this theory, which of our shelves is safe?

The slight vacuum in the left-hand case—two shelves from the ceiling—scarcely distinguishable but by the quick eye of a loser—was whilom the commodious resting place of Browne on Urn Burial. C. will hardly allege that he knows more about that treatise than I do, who introduced it to him, and was indeed the first (of the moderns) to discover its beauties —but so have I known a foolish lover to praise his mistress in the presence of a rival more qualified to carry her off than himself.—Just below, Dodsley's dramas want their fourth volume, where Vittoria Corombona is! The remainder nine are as distasteful as Priam's refuse sons, when the Fates *borrowed* Hector. Here stood the Anatomy of Melancholy, in sober state.—There loitered the Complete Angler; quiet as in life, by some stream side.—In yonder nook, John Buncle, a widower-volume, with "eyes closed," mourns his ravished mate.

One justice I must do my friend, that if he sometimes, like the sea, sweeps away a treasure, at another time, sea-like, he throws up as rich an equivalent to match it. I have a small under-collection of this nature (my friend's gatherings in his various calls), picked up, he has forgotten at what odd places, and deposited with as little memory at mine. I take in these orphans, the twice-deserted. These proselytes of the gate are welcome as the true Hebrews. There they stand in conjunction; natives, and naturalised. The latter seems as little disposed to inquire out their true lineage as I am.—I charge no warehouse-room for the deodands, nor shall ever put myself to the ungentlemanly trouble of advertising a sale of them to pay expenses.

To lose a volume to C. carries some sense and meaning in it. You are sure that he will make one hearty meal on your viands, if he can give no account of the platter after it. But what moved thee, wayward, spiteful K[enny], to be so importunate to carry off with thee, in spite of tears and adjurations to thee to forbear, the Letters of that princely woman, the thrice noble Margaret Newcastle?—knowing at the time, and knowing that I knew also, thou most assuredly wouldst never turn over one leaf of the illustrious folio;—what but the mere spirit of contradiction, and childish love of getting the better of thy friend?—Then, worst cut of all! to transport it with thee to the Gallican land—

> Unworthy land to harbour such a sweetness,
> A virtue in which all ennobling thoughts dwelt,
> Pure thoughts, kind thoughts, high thoughts, her sex's wonder!

——hadst thou not thy play-books, and books of jests and fancies, about thee, to keep thee merry, even as thou keepest all companies with thy quips and mirthful tales? Child of the Green-room, it was unkindly done of thee. Thy wife, too, that part-French, better-part-English-woman!—that *she* could fix upon no other treatise to bear away, in kindly token of remembering us, than the works of Fulke Greville, Lord Brook—of which no Frenchman, nor woman of France, Italy, or England, was ever by nature constituted to comprehend a tittle! *Was there not Zimmerman on Solitude?*

Reader, if haply thou art blessed with a moderate collection, be shy of showing it; or if thy heart overfloweth to lend them, lend thy books; but let it be to such a one as S. T. C.—he will return them (generally anticipating the time appointed) with usury; enriched with annotations, tripling their value. I have had experience. Many are these precious MSS. of his—(in *matter* oftentimes, and almost in *quantity* not infrequently, vying with the originals) in no very clerkly hand—legible in my Daniel; in old Burton; in Sir Thomas Browne; and those abstruser cogitations of the Greville, now, alas! wandering in Pagan lands.—I counsel thee, shut not thy heart, nor thy library, against S. T. C.

Another of Lamb's friends was John Bates Dibdin, who was employed in a shipping office in that part of London known as the "Old Jewry," and business often took him to the East India House, where he met Lamb. Dibdin was of a lively disposition, with a ready wit and interested in things literary. He it was who first penetrated Lamb's disguise, when the latter began to publish his essays under the pen-name of Elia.

LETTER TO DIBDIN

Friday, some day of June, 1826.

Dear D.,—My first impulse upon opening your letter was pleasure in seeing your old neat hand, nine parts gentlemanly, with a modest dash of the clerical: my second a thought, natural enough this hot weather—am I to answer all this? Why 'tis as long as those to the Ephesians and Galatians put together, I have counted the words for curiosity. But then Paul has nothing like the fun which is ebullient all over yours. I don't remember a good thing (good like yours) from the 1st Romans to the last of the Hebrews. I remember but one Pun in all the Evangely and that was made by his and our Master: Thou art Peter (that is Doctor Rock), and upon this Rock will I build etc., which sanctifies Punning with me against all gainsayers. I never knew an enemy to puns who was not an ill-natured man. Your fair critic in the coach reminds me of a Scotchman who assured me that he did not see much in Shakspeare. I replied, I daresay *not*. He felt the equivoke, look'd awkward and reddish, but soon return'd to the attack by saying that he thought Burns was as good as Shakspeare: I said that I had no doubt he was—to a *Scotchman*. We exchanged no more words that day. Your account of the fierce faces in the Hanging, with the presumed interlocution of the Eagle and the Tyger, amused us greatly. You cannot be so very bad while you can pick mirth off from rotten walls. May the Lord in the Fourth Person who clapt invisible wet blankets about the shoulders of Shadrack Meschek and Abednego, be with you in the Fiery Trial. But get out of the frying pan. Your business, I take it, is bathing, not baking.

Let me hear that you have clambered up to Lover's Seat; it is as fine in that neighbourhood as Juan Fernandez, as lonely, too, when the Fishing-boats are not out; I have sat for hours, staring upon a shipless sea. The salt sea is never so grand as when it is left to itself. One cock-boat spoils it. A sea-mew or two improves it. And go to the little church, which is a very Protestant Loretto, and seems dropt by some angel for the use of a hermit, who was at once parishioner and a whole parish. It is not too big. Go in the night, bring it away in your portmanteau, and I will plant it in my garden. It must have been erected in the very infancy of British Christianity, for the two or three first converts; yet with it all the appurtenances of a church of the first magnitude, its pulpit, its pews, its baptismal font; a cathedral in a nutshell. Seven people would crowd it like a Caledonian Chapel. The minister that divides the Word there, must give lumping penny-worths. It is built to the text of "two or three assembled in my name." It reminds me of the grain of mustard seed. If the glebe-land is proportionate, it may yield two potatoes. Tithes out of it could be no more split than a hair. Its First fruits must be its Last, for 'twould never produce a couple. It is truly the strait and narrow way, and few there be (of London visitants) that find it. The still small voice is surely to be found there, if anywhere. A sounding-board is merely there for ceremony. It is secure from earthquakes, not more from sanctity than size, for 'twould feel a mountain thrown upon it no more than a taper-worm would. *Go and see, but not without your spectacles*. By the way, there's a capital farm-house two-thirds of the way to the Lover's Seat, with incomparable plum cake, ginger-beer, etc. Mary bids me warn you not to read the *Anatomy of Melancholy* in your present *low way*. You'll fancy yourself a pipkin, or a headless bear, as Burton speaks of. You'll be lost in a maze of remedies for a labyrinth of diseasements; a plethora of cures. Read Fletcher; above all, the *Spanish Curate;* the *Thief, or Little Night Walker,* the *Wit Without Money,* and the *Lover's Pilgrimage*. Laugh, and come home fat. Neither do we think Sir T. Browne quite the thing for you just at present. Fletcher is as light as soda-water, Browne and Burton are two strong potions for an Invalid. And don't thumb or dirt the books. Take care of the bindings. Lay a leaf of silver paper under 'em as you read them. And don't smoke tobacco over 'em, the leaves will fall in and burn or dirty their namesakes. If you find any dusty atoms of the Indian weed crumbled up in the Beaumont and Fletcher, they are *mine*. But then, you know, so is the Folio also. A pipe and a comedy of Fletcher's the last thing of a night is the best recipe for light dreams and to scatter away Nightmares. *Probatum est*. But do as you like about the former. Only cut the Baker's. You will come home else all crust; Rankings must chip you, before you can appear in his counting-house. And, my dear Peter Fin, Junr., do contrive to see the sea at least once before you return. You'll be asked about it in the Old Jewry. It will appear singular not to have seen it. And rub up your Muse, the family Muse, and send us a rhyme or so. Don't waste your wit upon that damned Dry Salter. I never knew but one Dry Salter who could relish those mellow effusions, and he broke. You know Tommy Hill, the wittiest of dry salters. Dry Salters, what a word for this thirsty weather! I must drink after it. Here's to thee, my dear Dibdin, and to our having you again snug and well at Colebrooke. But our nearest hopes are to hear again from you shortly. An epistle only a quarter as agreeable as your last would be a treat.

Yours most truly,

C. LAMB.

LETTER TO DIBDIN

Saturday, September 9, 1826.

An answer is requested.

Dear D.:—

I have observed that a Letter is never more acceptable than when received upon a rainy day, especially a rainy Sunday;

which moves me to send you somewhat, however short. This will find you sitting after Breakfast, which you will have prolonged as far as you can with consistency to the poor handmaid that has the reversion of the Tea Leaves; making two nibbles of your last morsel of stale roll (you cannot have hot new ones on the Sabbath), and reluctantly coming to an end, because when that is done, what can you do till dinner? You cannot go to the Beach, for the rain is drowning the sea, turning rank Thetis fresh, taking the brine out of Neptune's pickles, while mermaids sit upon rocks with umbrellas, their ivory combs sheathed for spoiling in the wet of waters foreign to them. You cannot go to the library, for it's shut. You are not religious enough to go to church. O, it is worth while to cultivate piety to the gods, to have something to fill up the heart on a wet Sunday! You cannot cast accounts, for your ledger is being eaten with moths in the Ancient Jewry. You cannot play at draughts, for there is none to play with you, and besides there is not a draught-board in the house. You cannot go to market, for it closed last night. You cannot look into the shops, their backs are shut upon you. You cannot read the Bible, for it is not good reading for the sick and the hypochrondriacal. You cannot while away an hour with a friend, for you have no friend round that Wrekin. You cannot divert yourself with a stray acquaintance, for you have picked none up. You cannot bear the chiming of bells, for they invite you to a banquet where you are no visitant. You cannot cheer yourself with the prospect of to-morrow's letter, for none come on Mondays. You cannot count those endless vials on the mantlepiece with any hope of making a variation in their numbers. You have counted your spiders: your Bastile is exhausted. You sit and deliberately curse your hard exile from all familiar sights and sounds. Old Ranking poking in his head unexpectedly would just now be as good to you as Grimaldi. Anything to deliver you from this intolerable weight of Ennui. You are too ill to shake it off: not ill enough to submit to it, and to lie down as a lamb under it. The Tyranny of sickness is nothing to the Cruelty of Convalescence: 'tis to have Thirty Tyrants for one. That pattering rain drops on your brain. You'll be worse after dinner, for you must dine at one to-day, that Betty may go to afternoon service. She insists upon having her chopped hay. And then when she goes out, who was something to you, something to speak to—what an interminable afternoon you'll have to go through. You can't break yourself from your locality: you cannot say "to-morrow I set off for Banstead, by God:" for you are booked for Wednesday. Forseeing this, I thought a cheerful letter would come in opportunely. If any of the little topics for mirth I have thought upon would serve you in this utter extinguishment of sunshine, to make you a little merry, I shall have had my ends. I love to make things comfortable. . . . This, which is scratched out, was the most material thing I had to say, but on maturer thoughts I defer it.

P.S.—We are just sitting down to dinner with a pleasant party, Coleridge, Reynolds the dramatist, and Sam Bloxam: to-morrow (that is to-day), Liston, and Wyat of the Wells, dine with us. May this find you as jolly and freakish as we mean to be. C. LAMB.

Unquestionably the most eccentric of all Lamb's friends was George Dyer, or "G. D." as Lamb usually initialled him in his letters. He was an old Christ's Hospital boy, whose intellectual gifts attracted the attention of the physician to the school. The latter loaned him books and encouraged his Greek studies, with the result that Dyer went up to Cambridge with the distinction of "Grecian," a title which signified the highest honors.

From college he came out totally wrapped up in scholarly learning; but absolutely impractical. After acting for a time as schoolmaster and tutor, Dyer came up to London, and earned a slender living as hack-writer for the book-sellers.

Lamb took never-ending delight in Dyer's peculiarities, and his letters abound with amusing episodes in which Dyer was the chief figure. In *Oxford in the Vacation*, Lamb, who had been denied any years at college, relates his custom of wistfully visiting during his short summer holiday one or the other of the English university towns, and introduces George Dyer as the type of the absent-minded scholar.

OXFORD IN THE VACATION

Casting a preparatory glance at the bottom of this article— as the wary connoisseur in prints, with cursory eye (which, while it reads, seems as though it read not), never fails to consult the *quis sculpsit* in the corner, before he pronounces some rare piece to be a Vivares, or a Woollet—methinks I hear you exclaim, Reader, *Who is Elia?*

Because in my last I tried to divert thee with some half-forgotten humours of some old clerks defunct, in an old house of business, long since gone to decay, doubtless you have already set me down in your mind as one of the self-same college—a votary of the desk—a notched and cropt scrivener—one that sucks his sustenance, as certain sick people are said to do, through a quill.

Well, I do agonize something of the sort. I confess that it is my humour, my fancy—in the fore-part of the day, when the mind of your man of letters requires some relaxation (and none better than such as at first sight seems most abhorrent from his beloved studies)—to while away some good hours of my time in the contemplation of indigos, cottons, raw silks, piece-goods, flowered or otherwise. In the first place

. . . and then it sends you home with such increased appetite
to your books . . . not to say, that your outside sheets, and
waste wrappers of foolscap, do receive into them, most
kindly and naturally, the impression of sonnets, epigrams,
essays,—so that the very parings of a counting-house are, in
some sort, the settings up of an author. The enfranchised
quill that has plodded all the morning among the cart-rucks
of figures and ciphers, frisks and curvets so at its ease over the
flowery carpet-ground of a midnight dissertation.—It feels its
promotion. . . . So that you see, upon the whole, the literary
dignity of *Elia* is very little, if at all, compromised in the
condescension.

Not that, in my anxious detail of the many commodities
incidental to the life of a public office, I would be thought
blind to certain flaws, which a cunning carper might be able
to pick in this Joseph's vest. And here I must have leave,
in the fulness of my soul, to regret the abolition, and doing-
away-with altogether, of those consolatory interstices, and
sprinklings of freedom, through the four seasons,—the *red-
letter days*, now become, to all intents and purposes, *dead-
letter days*. There was Paul, and Stephen, and Barnabas—

Andrew and John, men famous in old times

—we were used to keep all their days holy, as long back as
when I was at school at Christ's. I remember their effigies,
by the same token, in the old *Baskett* Prayer Book. There
hung Peter in his uneasy posture—holy Bartlemy in the
troublesome act of flaying, after the famous Marsyas by
Spagnoletti.—I honoured them all, and could almost have
wept the defalcation of Iscariot—so much did we love to
keep holy memories sacred:—only methought I a little
grudged at the coalition of the *better Jude* with Simon—
clubbing (as it were) their sanctities together, to make up

one poor gaudy-day between them—as an economy unworthy of the dispensation.

These were bright visitations in a scholar's and a clerk's life—"far off their coming shone."—I was as good as an almanac in those days. I could have told you such a saint's day falls out next week, or the week after. Peradventure the Epiphany, by some periodical infelicity, would, once in six years, merge in a Sabbath. Now am I little better than one of the profane. Let me not be thought to arraign the wisdom of my civil superiors, who have judged the further observation of these holy tides to be papistical, superstitious. Only in a custom of such long standing, methinks, if their Holinesses the Bishops had, in decency, been first sounded—but I am wading out of my depths. I am not the man to decide the limits of civil and ecclesiastical authority—I am plain Elia—no Selden, nor Archbishop Usher—though at present in the thick of their books, here in the heart of learning, under the shadow of the mighty Bodley.

I can here play the gentleman, enact the student. To such a one as myself, who has been defrauded in his young years of the sweet food of academic institution, nowhere is so pleasant, to while away a few idle weeks at, as one or other of the Universities. Their vacation, too, at this time of the year, falls in so pat with *ours*. Here I can take my walks unmolested, and fancy myself of what degree or standing I please. I seem admitted *ad eundem*. I fetch up past opportunities. I can rise at the chapel-bell, and dream that it rings for *me*. In moods of humility I can be a Sizar, or a Servitor. When the peacock vein rises, I strut a Gentleman Commoner. In graver moments, I proceed Master of Arts. Indeed I do not think I am much unlike that respectable character. I have seen your dim-eyed vergers, and bed-makers in spectacles, drop a bow or curtsy, as I pass, wisely mistaking me for something of the sort. I go about in black, which favours the notion. Only in Christ Church reverend quadrangle I can be content to pass for nothing short of a Seraphic Doctor.

The walks at these times are so much one's own—the tall trees of Christ's, the groves of Magdalen! The halls deserted, and with open doors, inviting one to slip in unperceived, and pay a devoir to some Founder, or noble or royal Benefactress (that should have been ours) whose portrait seems to smile upon their overlooked beadsman, and to adopt me for their own. Then, to take a peep in by the way at the butteries, and sculleries, redolent of antique hospitality: the immense caves of kitchens, kitchen fire places, cordial recesses; ovens whose first pies were baked four centuries ago; and spits which have cooked for Chaucer. Not the meanest minister among the dishes but is hallowed to me through his imagination, and the Cook goes forth a Manciple.

Antiquity! thou wondrous charm, what art thou? that, being nothing, art everything! When thou *wert,* thou wert not antiquity—then thou wert nothing, but hadst a remoter *antiquity,* as thou called'st it, to look back to with blind veneration; thou thyself being to thyself flat, jejune, *modern!* What mystery lurks in this retroversion? or what half Januses are we, that cannot look forward with the same idolatry with which we forever revert! The mighty future is as nothing, being everything! the past is everything, being nothing!

What were thy *dark ages?* Surely the sun rose as brightly then as now, and man got him to his work in the morning. Why is it that we can never hear mention of them without an accompanying feeling, as though a palpable obscure had dimmed the face of things, and that our ancestors wandered to and fro groping!

Above all thy rarities, old Oxenford, what do most arride

and solace me, are thy repositories of mouldering learning, thy shelves——

What a place to be in is an old library! It seems as though all the souls of all the writers, that have bequeathed their labours to these Bodleians, were reposing here, as in some dormitory, or middle state. I do not want to handle, to profane the leaves, their winding-sheets. I could as soon dislodge a shade. I seem to inhale learning, walking amid their foliage; and the odour of their old-moth-scented coverings is fragrant as the first bloom of those sciential apples which grew amid the happy orchard.

Still less have I curiosity to disturb the elder repose of MSS. Those *variæ lectiones,* so tempting to the more erudite palates, do but disturb and unsettle my faith. I am no Herculanean raker. The credit of the three witnesses might have slept unimpeached for me. I leave these curiosities to Porson, and to G[eorge] D[yer]—whom, by the way, I found busy as a moth over some rotten archive, rummaged out of some seldom-explored press, in a nook at Oriel. With long poring, he is grown almost into a book. He stood as passive as one by the side of the old shelves. I longed to new-coat him in Russia, and assign him his place. He might have mustered for a tall Scapula.

D. is assiduous in his visits to these seats of learning. No inconsiderable portion of his moderate fortune, I apprehend, is consumed in journeys between them and Clifford's-inn—where, like a dove on the asp's nest, he has long taken up his unconscious abode, amid an incongruous assembly of attorneys, attorneys' clerks, apparitors, promoters, vermin of the law, among whom he sits, "in calm and sinless peace." The fangs of the law pierce him not—the winds of litigation blow over his humble chambers—the hard sheriff's officer moves his hat as he passes—legal nor illegal discourtesy

touches him—none thinks of offering violence or injustice
to him—you would as soon "strike an abstract idea."

D. has been engaged, he tells me, through a course of laborious years, in an investigation into all curious matter connected with the two Universities; and has lately lit upon a
MS. collection of charters, relative to C——, by which he
hopes to settle some disputed points—particularly that long
controversy between them as to priority of foundation. The
ardour with which he engages in these liberal pursuits, I am
afraid, has not met with all the encouragement it deserved,
either here, or at C——. Your caputs, and heads of colleges,
care less than anybody else about these questions.—Contented
to suck the milky fountains of their Alma Maters, without
inquiring into the venerable gentlewomen's years, they rather
hold such curiosities to be impertinent—unreverend. They
have their good glebe lands in *manu,* and care not much to
rake into the title-deeds. I gather at least so much from other
sources, for D. is not a man to complain.

D. started like an unbroke heifer, when I interrupted him.
A priori it was not very probable that we should have met
in Oriel. But D. would have done the same, had I accosted
him on the sudden in his own walks in Clifford's-inn, or in
the Temple. In addition to a provoking short-sightedness (the
effect of late studies and watchings at the midnight oil) D.
is the most absent of men. He made a call the other morning
at our friend M[ontague]'s in Bedford-square; and, finding
nobody at home, was ushered into the hall, where, asking for
pen and ink, with great exactitude of purpose he enters me
his name in the book—which ordinarily lies about in such
places, to record the failures of the untimely or unfortunate
visitor—and takes his leave with many ceremonies, and pro-
fessions of regret. Some two or three hours after, his walking
destinies returned him into the same neighbourhood again,

and again the quiet image of the fireside circle at M.'s—Mrs. M. presiding at it like a Queen Lar, with pretty A[nne] S[kepper] at her side—striking irresistibly on his fancy, he makes another call (forgetting that they were "certainly not to return from the country before that day week"), and disappointed a second time, inquires for pen and paper as before: again the book is brought, and in the line just above that in which he is about to print his second name (his rescript)—his first name (scarce dry) looks out upon him like another Sosia, or as if a man should suddenly encounter his own duplicate!—The effect may be conceived. D. made many a good resolution against any such lapses in future. I hope he will not keep them too rigorously.

For with G. D.—to be absent from the body, is sometimes (not to speak it profanely) to be present with the Lord. At the very time when, personally encountering thee, he passes on with no recognition——or, being stopped, starts like a thing surprised—at that moment, Reader, he is on Mount Tabor—or Parnassus—or co-sphered with Plato—or, with Harrington, framing "immortal commonwealths"—devising some plan of amelioration to thy country, or thy species—peradventure meditating some individual kindness or courtesy, to be done to *thee thyself*, the returning consciousness of which made him to start so guiltily at thy obtruded personal presence.

D. is delightful anywhere, but he is at the best in such places as these. He cares not much for Bath. He is out of his element at Buxton, at Scarborough, or Harrowgate. The Cam and the Isis are to him "better than all the waters of Damascus." On the Muses hill he is happy, and good, as one of the Shepherds on the Delectable Mountains; and when he goes about with you to show you the halls and colleges, you think you have with you the Interpreter at the House Beautiful.

LETTER TO MANNING

1800.

Dear Manning,—I am going to ask a favour of you, and am at a loss how to do it in the most delicate manner. For this purpose I have been looking into Pliny's letters, who is noted to have had the best grace in begging of all the ancients, (I read him in the elegant translation of Mr. Melmoth,) but not finding any case there exactly similar with mine, I am constained to beg in my own barbarian way. To come to the point then, and hasten into the middle of things: have you a copy of your Algebra to give away? I do not ask it for myself; I have too much reverence for the Black Arts ever to approach thy circle, illustrious Trismegist! But that worthy man, and excellent Poet, George Dyer, made me a visit yesternight, on purpose to borrow one; supposing, rationally enough, I must say, that you had made me a present of one before this; the omission of which I take to have proceeded only from negligence; but it is a fault. I could lend him no assistance. You must know he is just now diverted from the pursuit of the BELL LETTERS by a paradox, which he has heard his friend Frend, (that learned mathematician) maintain, that the negative quantities of mathematicians were *meræ nugæ*, things scarcely *in rerum natura*, and smacking too much of mystery for gentlemen of Mr. Frend's clear Unitarian capacity. However, the dispute once set a-going, has seized violently on George's pericranick; and it is necessary for his health that he should speedily come to a resolution of his doubts. He goes about teasing his friends with his new mathematics; he even frantically talks of purchasing Manning's Algebra, which shows him far gone; for, to my knowledge, he has not been master of seven shillings a good time. George's pockets and ——'s brains are two things in nature which do not abhor a vacuum. . . . Now, if you could step in, in his trembling suspense of his reason, and he should find on Saturday morning, lying for him at the Porter's Lodge, Clifford's Inn, (his safest address.) Manning's Algebra, with a neat manuscript in the blank leaf, running thus "FROM THE AUTHOR," it might save his wits, and restore the unhappy author to those studies of poetry and criticism which are at present suspended, to the infinite regret of the whole literary world. N. B.—Dirty backs, smeared leaves, and dogs' ears, will be rather a recommendation than otherwise. N. B.—He must have the book as soon as possible, or nothing can withhold him from madly purchasing the book on tick. . . . Then shall we see him sweetly restored to the chain of Longinus—to dictate in smooth and modest phrase the laws of verse; to prove that Theocritus first introduced the Pastoral, and Virgil and Pope brought it to its perfection; that Gray and Mason (who always hunt in couples in George's brain) have shown a great deal of poetical fire in their lyric poetry; that Aristotle's rules are not to be servilely followed, which George has shown to have imposed great shackles upon modern genius. His poems, I find, are to consist of two vols.—reasonable octavo; and a third book will exclusively contain criticisms, in which he asserts he has gone *pretty deeply* into the laws of blank verse and rhyme—epic poetry, dramatic and pastoral ditto— all which is to come out before Christmas. But above all, he has *touched* most *deeply* upon the Drama, comparing the English with the modern German stage, their merits and defects. Apprehending that his *studies* (not to mention his *turn,* which I take to be chiefly towards the lyrical poetry) hardly qualified him for these disquisitions, I modestly inquired what plays he had read? I found by George's reply that he *had* read Shakspeare, but that was a good while since:

he calls him a great but irregular genius, which I think to be an original and just remark. Beaumont and Fletcher, Massinger, Ben Jonson, Shirley, Marlowe, Ford, and the worthies of Dodsley's Collection—he confessed he had read none of them, but professed his *intention* of looking through them all, so as to be able to *touch* upon them in his book. So Shakspeare, Otway, and I believe Rowe, to whom he was naturally directed by Johnson's Lives, and these not read lately, are to stand in stead of a general knowledge of the subject. God bless his dear absurd head!

By the by, did I not write you a letter with something about an invitation in it? But let that pass; I suppose it is not agreeable.

N. B.—It would not be amiss if you were to accompany your *present* with a dissertation on negative quantities.

C. L.

LETTER TO MANNING

1800.

George Dyer is an Archimedes, and an Archimagus, and a Tycho Brahé, and a Corpernicus; and thou art the darling of the Nine; and midwife to their wandering babe also! We take tea with that learned poet and critic on Tuesday night, at half-past five, in his neat library. The repast will be light and Attic, with criticism. If thou couldst contrive to wheel up thy dear carcass on the Monday, and after dining with us on tripe, calves' kidneys, or whatever else the Cornucopia of St. Claire may be willing to pour out on the occasion, might we not adjourn together to the Heathen's—thou with thy Black Backs, and I with some innocent volume of the Bell Letters, Shenstone, or the like: it would make him wash his old flannel gown (that has not been washed to my knowledge since it has been *his*—Oh the long time!) with tears of

joy. Thou shouldst settle his scruples and unravel his cob-
webs, and sponge off the sad stuff that weighs upon his dear
wounded pia mater. Thou shouldst restore light to his eyes;
and him to his friends and the public. Parnassus should
shower her civic crowns upon thee for saving the wits of a
citizen! I thought I saw a lucid interval in George the other
night; he broke in upon my studies just at tea-time, and
brought with him Dr. Anderson, an old gentleman who
ties his breeches' knees with packthread, and boasts that he
has been disappointed by ministers. The Doctor wanted to
see *me;* for I being a Poet, he thought I might furnish him
with a copy of verses to suit his *Agricultural Magazine.* The
Doctor, in the course of the conversation, mentioned a poem
called the "Epigoniad," by one Wilkie, an epic poem, in
which there is not one tolerable good line all through, but
every incident and speech borrowed from Homer. George
had been sitting inattentive, seemingly, to what was going
on—hatching of negative quantities—when, suddenly, the
name of his old friend Homer stung his pericranicks, and,
jumping up, he begged to know where he could meet with
Wilkie's works. It was a curious fact, he said, that there
should be such an epic poem and he not know of it, and he
must get a copy of it, as he was going to touch pretty deeply
upon the subject of the Epic—and he was sure there must be
some things good in a poem of 8000 lines! I was pleased with
this transient return of his reason and recurrence to his old
ways of thinking: it gave me great hopes of a recovery,
which nothing but your book can completely insure. Pray
come on Monday, if you *can,* and stay your own time. I
have a good large room, with two beds in it, in the handsomest of which thou shalt repose a-nights, and dream of
Spheroides. I hope you will understand by the nonsense of
this letter that I am *not* melancholy at the thoughts of thy

coming: I thought it necessary to add this because you love *precision*. Take notice that our stay at Dyer's will not exceed eight o'clock; after which our pursuits will be our own. But indeed I think a little recreation among the Bell Letters and poetry will do you some service in the interval of severer studies. I hope we shall fully discuss with George Dyer what I have never yet heard done to my satisfaction, the reason of Dr. Johnson's malevolent strictures on the higher species of the Ode.

LETTER TO MANNING

December 27th, 1800.

At length George Dyer's phrenitis has come to a crisis; he is raging and furiously mad. I waited upon the Heathen, Thursday was a se'nnight. The first symptom which struck my eye, and gave me incontrovertible proof of the fatal truth, was a pair of nankeen pantaloons four times too big for him, which the said Heathen did pertinaciously affirm to be new.

They were absolutely ingrained with the accumulated dirt of ages; but he affirmed them to be clean. He was going to visit a lady that was nice about those things, and that's the reason he wore nankeen that day. And then he danced, and capered, and fidgeted, and pulled up his pantaloons, and hugged his intolerable flannel vestment closer about his poetic loins. Anon he gave it loose to the zephyrs which plentifully insinuate their tiny bodies through every crevice, door, window, or wainscot, expressly formed for the exclusion of such impertinents. Then he caught at a proof sheet, and catched up a laundress's bill instead—made a dart at Bloomfield's Poems, and threw them in agony aside. I could not bring him to one direct reply; he could not maintain his jumping mind

in a right line for the tithe of a moment by Clifford's Inn
clock. He must go to the printer's immediately: (the most
unlucky accident!) he had struck off five hundred impressions of his Poems, which were ready for delivery to subscribers, and the Preface must all be expunged. There were
eighty pages of Preface, and not till that morning had he
discovered that in the very first page of said Preface he had
set out with a principle of Criticism fundamentally wrong,
which vitiated all his following reasoning. The Preface must
be expunged, although it cost him £30, the lowest calculation,
taking in paper and printing! In vain have his real friends
remonstrated against this midsummer madness. George is
as obstinate as a Primitive Christian, and wards and parries
off all our thrusts with on unanswerable fence:—"Sir, 'tis
of great consequence that the *world* is not *misled!*"

As for the other Professor, he has actually begun to dive
into Tavernier and Chardin's *Persian* Travels for a story, to
form a new drama for the sweet tooth of this fastidious age.
Hath not Bethlehem College a fair action for non-residents
against such professors? Are poets so *few* in *this age,* that
he must write poetry? *Is morals* a subject so exhausted, that
he must quit that line? Is the metaphysic well (without a
bottom) drained dry?

If I can guess at the wicked pride of the Professor's heart,
I would take a shrewd wager that he disdains ever again to
dip his pen in *Prose.* Adieu, ye splendid theories! Farewell,
dreams of political justice! Lawsuits, where I was council
for Archbishop Fenelon *versus* my own mother, in the
famous fire cause!

Vanish from my mind, professors, one and all! I have
metal more attractive on foot.

Man of many snipes,—I will sup with thee (Deo
volente, et diabolo nolente,) on Monday night, the 5th

of January, in the new year, and crush a cup to the infant century.

A word or two of my progress: Embark at six o'clock in the morning, with a fresh gale, on a Cambridge one-decker; very cold till eight at night; land at St. Mary's light-house, muffins and coffee upon table, (or any other curious production of Turkey, or both Indies,) snipes exactly at nine, punch to commence at ten, with *argument;* difference of opinion is expected to take place about eleven; perfect unanimity, with some haziness and dimness, before twelve. N. B.—My single affection is not so singly wedded to snipes; but the curious and epicurean eye would also take pleasure in beholding a delicate and well-chosen assortment of teals, ortolans, the unctuous and palate-soothing flesh of geese, wild and tame, nightingales' brains, the sensorium of a young suckling pig, or any other Christian dish, which I leave to the judgment of you and the cook of Gonville.   C. LAMB.

In a letter to another friend, John Rickman, Lamb made George Dyer's behavior, while under the impression that he was nearly *in extremis,* the basis of a lively account.

LETTER TO RICKMAN

[Undated. Probably 1801.]

To
John Rickman, Esq.,
     Dublin Castle.

A letter from G. Dyer will probably accompany this. I wish I could convey to you any notion of the whimsical scenes I have been witness to in this fortnight past. 'Twas on Tuesday week that the poor heathen scrambled up to my door about breakfast time. He came thro' a violent rain with no neckcloth on, and a beard that made him a spectacle to men and angels, and tapped at the door. Mary opened it, and he stood stark still and held a paper in his hand importing that he had been ill with a fever. He neither wouldn't or couldn't speak except by signs. When you went to comfort him, he put his hand upon his heart and shook his head and told us his complaint lay where no medicines could reach it. I was dispatched for Dr. Dale, Mr. Phillins of St. Paul's Church yard and Mr. Frend, who is to be his executor. George solemnly delivered into Mr. Frend's hands and mine an old burnt preface that had been in the fire, with injunctions we solemnly vowed to obey that it should be printed after his death with his last corrections, and that some account should be given to the world why he had not fulfilled his engagement with subscribers. Having done this and borrowed two guineas of his bookseller to whom he imparted in confidence that he should leave a great many loose papers behind him which would only want methodizing and arranging to prove very lucrative to any bookseller after his death, he laid himself down on my bed in a mood of complacent resignation.

By the aid of meat and drink put into him (for I all along suspected a vacuum) he was enabled to sit up in the evening, but he had not got the better of his intolerable fear of dying; he expressed such philosophic indifference in his speech and such frightened apprehensions in his physiognomy that if he had been truly dying, and I had known it, I could not have kept my countenance. In particular, when the doctor came and ordered to take little white powders (I suppose of chalk or alum, to humour him), he eyed him with a suspicion which I could not account for; he has since explained that he took it for granted Dr. Dale knew his situation and had ordered him these powders to hasten his departure that he

might suffer as little pain as possible. Think what an aspect
the heathen put on with those fears upon a dirty face. To
recount all his freaks for two or three days while he thought
he was going, and how the fit operated, and sometimes the
man got uppermost and sometimes the author, and he had
this excellent person to serve, and he must correct some
proof sheets for Phillips, and he could not bear to leave his
subscribers unsatisfied, but he must not think of these things
now, he was going to a place where he should satisfy all his
debts—and when he got a little better he began to discourse
what a happy thing it would be if there was a place where all
the good men and women in the world might meet, meaning
heaven, and I really believe for a time he had doubts about
his soul, for he was very near, if not quite, light-headed.
The fact was he had not had a good meal for some days and
his little dirty niéce (whom he sent for with a still dirtier
nephew, and hugged him, and bid them farewell) told us
that unless he dines out he subsists on tea and gruels. And
he corroborated this tale by ever and anon complaining of
sensations of gnawing which he felt about his *heart*, which
he mistook his stomach to be, and sure enough these gnaw-
ings were dissipated after a meal or two, and he surely thinks
that he has been rescued from the jaws of death by Dr. Dale's
white powders. He is got quite well again by nursing, and
chirps of odes and lyric poetry the day long—he is to go
out of town on Monday, and with him goes the dirty train
of his papers and books which followed him to our house. I
shall not be sorry when he takes his nipt carcase out of my
bed, which it has occupied, and vanishes with all his lyric
lumber, but I will endeavor to bring him in future into a
method of dining at least once a day. I have proposed to
him to dine with me (and he has nearly come into it) whenever he does not go out; and pay me. I will take his money

beforehand and he shall eat it out. If I don't, it will go all over the world. Some worthless relations, of which the dirty little devil that looks after him and a still more dirty nephew are component particles, I have reason to think divide all his gains with some lazy worthless authors that are his constant satellites. The Literary Fund has voted him seasonably £20, and if I can help it, he shall spend it on his own carcase.

The unquestioned masterpiece of George Dyer's absentmindedness was the time he fell into New River as he was leaving Lamb's house. Lamb first indulged in an account of it in a letter to Mrs. Hazlitt, and then, unable to resist the essay possibilities of the incident, converted it into *Amicus Redivivus*.

LETTER TO MRS. HAZLITT

[Undated, 1823(?).]

Dear Mrs. H.,—Sitting down to write a letter is such a painful operation to Mary, that you must accept me as her proxy. You have seen our house. What I now tell you is literally true. Yesterday week George Dyer called upon us, at one o'clock, (*bright noonday,*) on his way to dine with Mrs. Barbauld at Newington. He sat with Mary about half an hour, and took leave. The maid saw him go out, from her kitchen window, but suddenly losing sight of him, ran up in a fright to Mary. G. D., instead of keeping the slip that leads to the gate, had deliberately, staff in hand, in broad open day, marched into the New River. He had not his spectacles on, and you know his absence. Who helped him out they can hardly tell, but between 'em they got him out, drenched thro' and thro'. A mob collected by that time, and accompanied him in. "Send for the Doctor," they said: and a one-eyed fellow, dirty and drunk, was fetched from the public house at the end, where it seems he lurks, for the sake of picking up water practice; having formerly had a medal from the Humane Society for some rescue. By his advice the patient was put between blankets; and when I came home at four to dinner, I found G. D. a-bed, and raving, light-headed, with the brandy and water which the doctor had administered. He sang, laughed, whimpered, screamed, bab-bled of guardian angels, would get up and go home; but we kept him there by force; and by next morning he departed sober, and seems to have received no injury. All my friends are open-mouth'd about having paling before the river; but I cannot see, that because a lunatic chooses to walk into a river with his eyes open at mid day, I am any the more likely to be drowned in it, coming home at midnight.

I had the honour of dining at the Mansion House on Thursday last by special card from the Lord Mayor, who never saw my face, nor I his; and all from being a writer in a magazine. The dinner costly, served on massy plate; cham-pagne, pines, &c.; 47 present, among whom the Chairman and two other directors of the India Company.

There's for you! and got away pretty sober. Quite saved my credit.

We continue to like our house prodigiously.

Does Mary Hazlitt go on with her novel? or has she begun another? I would not discourage her, though we continue to think it (so far) in its present state not saleable. Our kind remembrances to her and hers, and you and yours.

Yours truly,

C. LAMB.

I am pleased that H. liked my letter to Laureat.

Mrs. Hazlitt,
  Alpbington near Exeter.

AMICUS REDIVIVUS

Where were ye, Nymphs, when the remorseless deep
Clos'd o'er the head of your loved Lycidas?

I do not know when I have experienced a stranger sensation than on seeing my old friend G[eorge] D[yer], who
had been paying me a morning visit, a few Sundays back,
at my cottage at Islington, upon taking leave, instead of
turning down the right-hand path by which he had entered
—with staff in hand, and at noonday, deliberately march
right forwards into the midst of the stream that runs by
us, and totally disappear.

A spectacle like this at dusk would have been appalling
enough; but, in the broad, open daylight, to witness such
an unreserved motion towards self-destruction in a valued
friend, took from me all power of speculation.

How I found my feet I know not. Consciousness was
quite gone. Some spirit, not my own, whirled me to the spot.
I remember nothing but the silvery apparition of a good
white head emerging; nigh which a staff (the hand unseen
that wielded it) pointed upwards, as feeling for the skies.
In a moment (if time was in that time) he was on my shoulders, and I—freighted with a load more precious than his who
bore Anchises.

And here I cannot but do justice to the officious zeal of
sundry passers-by, who, albeit arriving a little too late to
participate in the honours of the rescue, in philanthropic
shoals came thronging to communicate their advice as to the
recovery; prescribing variously the application, or non-appli-
cation, of salt, etc., to the person of the patient. Life, meantime, was ebbing fast away, amidst the stifle of conflicting
judgments, when one, more sagacious than the rest, by a

bright thought, proposed sending for the Doctor. Trite as the counsel was, and impossible, as one should think, to be missed on,—shall I confess?—in this emergency it was to me as if an Angel had spoken. Great previous exertions—and mine had not been inconsiderable—are commonly followed by a debility of purpose. This was a moment of irresolution.

MONOCULUS—for so, in default of catching his true name, I choose to designate the medical gentleman who now appeared—is a grave, middle-aged person, who, without having studied at the college, or truckled to the pedantry of a diploma, hath employed a great portion of his valuable time in experimental processes upon the bodies of unfortunate fellow-creatures, in whom the vital spark, to mere vulgar thinking, would seem extinct and lost forever. He omitteth no occasion of obtruding his services, from a case of common surfeit-suffocation to the ignobler obstructions, sometimes induced by a too wilful application of the plant *Cannabis* outwardly. But though he declineth not altogether these drier extinctions, his occupation tendeth for the most part to water-practice; for the convenience of which, he hath judiciously fixed his quarters near the grand repository of the stream mentioned, where, day and night, from his little watch-tower, at the Middleton's Head, he listeneth to detect the wrecks of drowned mortality—partly, as he saith, to be upon the spot—and partly, because the liquids which he useth to prescribe to himself and his patients, on these distressing occasions, are ordinarily more conveniently to be found at these common hostelries than in the shops and phials of the apothecaries. His ear hath arrived to such finesse by practice, that it is reported he can distinguish a plunge at a half furlong distance; and can tell if it be casual or deliberate. He weareth a medal, suspended over a suit, originally of a sad brown, but which, by time, and frequency of nightly divings, has been dinged into a true professional sable. He passeth by the name of Doctor, and is remarkable for wanting his left eye. His remedy—after a sufficient application of warm blankets, friction, etc., is a simple tumbler, or more, of the purest Cognac, with water, made as hot as the convalescent can bear it. Where he findeth, as in the case of my friend, a squeamish subject, he condescendeth to be the taster; and showeth, by his own example, the innocuous nature of the prescription. Nothing can be more kind or encouraging than this procedure. It addeth confidence to the patient, to see his medical adviser go hand in hand with himself in the remedy. When the doctor swalloweth his own draught, what peevish invalid can refuse to pledge him in the potion? In fine, MONOCULUS is a humane, sensible man, who, for a slender pittance, scarce enough to sustain life, is content to wear it out in the endeavour to save the lives of others—his pretensions so moderate, that with difficulty I could press a crown upon him, for the price of restoring the existence of such an invaluable creature to society as G. D.

It was pleasant to observe the effect of the subsiding alarm upon the nerves of the dear absentee. It seemed to have given a shake to memory, calling up notice after notice, of all the providential deliverances he had experienced in the course of his long and innocent life. Sitting up on my couch—my couch which, naked and void of furniture hitherto, for the salutary repose which it administered, shall be honoured with costly valance, at some price, and henceforth be a state-bed at Colebrook,—he discoursed of marvellous escapes—by carelessness of nurses—by pails of gelid, and kettles of the boiling element, in infancy—by orchard pranks, and snapping twigs, in schoolboy frolics—by descent of tiles at Trumpington, and of heavier tomes at Pembroke—by studi-

ous watchings, inducing frightful vigilance—by want, and
the fear of want, and all the sore throbbings of the learned
head.—Anon, he would burst out into little fragments of
chanting—of songs long ago—ends of deliverance hymns,
not remembered before since childhood, but coming up now,
when his heart was made tender as a child's—for the *tremor
cordis,* in the retrospect of a recent deliverance, as in a case
of impending danger, acting upon an innocent heart, will
produce a self-tenderness, which we should do ill to christen
cowardice; and Shakspeare, in the latter crisis, has made his
good Sir Hugh to remember the sitting by Babylon, and to
mutter of shallow rivers.

Waters of Sir Hugh Middleton—what a spark you were
like to have extinguished forever! Your salubrious streams
to this City, for now near two centuries, would hardly have
atoned for what you were in a moment washing away. Mockery of a river—liquid artifice—wretched conduit! henceforth
rank with canals and sluggish aqueducts. Was it for this that,
smit in boyhood with the explorations of that Abyssinian
traveller, I paced the vales of Amwell to explore your tributary springs, to trace your salutary waters sparkling through
green Hertfordshire, and cultured Enfield parks?—Ye have
no swans—no Naïads—no river God—or did the benevolent
hoary aspect of my friend tempt ye to suck him in, that
ye also might have the tutelary genius of your waters?

Had he been drowned in Cam, there would have been
some consonancy in it; but what willows had ye to wave
and rustle over his moist sepulture?—or, having no *name,*
besides that unmeaning assumption of *eternal novity,* did ye
think to get one by the noble prize, and henceforth to be
termed the STREAM DYERIAN?

> And could such spacious virtue find a grave
> Beneath the imposthumed bubble of a wave?

I protest, George, you shall not venture out again—no, not by daylight—without a sufficient pair of spectacles—in your musing moods especially. Your absence of mind we have borne, till your presence of body came to be called in question by it. You shall not go wandering into Euripus with Aristotle, if you can help it. Fie, man, to turn dipper at your years, after your many tracts in favour of sprinkling only!

I have nothing but water in my head o'nights since this frightful accident. Sometimes I am with Clarence in his dream. At others, I behold Christian beginning to sink, and crying out to his good brother Hopeful (that is, to me), "I sink in deep waters; the billows go over my head, all the waves go over me. Selah." Then I have before me Palinurus, just letting go the steerage. I cry out too late to save. Next follow—a mournful procession—*suicidal faces,* saved against their will from drowning; dolefully trailing a length of reluctant gratefulness, with ropy weeds pendent from locks of watchet hue—constrained Lazari—Pluto's half-subjects—stolen fees from the grave—bilking Charon of his fare. At their head Arion—or is it G. D.?—in his singing garments marcheth singly, with harp in hand, and votive garland, which Machaon (or Dr. Hawes) snatcheth straight, intending to suspend it to the stern God of Sea. Then follow dismal streams of Lethe, in which the half-drenched on earth are constrained to drown downright, by wharfs where Ophelia twice acts her muddy death.

And, doubtless, there is some notice in that invisible world when one of us approacheth (as my friend did so lately) to their inexorable precincts. When a soul knocks once, twice, at Death's door, the sensation aroused within the palace must be considerable; and the grim Feature, by modern science so often dispossessed of his prey, must have learned by this time to pity Tantalus.

A pulse assuredly was felt along the line of the Elysian shades, when the near arrival of G. D. was announced by no equivocal indications. From their seats of Asphodel arose the gentler and the graver ghosts—poet, or historian—of Grecian or of Roman lore—to crown with unfading chaplets the half-finished love-labours of their unwearied scholiast. Him Markland expected—him Tyrwhitt hoped to encounter—him the sweet lyrist of Peter House, whom he had barely seen upon earth, with newest airs prepared to greet——; and, patron of the gentle Christ's boy,—who should have been his patron through life—the mild Askew, with long aspirations, leaned foremost from his venerable Æsculapian chair, to welcome into that happy company the matured virtues of the man, whose tender scions in the boy he himself upon earth had so prophetically fed and watered.

George Dyer's "tender conscience," as Lamb designated it, had gotten into activity years after the event in regard to two lines in his poem *The Poet's Fate*, which seemingly reflected on Samuel Rogers, the poet. When he mentioned his perturbation in a letter to Lamb, the latter replied suggesting that he was making a mountain out of a mole-hill. He also used the opportunity to hearten his old friend against the infirmities of age and disabuse his fears that eyesight and penmanship were suffering from the ravages of time.

LETTER TO DYER

Feb. 22nd, 1832.

Dear Dyer,—Mr. Rogers, and Mr. Rogers's friends, are perfectly assured that you never intended any harm by an innocent couplet, and that in the revivification of it by blundering Barker you had no hand whatever. To imagine that at this time of day Rogers broods over a fantastic expres-

sion of more than thirty years' standing, would be to suppose
him indulging his Pleasures of Memory with a vengeance.
You never penned a line which for its own sake you need,
dying, wish to blot. You mistake your heart if you think
you *can* write a lampoon. Your whips are rods of roses. Your
spleen has ever had for its object vices, not the vicious;
abstract offenses, not the concrete sinner. But you are sensi-
tive, and wince as much at the consciousness of having committed a compliment, as another man would at the perpetra-
tion of an affront. But do not lug me into the same soreness
of conscience with yourself. I maintain, and will to the last
hour, that I never writ of you but *con amore;* that if any
allusion was made to your near-sightedness, it was not for
the purpose of mocking an infirmity, but of connecting it
with scholar-like habits: for is it not erudite and scholarly
to be somewhat near of sight before age naturally brings on
the malady? You could not then plead the *obrepens senectus!*
Did I not moreover make it an apology for a certain *absence,*
which some of our friends may have experienced, when you
have not on a sudden made recognition of them in a casual
street-meeting? And did I not strengthen your excuse for
this slowness of recognition, by further accounting morally
for the present engagement of your mind in worthy objects?
Did I not, in your person, make the handsomest apology for
absent-of-mind people that was ever made? If these things
be not so, I never knew what I wrote, or meant by my
writing, and have been penning libels all my life without
being aware of it. Does it follow that I should have exprest
myself exactly in the same way of those dear old eyes of
yours *now,* now that Father Time has conspired with a hard
task-master to put a last extinguisher upon them? I should
as soon have insulted the Answerer of Salmasius when he
awoke up from his ended task and saw no more with mortal

vision. But you are many films removed yet from Milton's calamity. You write perfectly intelligibly. Marry, the letters are not all of the same size or tallness; but that only shows your proficiency in the *hands*, text, german-hand, court-hand, sometimes law-hand, and affords variety. You pen better than you did a twelvemonth ago; and if you continue to improve, you bid fair to win the golden pen which is the prize at your young gentlemen's academy. But you must be aware of Valpy, and his printing-house, that hazy cave of Trophonius, out of which it was a mercy that you escaped with a glimmer. Beware of MSS. and Variæ Lectiones. Settle the text for once in your mind, and stick to it. You have some years' good sight in you yet, if you do not tamper with it. It is not for you (for *us* I should say) to go poring into Greek contractions, and star-gazing upon slim Hebrew points. We have yet the sight

> Of sun, and moon, and star, throughout the year
> And man and woman.

You have vision enough to discern Mrs. Dyer from the other comely gentlewoman who lives up at staircase No. 5; or, if you should make a blunder in the twilight, Mrs. Dyer has too much good sense to be jealous for a mere effect of imperfect optics. But don't try to write the Lord's Prayer, Creed, and Ten Commandments in the compass of a half-penny; nor run after a midge, or a mote, to catch it; and leave off hunting for needles in bundles of hay, for all these things strain the eyes. The snow is six feet deep in some parts here. I must put on jack-boots to get at the Post-Office with this. It is not good for weak eyes to pore upon snow too much. It lies in drifts. I wonder what its drift is; only that it makes good pancakes, remind Mrs. Dyer. It turns a pretty green world into a white one. It glares too much for an innocent colour methinks. I wonder why you think I dislike gilt edges. They set off a letter marvellously. Yours, for instance, looks for all the world like a tablet of curious *hieroglyphics* in a gold frame. But don't go and lay this to your eyes. You always wrote hieroglyphically, yet not to come up to the mystical notations and conjuring characters of Dr. Parr. You never wrote what I call a school-master's hand, like Mrs. Clarke; nor a woman's hand, like Southey; nor a missal hand, like Porson; nor an all-of-the-wrong-side sloping hand, like Miss Hayes; nor a dogmatic, Mede-and-Persian, peremptory hand, like Rickman; but you ever wrote what I call a Grecian's hand; what the Grecians write (or used) at Christ's Hospital; such as Whalley would have admired, and Boyer have applauded, but Smith or Atwood (writing-masters) would have horsed you for. Your boy-of-genius hand and your mercantile hand are various. By your flourishes, I should think you never learned to make eagles or corkscrews, or flourish the governors' names in the writing-school; and by the tenour and cut of your letters, I suspect you were never in it at all. By the length of this scrawl you will think I have a design upon your optics; but I have writ as large as I could, out of respect to them; too large, indeed, for beauty. Mine is a sort deputy Grecian's hand; a little better, and more of a worldly hand than a Grecian's, but still remote from the mercantile. I don't know how it is, but I keep my rank in fancy still since school-days. I can never forget I was a deputy Grecian! And writing to you, or to Coleridge, besides affection, I feel a reverential deference as to Grecians still. I keep my soaring way above the Great Erasmians, yet far beneath the other. Alas! what am I now? What is a Leadenhall clerk, or India pensioner, to a deputy Grecian? How art thou fallen, O Lucifer! Just room for our loves to Mrs. D., &c. C. LAMB.

Lamb's friendships often had to survive separation and distance. Among his correspondents were several to whom he wrote for years, although he saw them but seldom in the meanwhile. His ideas about what should go into letters intended for "distant correspondents," Lamb gave in the essay that follows. It is itself in the form of a letter to Barron Field, who, at the time, was judge of the supreme court of New South Wales.

DISTANT CORRESPONDENTS

IN A LETTER TO B[ARRON] F[IELD] ESQ., AT SYDNEY, NEW SOUTH WALES

My Dear F.—When I think how welcome the sight of a letter from the world where you were born must be to you in that strange one to which you have been transplanted, I feel some compunctious visitings at my long silence. But, indeed, it is no easy effort to set about a correspondence at our distance. The weary world of waters between us oppresses the imagination. It is difficult to conceive how a scrawl of mine should ever stretch across it. It is a sort of presumption to expect that one's thoughts should live so far. It is like writing for posterity; and reminds me of one of Mrs. Rowe's superscriptions, "Alcander to Strephon in the shades." Cowley's Post-Angel is no more than would be expedient in such an intercourse. One drops a packet at Lombard-street, and in twenty-four hours a friend in Cumberland gets it as fresh as if it came in ice. It is only like whispering through a long trumpet. But suppose a tube let down from the moon, with yourself at one end and *the man* at the other; it would be some balk to the spirit of conversation, if you knew that the dialogue exchanged with that interesting theosophist would take two or three revolutions of a higher luminary in its passage. Yet for aught I know, you may be some parasangs nigher that primitive idea—Plato's man—than we in England here have the honour to reckon ourselves.

Epistolary matter usually compriseth three topics; news, sentiment, and puns. In the latter, I include all non-serious subjects; or subjects serious in themselves, but treated after my fashion, non-seriously.—And first, for news. In them the most desirable circumstance, I suppose, is that they shall be true. But what security can I have that what I now send you for truth shall not, before you get it, unaccountably turn into a lie? For instance, our mutual friend P. is at this present writing—*my Now*—in good health, and enjoys a fair share of worldly reputation. You are glad to hear it. This is natural and friendly. But at this present reading—*your Now*—he may possibly be in the Bench, or going to be hanged, which in reason ought to abate something of your transport (*i e.,* at hearing he was well, etc.), or at least considerably to modify it. I am going to the play this evening, to have a laugh with Munden. You have no theatre, I think you told me, in youd land of d——d realities. You naturally lick your lips, and envy me my felicity. Think but a moment, and you will correct the hateful emotion. Why, it is Sunday morning with you, and 1823. This confusion of tenses, this grand solecism of *two presents,* is in a degree common to all postage. But if I sent you word to Bath or the Devizes, that I was expecting the aforesaid treat this evening, though at the moment you received the intelligence my full feast of fun would be over, yet there would be for a day or two after, as you would well know, a smack, a relish left upon my mental palate, which would give rational encouragement for you to foster a portion at least of the disagreeable passion, which it was in part my intention to produce. But ten months hence, your envy or your sympathy would be as useless as a passion spent upon the dead. Not only does truth, in these long intervals, unessence herself, but (what is harder) one cannot venture a crude fiction for the fear that it may ripen into a truth upon the voyage. What a wild improbable banter I put upon you some three years since,——— of Will Weatherall having married a servant-maid! I remember gravely consulting you how we were to receive her—for Will's wife was in no case to be rejected; and your no less serious replication in the matter; how tenderly you advised an abstemious introduction of literary topics before the lady, with a caution not to be too forward in bringing on the carpet matters more within the sphere of her intelligence; your deliberate judgment, or rather wise suspension of sentence, how far jacks, and spits, and mops, could, with propriety, be introduced as subjects; whether the conscious avoiding of all such matters in discourse would not have a worse look than the taking of them casually in our way; in what manner we should carry ourselves to our maid Becky, Mrs. William Weatherall being by; whether we should show more delicacy, and a truer sense of respect for Will's wife, by treating Becky with our customary chiding before her, or by an unusual deferential civility paid to Becky as to a person of great worth, but thrown by the caprice of fate into a humble station. There were difficulties, I remember, on both sides, which you did me the favour to state with the precision of a lawyer, united to the tenderness of a friend. I laughed in my sleeve at your solemn pleadings, when lo! while I was valuing myself upon this flam put upon you in New South Wales, the devil in England, jealous possibly of any lie-children not his own, or working after my copy, has actually instigated our friend (not three days since) to the commission of matrimony, which I had only conjured up for your diversion. William Weatherall has married Mrs. Cotterel's maid. But to take it in its truest sense, you will see, my dear F., that news from me must become history to you; which I neither profess to write, nor indeed care much for reading. No person, under a diviner, can, with any prospect of veracity, conduct a correspondence at such an arm's length. Two prophets, indeed, might thus interchange intelligence with effect; the epoch of the writer (Habakkuk) falling in with the true present time of the receiver (Daniel); but then we are no prophets.

Then as to sentiment. It fares little better with that. This kind of dish, above all, requires to be served up hot; or sent off in water-plates, that your friend may have it almost as warm as yourself. If it have time to cool, it is the most tasteless of all cold meats. I have often smiled at a conceit of the late Lord C[amelford]. It seems that travelling somewhere about Geneva, he came to some pretty green spot, or nook, where a willow, or something, hung so fantastically and invitingly over a stream—was it?—or a rock?—no matter—but the stillness and the repose, after a weary journey, 'tis likely, in a languid moment of his Lordship's hot, restless life, so took his fancy that he could imagine no place so proper, in the event of his death, to lay his bones in. This was all very natural and excusable as a sentiment, and shows his character in a very pleasing light. But when from a passing sentiment it came to be an act; and when, by a positive testamentary disposal, his remains were actually carried all that way from England; who was there, some desperate sentimentalists excepted, that did not ask the question, Why could not his Lordship have found a spot as solitary, a nook as romantic, a tree as green and pendent, with a stream as emblematic to his purpose, in Surrey, in Dorset, or in Devon? Conceive the sentiment boarded up, freighted, entered at the Custom House (startling the tide-waiters with the novelty), hoisted into a ship. Conceive it pawed about and handled between the rude jests of tarpaulin ruffians—a thing of its delicate texture—the salt bilge wetting it till it became as vapid as a damaged lustring. Suppose it in material danger (mariners have some superstition about sentiments) of being tossed over in a fresh gale to some propitiatory shark (spirit of Saint Gothard, save us from a quietus so foreign to the deviser's purpose!) but it has happily evaded a fishy consummation. Trace it then to its lucky landing—at Lyons shall we say?—I have not the map before me—jostled upon four men's shoulders—baiting at this town—stopping to refresh at t'other village—waiting a passport here, a license there; the sanction of the magistracy in this district, the concurrence of the ecclesiastics in that canton; till at length it arrives at its destination, tired out and jaded, from a brisk sentiment into a feature of silly pride or tawdry senseless affectation. How few sentiments, my dear F., I am afraid we can set down, in the sailor's phrase, as quite seaworthy.

Lastly, as to the agreeable levities, which though contemptible in bulk, are the twinkling corpuscula which should irradiate a right friendly epistle—your puns and small jests are, I apprehend, extremely circumscribed in their sphere of action. They are so far from a capacity of being packed up and sent beyond sea, they will scarce endure to be transported by hand from this room to the next. Their vigour is as the instant of their birth. Their nutriment for their brief existence is the intellectual atmosphere of the bystanders: or this last is the fine slime of Nilus—the *melior lutus*,—whose maternal recipiency is as necessary as the *sol pater* to their equivocal generation. A punt hath a hearty kind of present ear-kissing smack with it; you can no more transmit it in its pristine flavour than you can send a kiss.—Have you not tried in some instances to palm off a yesterday's pun upon a gentleman, and has it answered? Not but it was new to his hearing, but it did not seem to come new from you. It did not hitch in. It was like picking up at a village ale house a two-days-old newspaper. You have not seen it before, but you resent the stale thing as an affront. This sort of merchandise above all requires a quick return. A pun, and its recognitory laugh, must be co-instantaneous. The one is the brisk lightning, the other the fierce thunder. A moment's interval, and the link is snapped. A pun is reflected from a friend's face as from a mirror. Who would consult his sweet visnomy, if the polished surface were two or three minutes (not to speak of twelvemonths, my dear F.) in giving back its copy?

I cannot image to myself whereabout you are. When I try to fix it, Peter Wilkins's island comes across me. Sometimes you seem to be in the *Hades of Thieves*. I see Diogenes prying among you with his perpetual fruitless lantern. What must you be willing by this time to give for the sight of an honest man! You must almost have forgotten how *we* look. And tell me what your Sydneyites do? are they th . . . v . . . ng all day long? Merciful Heaven! what property can stand against such a depredation! The kangaroos—your Aborigines—do they keep their primitive simplicity un-Europe-tainted, with those little short fore puds, looking like a lesson framed by nature to the pickpocket! Marry, for diving into fobs they are rather lamely provided *à priori*; but if the hue and cry were once up, they would show as fair a pair of hind-shifters as the expertest locomotor in the colony. We hear the most improbable tales at this distance. Pray, is it true that the young Spartans among you are born with six fingers, which spoils their scanning?—It must look very odd; but use reconciles. For their scansion, it is less to be regretted; for if they take it into their heads to be poets, it is odds but they turn out, the greater part of them, vile plagiarists.—Is there much difference to see, too, between the son of a th . . . f and the grandson? or where does the taint stop? Do you bleach in three or in four generations? I have many questions to put, but ten Delphic voyages can be made in a shorter time than it will take to satisfy my scruples. Do you grow your own hemp?—What is your staple trade,—exclusive of the national profession, I mean? Your locksmiths, I take it, are some of your great capitalists.

I am insensibly chatting to you as familiarly as when we used to exchange good-morrows out of our old contiguous windows, in pump-famed Hare Court in the Temple. Why did you ever leave that quiet corner?—Why did I?—with its complement of four poor elms, from whose smoke-dyed barks, the theme of jesting ruralists, I picked my first lady-birds! My heart is as dry as that spring sometimes proves in a thirsty August, when I revert to the space that is between us; a length of passage enough to render obsolete the phrases of our English letters before they can reach you. But while I talk I think you hear me,—thoughts dallying with vain surmise—

> Aye me! while thee the seas and sounding shores
> Hold far away.

Come back, before I am grown into a very old man, so as you shall hardly know me. Come, before Bridget walks on crutches. Girls whom you left children have become sage matrons while you are tarrying there. The blooming Miss W[inte]r (you remember Sally W[inte]r) called upon us yesterday, an aged crone. Folks whom you knew die off every year. Formerly, I thought that death was wearing out,—I stood ramparted about with so many healthy friends. The departure of J[ohn] W[hite], two springs back, corrected my delusion. Since then the old divorcer has been busy. If you do not make haste to return, there will be little left to greet you, of me, or mine.

Among Lamb's distant correspondents was his best-loved friend, Thomas Manning. Manning was a Cambridge scholar, who was especially interested in mathematics and Chinese. In 1806 he went as a doctor to Canton, and remained in the East until 1817, when he returned to England. During his stay abroad he did some exploring, being the first Englishman to enter Lhasa, the holy city of Tibet. It was to Manning that Lamb wrote some of his finest letters, for something about Manning called forth from Lamb in abundant measure his characteristic foolishness and practical joking. The first letter below is a heart-wringing account of the changes time had brought among their mutual friends. This letter was sent so that Manning would receive it before leaving China for England. The next letter is a corrective to the first one, telling about these old acquaintances; but this second letter was sent so as to await Manning's arrival at St. Helena, after he had made most of the journey back to England under the disconcerting impression that he would find many astounding changes on his return.

LETTER TO MANNING

Dec. 25th, 1815.

Dear old friend and absentee,—This is Christmas Day 1815 with us; what it may be with you I don't know, the 12th of June next year perhaps; and if it should be the consecrated season with you, I don't see how you can keep it. You have no turkeys; you would not desecrate the festival by offering up a withered Chinese Bantam, instead of the savoury grand Norfolcian holocaust, that smokes all around my nostrils at this moment from a thousand firesides. Then what puddings have you? Where will you get holly to stick in your churches, or churches to stick your dried tea-leaves (that must be the substitute) in? What memorials you can have of the holy time, I see not. A chopped missionary or two may keep up the thin idea of Lent and the wilderness; but what standing evidence have you of the Nativity? 'Tis our rosy-cheeked, homestalled divines, whose faces shine to the tune of "Unto us a child was born," faces fragrant with the mince-pies of half a century, that alone can authenticate the cheerful mystery. I feel my bowels refreshed with the holy tide; my zeal is great against the unedified heathen. Down with the Pagodas—down with the idols—Ching-chong-fo—and his foolish priesthood! Come out of Babylon, O my friend! for her time is come; and the child that is native, and the Proselyte of her gates, shall kindle and smoke together! And in sober sense what makes you so long from among us, Manning? You must not expect to see the same England again which you left.

Empires have been overturned, crowns trodden into dust, the face of the western world quite changed. Your friends have all got old—those you left blooming; myself, (who am one of the few that remember you), those golden hairs which you recollect my taking a pride in, turned to silvery and grey. Mary has been dead and buried many years: she desired to be buried in the silk gown you sent her. Rickman, that you remember active and strong, now walks out supported by a servant maid and a stick. Martin Burney is a very old man. The other day an aged woman knocked at my door, and pretended to my acquaintance. It was long before I had the most distant cognition of her; but at last, together, we made her out to be Louisa, the daughter of Mrs. Topham, formerly Mrs. Morton, who had been Mrs. Reynolds formerly Mrs. Kenney, whose first husband was Holcroft, the dramatic writer of the last century. St. Paul's church is a heap of ruins; the Monument isn't half so high as you knew it, divers parts being successively taken down which the ravages of time had rendered dangerous; the horse at Charing Cross is gone, no one knows whither; and all this has taken place while you have been settling whether Ho-hing-tong should be spelt with a ——, or a ——. For aught I see you might almost as well remain where you are, and not come like a Struldbrug into a world where few were born when you went away. Scarce here and there one will be able to make out your face. All your opinions will be out of date, your jokes obsolete, your puns rejected with fastidiousness as wit of the last age. Your way of mathematics has already given way to a new method, which after all is I believe the old doctrine of Maclaurin, new-vamped up with what he borrowed of the negative quantity of fluxions from Euler.

Poor Godwin! I was passing his tomb the other day in Cripplegate churchyard. There are some verses upon it written by Miss ——, which if I thought good enough I would send you. He was one of those who would have hailed your return, not with boisterous shouts and clamours, but with the complacent gratulations of a philosopher anxious to promote knowledge as leading to happiness; but his systems and his theories are ten feet deep in Cripplegate mould. Coleridge is just dead, having lived just long enough to close the eyes of Wordsworth, who paid the debt to Nature but a week or two before. Poor Col., but two days before he died he wrote to a bookseller, purposing an epic poem on the "Wanderings of Cain," in twenty-four books. It is said he has left behind him more than forty thousand treatises in criticism, metaphysics, and divinity, but few of them in a state of completion. They are now destined, perhaps, to wrap up spices. You see what mutations the busy hand of Time has produced, while you have consumed in foolish voluntary exile that time which might have gladdened your friends —benefited your country; but reproaches are useless. Gather up the wretched reliques, my friend, as fast as you can, and come to your old home. I will rub my eyes and try to recognise you. We will shake withered hands together, and talk of old things—of St. Mary's Church and the barber's opposite, where the young students in mathematics used to assemble. Poor Crips, that kept it afterwards, set up a fruiterer's shop in Trumpington Street, and for aught I know resides there still, for I saw the name up in the last journey I took there with my sister just before she died. I suppose you heard that I had left the India House, and gone into the Fishmongers' Almshouses over the bridge. I have a little cabin there, small and homely, but you shall be welcome to it. You like oysters, and to open them yourself; I'll get you some if you come in oyster time. Marshall, Godwin's old friend, is still alive, and talks of the faces you used to make.

Come as soon as you can.   C. LAMB.

LETTER TO MANNING

Dec. 26th, 1815.

Dear Manning,—Following your brother's example, I have just ventured one letter to Canton, and am now hazarding another (not exactly a duplicate) to St. Helena. The first was full of unprobable romantic fictions, fitting the remoteness of the mission it goes upon; in the present I mean to confine myself nearer to truth as you come nearer home. A correspondence with the uttermost parts of the earth necessarily involves in it some heat of fancy, it sets the brain agoing, but I can think on the half-way house tranquilly. Your friends then are not all dead or grown forgetful of you through old age, as that lying letter asserted, anticipating rather what must happen if you kept tarrying on for ever on the skirts of creation, as there seemed a danger of your doing; but they are all tolerably well and in full and perfect comprehension of what is meant by Manning's coming home again. Mrs. Kenney never lets her tongue run riot more than in remembrances of you. Fanny expends herself in phrases that can only be justified by her romantic nature. Mary reserves a portion of your silk, not to be buried in, (as the false nuncio asserts,) but to make up spick and span into a bran-new gown to wear when you come. I am the same as when you knew me, almost to a surfeiting identity. This very night I am going to *leave off tobacco!* Surely there must be some other world in which this unconquerable purpose shall be realised. The soul hath not her generous aspirings implanted in her in vain. One that you knew, and I think the only one of those friends we knew much of in common, has died in earnest. Poor Priscilla! Her brother Robert is also dead, and several of the grown-up brothers and sisters, in the compass of a very few years. Death has not otherwise meddled much in families that I know. Not but he has his eye upon us, and is whetting his feathered dart every instant, as you see him truly pictured in that impressive moral picture, "The good man at the hour of death." I have in trust to put in the post four letters from Diss, and one from Lynn, to St. Helena, which I hope will accompany this safe, and one from Lynn, and the one before spoken of from me, to Canton. But we all hope that these letters may be waste paper. I don't know why I have forborne writing so long; but it is such a forlorn hope to send a scrap of paper straggling over wide oceans! And yet I know, when you come home, I shall have you sitting before me at our fire-side as if you had never been away. In such an instant does the return of a person dissipate all the weight of imaginary perplexity from distance of time and space! I'll promise you good oysters. Cory is dead that kept the shop opposite St. Dunstan's; but the tougher materials of the shop survive the perishing frame of its keeper. Oysters continue to flourish there under as good auspices. Poor Cory! But if you will absent yourself twenty years together, you must not expect numerically the same population to congratulate your return which whetted the sea-beach with their tears when you went away. Have you recovered the breathless stone-staring astonishment into which you must have been thrown upon learning at landing that an Emperor of France was living in St. Helena. What an event in the solitude of the seas! like finding a fish's bone at the top of Plinlimmon; but these things are nothing in our western world. Novelties cease to affect. Come and try what your presence can.

God bless you.—Your old friend,

C. LAMB.

At another time Lamb played a similar practical joke on another of his friends. His target this time was Henry Crabb Robinson, a retired lawyer who was, in the apt description of E. V. Lucas, "an amateur in friendship." His acquaintance among the literary lights of the time was extensive, and his *Diary* is an invaluable mine of information about Lamb and others. Knowing that Robinson was suffering from an attack of rheumatism, Lamb jokingly wrote the first letter below; then in about a week's time he followed it with an ample confession of the hoax.

LETTER TO ROBINSON

[Undated. April(?) 1829.]

Dear Robinson,

We are afraid you will slip from us from England without again seeing us. It would be a charity to come and see me. I have these three days been laid up with strong rheumatic pains, in loins, back, shoulders. I shriek sometimes from the violence of them. I get scarce any sleep, and the consequence is, I am restless, and want to change sides as I lie, and I cannot turn without resting on my hands, and so turning all my body all at once, like a log with a lever. While this rainy weather lasts, I have no hope of alleviation. I have tried flannels and embrocation in vain. Just at the hip joint the pangs sometimes are so excruciating, that I cry out. It is as violent as the cramp, and far more continuous. I am ashamed to whine about these complaints to you, who can ill enter into them; but indeed they are sharp. You go about, in rain or fine, at all hours, without discommodity. I envy you your immunity at a time of life not much removed from my own. But you owe your exemption to temperance, which it is too late for me to pursue. I, in my lifetime, have had my good things. Hence my frame is brittle—yours strong as brass. I never knew any ailment you had. You can go out at night in all weathers, sit up all hours. Well, I don't want to moralize; I only wish to say that if you are inclined to a game at double-dummy, I would try and bolster myself in a chair for a rubber or so. My days are tedious, but less so, and less painful than my nights. May you never know the pain and difficulty I have in writing so much! Mary, who is most kind, joins in the wish.   C. Lamb.

LETTER TO ROBINSON

April 17, 1829.

I do confess to mischief. It was the subtlest diabolical piece of malice heart of man has contrived. I have no more rheumatism than that poker. Never was freer from all pains and aches. Every joint sound, to the tip of the ear from the extremity of the lesser toe. The report of thy torments was blown circuitously here from Bury. I could not resist the jeer. I conceived you writhing when you should just receive my congratulations. How mad you'd be! Well, it is not in my method to inflict pangs. I leave that to Heaven: but in the existing pangs of a friend I have a share. His disquietude crowns my exemption. I imagine you howling, and pace across the room, shooting out my free arms, legs, &c., this way and that way, with an assurance of not kindling a spark of pain from them. I deny that Nature meant us to sympathize with agonies. Those face-contortions, retortions, distortions have the merriness of antics. Nature meant them for farce—not so pleasant to the actor, indeed; but Grimaldi cries when we laugh, and 'tis but one that suffers to make thousands rejoice.

You say that shampooing is ineffectual; but, *per se,* it is good, to show the introvolutions, extravolutions, of which the animal frame is capable—to show what the creature is receptible of, short of dissolution.

You are worst of nights, an't you? You never was rack'd, was you? I should like an authentic map of those feelings.

You seem to have the flying gout. You can scarcely screw a smile out of your face, can you? I sit at immunity and sneer *ad libitum.* 'Tis now the time for you to make good resolutions. I may go on breaking 'em for any thing the worse I find myself. Your doctor seems to keep you on the long cure. Precipitate healings are never good. Don't come while you are so bad; I shan't be able to attend to your throes and the dumby at once. I should like to know how slowly the pain goes off. But don't write, unless the motion will be likely to make your sensibility more exquisite.

Your affectionate and truly healthy friend,

C. LAMB.

Mary thought a letter from me might amuse you in your torment.

The latter part of his life Lamb developed a warm friendship with the Quaker poet, Bernard Barton, who, like Lamb, was earning a living by clerking in a bank at Suffolk, and trying to write poetry in his spare time. Once when Barton was thinking of throwing off his irksome clerkship and making an attempt to earn a living by writing, Lamb sent him the following letter of advice. The second letter to Barton is a delightful complaint about the disagreeableness of a severe cold.

LETTER TO BARTON

January 9, 1823.

"Throw yourself on the world without any rational plan of support, beyond what the chance employ of booksellers would afford you!!!"

Throw yourself rather, my dear sir, from the steep Tarpeian rock, slap-dash headlong upon iron spikes. If you had but five consolatory minutes between the desk and the bed, make much of them, and live a century in them, rather than turn slave to the booksellers. They are Turks and Tartars when they have poor authors at their beck. Hitherto you have been at arm's length from them. Come not within their grasp. I have known many authors for bread, some repining, others envying the blessed security of a counting-house, all agreeing they would rather have been tailors, weavers,— what not, rather than the things they were. I have known some starved, some to go mad, one dear friend literally dying in a workhouse. You know not what a rapacious, dishonest set these booksellers are. Ask even Southey, who (a single case almost) has made a fortune by book drudgery, what he has found them. Oh, you know not (may you never know!) the miseries of subsisting by authorship. 'Tis a pretty appendage to a situation like yours or mine; but a slavery, worse than all slavery, to be a bookseller's dependent, to drudge your brains for pots of ale and breasts of mutton, to change your free thoughts and voluntary numbers for ungracious task-work. Those fellows hate *us*. The reason I take to be, that contrary to other trades, in which the master gets all the credit (a jeweller or silversmith for instance), and the journeyman, who really does the fine work, is in the background,—in *our* work the world gives all the credit to us, whom *they* consider as *their* journeymen, and therefore do they hate us, and cheat us, and oppress us, and would wring the blood of us out, to put another sixpence in their mechanic pouches! I contend that a bookseller has a *relative honesty* towards Authors, not like his honesty to the rest of the world. B., who first engaged me as "Elia," has not paid me up yet (nor any of us without repeated mortifying appeals), yet how the Knave fawned when I was of service to him! Yet I dare say the fellow is punctual in settling his milk-score, etc.

Keep to your bank, and the bank will keep you. Trust not to the Public; you may hang, starve, drown yourself, for anything that worthy *Personage* cares. I bless every star that Providence, not seeing good to make me independent, has seen it next good to settle me upon the stable foundation of Leadenhall. Sit down, good B. B., in the banking-office. What! is there not from six to eleven P.M. six days in the week, and is there not all Sunday? Fie, what a superfluity of man's time, if you could think so!—enough for relaxation, mirth, converse, poetry, good thoughts, quiet thoughts. Oh the corroding, torturing, tormenting thoughts, that disturb the brain of the unlucky wight who must draw upon it for daily sustenance. Henceforth I retract all my fond complaints of mercantile employment; look upon them as lovers' quarrels. I was but half in earnest. Welcome dead timber of a desk, that makes me live. A little grumbling is a wholesome medicine for the spleen; but in my inner heart do I approve and embrace this our close but unharassing way of life. I am quite serious. If you can send me Fox, I will not keep it *six weeks*, and will return it, with warm thanks to yourself and friend, without blot or dog's ear. You will much oblige me by this kindness.   Yours truly,   C. LAMB.

To Barton was sent this humorous description of an afflictive bad cold.

LETTER TO BARTON

Dear B. B.:—   January 9, 1824.

Do you know what it is to succumb under an insurmount-able day-mare,—a whoreson lethargy, Falstaff calls it,—an indisposition to do any thing, or to be any thing,—a total deadness and distaste—a suspension of vitality,—an indiffer-ence to locality,—a numb, soporifical, good-for-nothingness —an ossification all over,—an oyster-like insensibility to the passing events,—a mind-stupor,—a brawny defiance to the needles of a thrusting-in conscience—did you ever have a very bad cold with a total irresolution to submit to water-gruel processes? this has been for many weeks my lot and my excuse—my fingers drag heavily over this paper, and to my thinking it is three-and-twenty furlongs from here to the end of this demi-sheet—I have not a thing to say—no thing is of a more importance than another—I am flatter than a denial or a pancake—emptier than Judge Park's wig when the head is in it—duller than a country stage when the actors are off it—a cipher an 0—I acknowledge life at all only by an occasional convulsional cough, and a perma-nent phlegmatic pain in the chest—I am weary of the world —Life is weary of me. My day is gone into Twilight, and

I don't think it worth the expense of candles—my wick hath a thief in it, but I can't muster courage to snuff it—I inhale suffocation—I can't distinguish veal from mutton—nothing interests me—'tis 12 o'clock, and Thurtell is just now coming out upon the New Drop—Jack Ketch alertly tucking up his greasy sleeves to do the last office of mortality, yet cannot I elicit a groan or a moral reflection—if you told me the world will be at an end to-morrow, I should just say, "will it?"— I have not volition enough left to dot my i's—much less to comb my eyebrows—my eyes are set in my head—my brains are gone out to see a poor relation in Moorfields, and they did not say when they'd come back again—my skull is a Grub Street Attic, to let—not so much as a joint-stool or a crack'd jordan left in it—my hand writes, not I, from habit, as chickens run about a little when their heads are off—O for a vigorous fit of gout, cholic, toothache,—an earwig in my auditory, a fly in my visual organs—pain is life—the sharper, the more evidence of life—but this apathy, this death—did you ever have an obstinate cold, a six or seven weeks' un-intermitting chill and suspension of hope, fear, conscience, and everything—yet do I try all I can to cure it. I try wine, and spirits, and smoking, and snuff in unsparing quantities, but they all only seem to make me worse, instead of better— I sleep in a damp room, but it does me no good; I come home late o'nights, but do not find any visible amendment.

Who shall deliver me from the body of this death?

It is just 15 minutes after 12. Thurtell is by this time a good way on his journey, baiting at Scorpion perhaps, Ketch is bargaining for his cast coat and waistcoat, the Jew demurs at first at three half-crowns, but on consideration that he may get somewhat by showing 'em in the Town, finally closes.   C. L.

VI

RETIREMENT AND DEATH

As the years went by, Lamb's duties at the East India House became more and more irksome to him. By 1825 he was receiving a salary of £700 a year, and the income from his writings was reasonably good. So, under the circumstances, Lamb felt justified in retiring upon the handsome terms the directors offered in appreciation of his long and faithful service, his retiring allowance being two-thirds of his salary, with a provision that something would be paid to his sister if she should survive him.

The account of his feelings at this great change in his life when he was fifty is in his essay *The Superannuated Man*. But in connection with this essay, it is interesting to read some of the less formal things he said about his retirement in letters to his friends. One of the first to whom he wrote about his approaching release was Manning. A few weeks later, when everything was finally settled, he wrote more at length about it to Wordsworth, and also to Wordsworth's sister-in-law, Miss Hutchinson.

LETTER TO MANNING

[Undated. February, 1825 (?).]

My dear M.,—You might have come inopportunely a week since, when we had an inmate. At present and for as long as *ever* you like our castle is at your service. I saw Tuthill yesternight, who has done for me what may

To all my nights and days to come,
Give solely sovran sway and masterdom.

But I dare not hope, for fear of disappointment. I cannot be more explicit at present. But I have it under his own hand, that I am *non*-capacitated (I cannot write it *in*-) for business. O joyous imbecility! Not a susurration of this to *anybody!*   Mary's love,   C. LAMB.

LETTER TO WORDSWORTH

Colebrook Cottage, April 6, 1825.

Dear Wordsworth—I have been several times meditating a letter to you concerning the good thing which has befallen me, but the thought of poor Monkhouse came across me. He was one that I had exulted in the prospect of congratulating me. He and you were to have been the first participators, for indeed it has been ten weeks since the first motion of it. Here am I then, after thirty-three years' slavery, sitting in my own room at eleven o'clock this finest of all April mornings, a freed man, with £441 a year for the remainder of my life, live I as long as John Dennis, who outlived his annuity and starved at ninety; £441, *i. e.* £450, with a deduction of £9 for a provision secured to my sister, she being survivor, the pension guaranteed by Act Georgii Tertii, etc.

I came home FOR EVER on Tuesday in last week. The incomprehensibleness of my condition overwhelmed me. It was like passing from life into eternity. Every year to be as long as three, *i. e.* to have three times as much real time (time that is my own) in it! I wandered about thinking I was happy, but feeling I was not. But that tumultuousness is passing off, and I begin to understand the nature of the gift. Holydays, even the annual month, were always uneasy joys; their conscious fugitiveness; the craving after making the most of them. Now, when all is holyday, there are no holydays. I can sit at home, in rain or shine, without a restless impulse for walkings. I am daily steadying, and shall soon find it as natural to me to be my own master, as it has been irksome to have had a master. Mary wakes every morning with an obscure feeling that some good has happened to us.

Leigh Hunt and Montgomery, after their releasements, describe the shock of their emancipation much as I feel mine. But it hurt their frames. I eat, drink, and sleep as sound as ever. I lay no anxious schemes for going hither and thither, but take things as they occur. Yesterday I excursioned twenty miles; to-day I write a few letters. Pleasuring was for fugitive play-days; mine are fugitive only in the sense that life is fugitive. Freedom and life co-existent!

At the foot of such a call upon you for gratulation, I am ashamed to avert to that melancholy event. Monkhouse was a character I learned to love slowly, but it grew upon me, yearly, monthly, daily. What a chasm has it made in our pleasant parties! His noble friendly face was always coming before me, till this hurrying event in my life came, and for the time has absorbed all interest; in fact it has shaken me a little. My old desk companions, with whom I have had such merry hours, seem to reproach me for removing my lot from among them. They were pleasant creatures; but to the anxieties of business, and a weight of possible worse ever impending, I was not equal. Tuthill and Gillman gave me my certificates. I laughed at the friendly lie implied in them; but my sister shook her head, and said it was all true. Indeed, this last Winter I was jaded out: Winters were always worse than other parts of the year, because the spirits are worse, and I had no daylight. In Summer I had daylight evenings. The relief was hinted to me from a superior Power, when I, poor slave, had not a hope but that I must wait another seven years with Jacob: and lo! the Rachel which I coveted is brought to me!

Have you read the noble dedication of Irving's "Missionary Orations" to S. T. C.? Who shall call this man a quack hereafter? What the Kirk will think of it neither I nor Irving care. When somebody suggested to him that it would not be likely to do him good, videlicet, among his own people, "That is a reason for doing it," was his noble answer. That Irving thinks he has profited mainly by S. T. C., I have no doubt. The very style of the Dedication shows it.

Communicate my news to Southey, and beg his pardon for my being so long acknowledging his kind present of the "Church," which circumstances, having no reference to himself, prevented at the time. Assure him of my deep respect and friendliest feelings.

Divide the same, or rather each take the whole to you—I mean you and all yours. To Miss Hutchinson I must write separate.

Farewell! and end at last, long selfish letter.

C. LAMB.

LETTER TO MISS HUTCHINSON

April 18, 1825.

Dear Miss Hutchinson:—

You want to know all about my gaol delivery. Take it then. About twelve weeks since I had a sort of intimation that a resignation might be well accepted from me. This was a kind bird's whisper. On that hint I spake. Gilman and Tuthill furnished me with certificates of wasted health and sore spirits—not much more than the truth, I promise you—and for nine weeks I was kept in a fright. I had gone too far to recede, and they might take advantage, and dismiss me with a much less sum than I had reckoned on. However, liberty came at last, with a liberal provision. I have given up what I could have lived on in the country; but have enough to live here, by management and scribbling occasionally. I would not go back to my prison for seven years longer for £10,000 a year; seven years after one is fifty, is no trifle to give up. Still I am a young pensioner, and have served but thirty-three years; very few, I assure you, retire before forty, forty-five or fifty years' service.

You will ask how I bear my freedom? Faith, for some days I was staggered; could not comprehend the magnitude of my deliverance; was confused, giddy; knew not whether I was on my head or my heel, as they say. But those giddy feelings have gone away, and my weather-glass stands at a degree or two above

CONTENT.

I go about quiet, and have none of that restless hunting after recreation which made holydays formerly uneasy joys. All being holydays, I feel as if I had none, as they do in heaven, where 'tis all red-letter days. I have a kind letter from the Wordsworths, congratulatory not a little. It is a damp, I do assure you, amid all my prospects, that I can receive none from a quarter upon which I had calculated, almost more than from any, upon receiving congratulations. I had grown to like poor Monkhouse more and more. I do not esteem a soul living or not living more warmly than I had grown to esteem and value him. But words are vain. We have none of us to count upon many years. That is the only cure for sad thoughts. If only some died, and the rest were permanent on earth, what a thing a friend's death would be then!

I must take leave, having put off answering a load of letters

to this morning; and this, alas! is the first. Our kindest remembrances to Mrs. Monkhouse.

And believe us yours most truly,

C. LAMB.

THE SUPERANNUATED MAN

Sera tamen respexit
Libertas.   VIRGIL.
A Clerk I was in London gay.—O'KEEFE.

If peradventure, Reader, it has been thy lot to waste the
golden years of thy life—thy shining youth—in the irksome
confinement of an office; to have thy prison days prolonged
through middle age down to decreptitude and silver hairs,
without hope of release or respite; to have lived to forget
that there are such things as holidays, or to remember them
but as the prerogatives of childhood; then, and then only,
will you be able to appreciate my deliverance.

It is now six and thirty years since I took my seat at the
desk in Mincing-lane. Melancholy was the transition at fourteen from the abundant playtime, and the frequently-inter-
vening vacations of school days, to the eight, nine, and
sometimes ten hours a day attendance at the counting-house.
But time partially reconciles us to anything. I gradually became content—doggedly contented, as wild animals in cages.

It is true I had my Sundays to myself; but Sundays, admirable as the institution of them is for purposes of worship,
are for that very reason the very worst adapted for days of
unbending and recreation. In particular, there is a gloom for
me attendant upon a city Sunday, a weight in the air.
I miss the cheerful cries of London, the music, and the ballad-
singers—the buzz and stirring murmur of the streets. Those
eternal bells depress me. The closed shops repel me. Prints,

pictures, all the glittering and endless succession of knacks and gewgaws, and ostentatiously displayed wares of tradesmen, which make a weekday saunter through the less busy parts of the metropolis so delightful—are shut out. No bookstalls deliciously to idle over—no busy faces to recreate the idle man who contemplates them ever passing by—the very face of business a charm by contrast to his temporary relaxation from it. Nothing to be seen but unhappy countenances —or half-happy at best—of emancipated 'prentices and little tradesfolks, with here and there a servant-maid that has got leave to go out, who, slaving all the week, with the habit has lost almost the capacity of enjoying a free hour; and livelily expressing the hollowness of a day's pleasuring. The very strollers in the fields on that day look anything but comfortable.

But besides Sundays I had a day at Easter, and a day at Christmas, with a full week in the summer to go and air myself in my native fields of Hertfordshire. This last was a great indulgence; and the prospect of its recurrence, I believe, alone kept me up through the year, and made my durance tolerable. But when the week came round, did the glittering phantom of the distance keep touch with me? or rather was it not a series of seven uneasy days, spent in restless pursuit of pleasure, and a wearisome anxiety to find out how to make the most of them? Where was the quiet, where the promised rest? Before I had a taste of it, it was vanished. I was at the desk again, counting upon the fifty-one tedious weeks that must intervene before such another snatch would come. Still the prospect of its coming threw something of an illumination upon the darker side of my captivity. Without it, as I have said, I could scarcely have sustained my thraldom.

Independently of the rigours of attendance, I have ever

been haunted with a sense (perhaps a mere caprice) of incapacity for business. This, during my latter years, had increased to such a degree, that it was visible in all the lines of my countenance. My health and my good spirits flagged. I had perpetually a dread of some crisis, to which I should be found unequal. Besides my daylight servitude, I served over again all night in my sleep, and would awake with terrors of imaginary false entries, errors in my accounts, and the like. I was fifty years of age, and no prospect of emancipation presented itself. I had grown to my desk, as it were; and the wood had entered into my soul.

My fellows in the office would sometimes rally me upon the trouble legible in my countenance; but I did not know that it had raised the suspicions of any of my employers, when, on the 5th of last month, a day ever to be remembered by me, L——, the junior partner in the firm, calling me on one side, directly taxed me with my bad looks, and frankly inquired the cause of them. So taxed, I honestly made confession of my infirmity, and added that I was afraid I should eventually be obliged to resign his service. He spoke some words of course to hearten me, and there the matter rested. A whole week I remained labouring under the impression that I had acted imprudently in my disclosure; that I had foolishly given a handle against myself, and had been anticipating my own dismissal. A week passed in this manner, the most anxious one, I verily believe, in my whole life, when on the evening of the 12th of April, just as I was about quitting my desk to go home (it might be about eight o'clock), I received an awful summons to attend the presence of the whole assembled firm in the formidable back parlour. I thought, now my time is surely come, I have done for myself, I am going to be told that they have no longer occasion for me. L[acy], I could see, smiled at the terror I was in, which was a little relief to me,—when to my utter astonishment B[osanquet], the eldest partner, began a formal harangue to me on the length of my services, my very meritorious conduct during the whole of the time (the deuce, thought I, how did he find out that? I protest I never had the confidence to think as much). He went on to descant on the expediency of retiring at a certain time of life (how my heart panted!) and asking me a few questions as to the amount of my own property, of which I have a little, ended with a proposal, to which his three partners nodded a grave assent, that I should accept from the house, which I had served so well, a pension for life to the amount of two-thirds of my accustomed salary—a magnificent offer! I do not know what I answered between surprise and gratitude, but it was understood that I accepted their proposal, and I was told that I was free from that hour to leave their service. I stammered out a bow, and at just ten minutes after eight I went home—for ever. This noble benefit —gratitude forbids me to conceal their names—I owe to the kindness of the most munificent firm in the world—the house of Boldero, Merryweather, Bosanquet, and Lacy.

Esto perpetua!

For the first day or two I felt stunned, overwhelmed. I could only apprehend my felicity; I was too confused to taste it sincerely. I wandered about, thinking I was happy, and knowing that I was not. I was in the condition of a prisoner in the old Bastile, suddenly let loose after a forty years confinement. I could scarce trust myself with myself. It was like passing out of Time into Eternity—for it is a sort of Eternity for a man to have all his Time to himself. It seemed to me that I had more time on my hands than I could ever manage. From a poor man, poor in Time, I was suddenly lifted up into a vast revenue; I could see no end of my possessions; I wanted some steward, or judicious bailiff, to manage my estates in Time for me. And here let me caution persons grown old in active business, not lightly, nor without weighing their own resources, to forego their customary employment all at once, for there may be danger in it. I feel it by myself, but I know that my resources are sufficient; and now that those first giddy raptures have subsided, I have a quiet home-feeling of the blessedness of my condition. I am in no hurry. Having all holidays, I am as though I had none. If Time hung heavy upon me, I could walk it away; but I do *not* walk all day long, as I used to do in those old transient holidays, thirty miles a day to make the most of them. If Time were trouble-some, I could read it away; but I do *not* read in that violent measure, with which, having no Time my own but candle-light Time, I used to weary out my head and eyesight in by-gone winters. I walk, read, or scribble (as now) just when the fit seizes me. I no longer hunt after pleasure; I let it come to me. I am like the man

——that's born, and has his years come to him,
   In some green desert.

"Years!" you will say; "what is this superannuated simpleton calculating upon? He has already told us he is past fifty."

I have indeed lived nominally fifty years, but deduct out of them the hours which I have lived to other people, and not to myself, and you will find me still a young fellow. For *that* is the only true Time, which a man can properly call his own, that which he has all to himself; the rest, though in some sense he may be said to live it, is other people's Time, not his. The remnant of my poor days, long or short, is at least multiplied for me threefold. My ten next years, if I stretch so far, will be as long as any preceding thirty. 'Tis a fair rule-of-three sum.

Among the strange fantasies which beset me at the commencement of my freedom, and of which all traces are not yet gone, one was, that a vast tract of time had intervened since I quitted the Counting-House. I could not conceive of it as an affair of yesterday. The partners, and the clerks, with whom I had for so many years, and for so many hours in each day of the year, been closely associated—being suddenly removed from them—they seemed as dead to me. There is a fine passage, which may serve to illustrate this fancy, in a Tragedy by Sir Robert Howard, speaking of a friend's death:

> ————'Twas but just now he went away;
> I have not since had time to shed a tear;
> And yes the distance does the same appear
> As if he had been a thousand years from me.
> Time takes no measure in Eternity.

To dissipate this awkward feeling, I have been fain to go among them once or twice since; to visit my old desk-fellows—my co-brethren of the quill—that I had left below in the state militant. Not all the kindness with which they received me could quite restore me that pleasant familiarity, which I had heretofore enjoyed among them. We cracked some of our old jokes, but methought they went off but faintly. My old desk; the peg where I hung my hat, were appropriated to another. I knew it must be, but I could not take it kindly. D——l take me, if I did not feel some remorse—beast, if I had not,—at quitting my old compeers, the faithful partners of my toils for six and thirty years, that soothed for me with their jokes and conundrums the ruggedness of my professional road. Had it been so rugged then after all? or was I a coward simply? Well, it is too late to repent; and I also know that these suggestions are a common fallacy of the mind on such occasions. But my heart smote me. I had vio-

lently broken the bands betwixt us. It was at least not courteous. I shall be some time before I get quite reconciled to the
separation. Farewell, old cronies, yet not for long, for again
and again I will come among ye, if I shall have your leave.
Farewell, Ch[ambers], dry, sarcastic, and friendly! Do[d-
well], mild, slow to move, and gentlemanly! Pl[umley], officious to do, and to volunteer, good services!—and thou,
thou dreary pile, fit mansion for a Gresham or a Whittington
of old, stately House of Merchants; with thy labyrinthine
passages, and light-excluding, pent-up offices, where candles
for one half the year supplied the place of the sun's light;
unhealthy contributor to my weal, stern fosterer of my living, farewell! In thee remain, and not in the obscure collection of some wandering bookseller, my "works!" There let
them rest, as I do from my labours, piled on thy massy
shelves, more MSS. in folio than ever Aquinas left, and full
as useful! My mantle I bequeath among ye.

A fortnight has passed since the date of my first communication. At that period I was approaching to tranquillity, but
had not reached it. I boasted of a calm indeed, but it was
comparative only. Something of the first flutter was left; an
unsettling sense of novelty; the dazzle to weak eyes of un-
accustomed light. I missed my old chains, forsooth, as if they
had been some necessary part of my apparel. I was a poor
Carthusian, from strict cellular discipline suddenly by some
revolution returned upon the world. I am now as if I had
never been other than my own master. It is natural for me to
go where I please, to do what I please. I find myself at 11
o'clock in the day in Bond-street, and it seems to me that I
have been sauntering there at that very hour for years past.
I digress into Soho, to explore a bookstall. Methinks I have
been thirty years a collector. There is nothing strange nor
new in it. I find myself before a fine picture in the morning.

Was it ever otherwise? What is become of Fish-street Hill? Where is Fenchurch-street? Stones of old Mincing-lane, which I have worn with my daily pilgrimage for six and thirty years, to the footsteps of what toil-worn clerk are your ever-lasting flints now vocal? I indent the gayer flags of Pall Mall. It is 'Change time, and I am strangely among the Elgin marbles. It was no hyperbole when I ventured to compare the change in my condition to passing into another world. Time stands still in a manner to me. I have lost all distinction of season. I do not know the day of the week, or of the month. Each day used to be individually felt by me in its reference to the foreign post days; in its distance from, or propinquity to, the next Sunday. I had my Wednesday feelings, my Saturday nights' sensations. The genius of each day was upon me distinctly during the whole of it, affecting my appe-tite, spirits, etc. The phantom of the next day, with the dreary five to follow, sate as a load upon my poor Sabbath recreations. What charm has washed that Ethiop white? What is gone of Black Monday? All days are the same. Sunday itself—that unfortunate failure of a holyday as it too often proved, what with my sense of its fugitiveness, and over-care to get the greatest quantity of pleasure out of it—is melted down into a week-day. I can spare to go to church now, without grudging the huge cantle which it used to seem to cut out of the holiday. I have time for everything. I can visit a sick friend. I can interrupt the man of much occupa-tion when he is busiest. I can insult over him with an invi-tation to take a day's pleasure with me to Windsor this fine May-morning. It is Lucretian pleasure to behold the poor drudges, whom I have left behind in the world, carking and caring; like horses in a mill, drudging on in the same eternal round—and what is it all for? A man can never have too much Time to himself, nor too little to do. Had I a little son, I would christen him NOTHING-TO-DO; he should do nothing. Man, I verily believe, is out of his element as long as he is operative. I am altogether for the life contemplative. Will no kindly earthquake come and swallow up those accursed cotton-mills? Take me that lumber of a desk there, and bowl it down

> As low as to the fiends.

I am no longer —————, clerk to the Firm of, &c. I am Retired Leisure. I am to be met with in trim gardens. I am already come to be known by my vacant face and careless gesture, perambulating at no fixed pace, nor with any settled purpose. I walk about; not to and from. They tell me, a certain *cum dignitate* air, that has been buried so long with my other good parts, has begun to shoot forth in my person. I grow into gentility perceptibly. When I take up a newspaper, it is to read the state of the opera. *Opus operatum est.* I have done all that I came into this world to do. I have worked task-work, and have the rest of the day to myself.

Lamb, however, was not entirely happy in his retirement. He missed his regular occupation more than he had anticipated, and he tended to worry excessively over his sister's condition, the attacks of her malady having become more frequent. A feeling of loneliness crept upon him as he became called upon to mourn the loss of many of the friends connected with his early life. He was deeply affected by the death of Randal Norris, for many years sub-treasurer and librarian of the Inner Temple, who had been as Lamb said truthfully, "mine and my father's friend for nearly half a century." The letter that Lamb wrote to Crabb Robinson to tell him that this old friend is dying is a pathetic reflection of Lamb's feeling about the toll death was taking among his friends, as well as his wish to be helpful to the dependents of this life-long friend.

LETTER TO ROBINSON

Saturday, 20th Jan., 1827.
Colebrook Row, Islington.

Dear Robinson.—I called upon you this morning, and found that you were gone to visit a dying friend. I had been upon a like errand. Poor Norris has been lying dying for now almost a week, such is the penalty we pay for having enjoyed a strong constitution! Whether he knew me or not, I know not, or whether he saw me through his poor glazed eyes; but the group I saw about him I shall not forget. Upon the bed, or about it, were assembled his wife and two daughters, and poor deaf Richard, his son, looking doubly stupefied. There they were, and seemed to have been sitting all the week. I could only reach out a hand to Mrs. Norris. Speaking was impossible in that mute chamber. By this time I hope it is all over with him. In him I have a loss the world cannot make up. He was my friend and my father's friend all the life I can remember. I seem to have made foolish friendships ever since. Those are friendships which outlive a second generation. Old as I am waxing, in his eyes I was still the child he first knew me. To the last he called me Charley. I have none to call me Charley now. He was the last link that bound me to the Temple. You are but of yesterday. In him seemed to have died the old plainness of manners and singleness of heart. Letters he knew nothing of, nor did his reading extend beyond the pages of the Gentleman's Magazine. Yet there was a pride of literature about him from being amongst books (he was librarian), and from some scraps of doubtful Latin which he had picked up in his office of entering students, that gave him very diverting airs of pedantry. Can I forget the erudite look with which, when he had been in vain

trying to make out a black-letter text of Chaucer in the
Temple Library, he laid it down and told me that—"in
those old books, Charley, there is sometimes a deal of very
indifferent spelling;" and seemed to console himself in the
reflection! His jokes, for he had his jokes, are now ended,
but they were old trusty perennials, staples that pleased after
decies repetita, and were always as good as new. One song
he had, which was reserved for the night of Christmas-day,
which we always spent in the Temple. It was an old thing,
and spoke of the flat bottoms of our foes and the possibility
of their coming over in darkness, and alluded to threats of
an invasion many years blown over; and when we came to
the part

> We'll still make 'em run, and we'll still make 'em sweat,
> In spite of the devil and Brussels Gazette!

his eyes would sparkle as with the freshness of an impending
event. And what is the Brussels Gazette now? I cry while I
enumerate these trifles. "How shall we tell them in a
stranger's ear?." His poor good girls will now have to receive their afflicted mother in an inaccessible hovel in an obscure village in Herts, where they have been long struggling
to make a school without effect; and poor deaf Richard—
and the more helpless for being so—is thrown on the wild
world.

My first motive in writing, and, indeed, in calling on you,
was to ask if you were enough acquainted with any of the
Benchers, to lay a plain statement before them of the circumstances of the family. I almost fear not, for you are of another hall. But if you can oblige me and my poor friend,
who is now insensible to any favours, pray exert yourself.
You cannot say too much good of poor Norris and his poor
wife.

                    Yours ever,   CHARLES LAMB.

In 1827 Lamb and his sister removed from Islington, to Enfield, another suburb of London, and thence in 1833 to the
little cottage at Edmonton, in which he died. In these last years,
there was but little writing. He felt his period of literary activity was over, and he even was disinclined to write letters to
his friends. His time was spent in reading, walking, and visiting. Glimpses of this last scene of all are to be found in letters
to Bernard Barton, written in 1829, and to Wordsworth, written
in 1830.

LETTER TO BERNARD BARTON

Enfield Chase Side,
Saturday, 25th July, A.D. 1829, 11 a.m.

There—a fuller, plumper, juicier date never dropt from
Iduean palm. Am I in the date-ive case now? If not, a fig
for dates, which is more than a date is worth. I never stood
much affected to these limitary specialties. Least of all since
the date of my superannuation.

What have I with Time to do?   ⎧ Dear B. B.—Your hand-
Slaves of desks, 'twas meant for you. ⎨ writing has conveyed much
                                     ⎩ pleasure to me

in report of Lucy's restoration. Would I could send you as
good news of my poor Lucy. But some wearisome weeks I
must remain lonely yet. I have had the loneliest time, near
ten weeks, broken by a short apparition of Emma for her
holidays, whose departure only deepened the returning solitude, and by ten days I have past in Town. But Town, with
all my native hankering after it, is not what it was. The
streets, the shops are left, but all old friends are gone. And
in London I was frightfully convinced of this as I past houses
and places—empty caskets now—I have ceased to care almost
about any body. The bodies I cared for are in graves, or dis-

persed. My old Clubs, that lived so long, and flourish'd so steadily, are crumbled away. When I took leave of our adopted young friend at Charing Cross, 'twas heavy unfeeling rain, and I had no where to go. Home have I none—and not a sympathizing house to turn to in the great city. Never did the waters of the heaven pour down on a forlorner head. Yet I tried ten days at a sort of friend's house, but it was large and straggling—one of the individuals of my old long knot of friends, card-players, pleasant companions—that have tumbled to pieces into dust and other things—and I got home on Thursday, convinced that I was better to get home to my hole at Enfield, and hide like a sick cat in my corner. Less than a month, I hope, will bring home Mary. She is at Fulham, looking better in her health than ever, but sadly rambling, and scarce showing any pleasure in seeing me, or curiosity when I should come again. But the old feelings will come back again, and we shall drown old sorrows over a game at Picquet again. But 'tis a tedious cut out of a life of sixty-four, to lose twelve or thirteen weeks every year or two. And to make me more alone, our ill-temper'd maid is gone, who, with all her airs, was yet a home-piece of furniture, a record of better days; the young thing that has succeeded her is good and attentive, but she is nothing—and I have no one here to talk over old matters with. Scolding and quarrelling have some thing of familiarity, and a community of interest—they imply acquaintance—they are of resentment, which is of the family of dearness. I can neither scold nor quarrel at this insignificant implement of necessary services; she is less than a cat, and just better than a deal Dresser. What I can do, and do over-do, is to walk, but deadly long are the days—these summer all-day days, with but a half hour's candle-light and no fire-light. I do not write, tell your kind inquisitive Eliza, and can hardly read.

In the ensuing *Blackwood* will be an old rejected farce of mine, which may be new to you, if you see that same dull medley. What things are all the Magazines now—I contrive studiously not to see them. The popular *New Monthly* is perfect trash. Poor Hessey, I suppose you see, has failed; Hunt and Clarke too. Your "Vulgar Truths" will be a good name; and I think your prose must please—me at least; but 'tis useless to write poetry with no purchasers. 'Tis cold work Authorship without some thing to puff one into fashion. Could you not write something on Quakerism—for Quakers to read—but nominally addrest to Non-Quakers? explaining your dogmas—waiting on the Spirit—by the analogy of human calmness and patient waiting on the judgment? I scarcely know what I mean; but to make Non-Quakers reconciled to your doctrines, by showing something like them in mere human operations—but I hardly understand myself, so let it pass for nothing. I pity you for overwork, but I assure you no-work is worse. The mind preys on itself, the most unwholesome food. I brag'd formerly that I could not have too much time. I have a surfeit. With few years to come, the days are wearisome. But weariness is not eternal. Something will shine out to take the load off, that flags me, which is at present intolerable. I have killed an hour or two in this poor scrawl. I am a sanguinary murderer of Time, and would kill him inch-meal just now. But the snake is vital. Well, I shall write merrier anon. 'Tis the present copy of my countenance I send, and to complain is a little to alleviate. May you enjoy yourself as far as the wicked world will let you—and think that you are not quite alone, as I am! Health to Lucia and to Anna, and kind remembrances.

Yours forlorn,

C. L.

LETTER TO WORDSWORTH

January 22, 1830.

And is it a year since we parted from you at the steps of Edmonton stage? There are not now the years that there used to be. The tale of the dwindled age of men, reported of successional mankind, is true of the same man only. We do not live a year in a year now. 'Tis a *punctum stans*. The seasons pass us with indifference. Spring cheers not, nor Winter heightens our gloom; Autumn hath foregone its moralities,—they are "hey-pass re-pass," as in a show-box. Yet, as far as last year occurs back,—for they scarce show a reflex now, they make no memory as heretofore,—'twas sufficiently gloomy. Let the sullen nothing pass. Suffice it that after sad spirits, prolonged through many of its months, as it called them, we have cast our skins; have taken a farewell of the pompous, troublesome trifle, called housekeeping, and are settled down into poor boarders and lodgers at next door with an old couple, the Baucis and Baucida of dull Enfield. Here we have nothing to do with our victuals but to eat them; with the garden but to see it grow; with the tax-gatherer but to hear him knock; with the maid but to hear her scolded. Scot and lot, butcher, baker, are things unknown to us, save as spectators of the pageant. We are fed we know not how; quietists—confiding ravens. We have *'otium pro dignitate*, a respectable insignificance.

Yet in the self-condemned obliviousness, in the stagnation, some molesting yearnings of life, not quite killed, rise, prompting me that there was a London, and that I was of that old Jerusalem. In dreams I am in Fleet Market, but I wake and cry to sleep again. I die hard, a stubborn Eloisa in this detestable Paraclete. What have I gained by health? Intolerable dulness. What by early hours and moderate meals?

A total bland. O never let the lying poets be believed, who 'tice men from the cheerful haunts of streets, or think they mean it not of a country village. In the ruins of Palmyra I could gird myself up to solitude, or muse to the snorings of the Seven Sleepers; but to have a little teazing image of a town about one; country folks that do not look like country folks; shops two yards square, half-a-dozen apples, and two penn'orth of overlooked ginger-bread for the lofty fruiterers of Oxford Street; and, for the immortal book and print stalls a circulating library that stands still, where the show-picture is a last year's Valentine, and whither the fame of the last ten Scotch novels has not yet travelled,—(marry, they just begin to be conscious of the Redgauntlet.)—to have a new plastered flat church, and to be wishing that it was but a Cathedral! The very blackguards here are degenerate; the topping gentry stock-brokers; the passengers too many to insure your quiet, or let you go about whistling or gaping, too few to be the fine indifferent pageants of Fleet Street. Confiding, room-keeping, thickest Winter, is yet more bearable here than the gaudy months. Among one's books at one's fire by candle, one is soothed into an oblivion that one is not in the country; but with the light the green fields return, till I gaze, and in a calenture can plunge myself into St. Giles's. O let no native Londoner imagine that health, and rest, and innocent occupation, interchange of converse sweet, and recreative study, can make the country anything better than altogether odious and detestable! A garden was the primitive prison, till man, with Promethean felicity and boldness, luckily sinned himself out of it. Thence followed Babylon, Nineveh, Venice, London, haberdashers, goldsmiths, taverns, playhouses, satires, epigrams, puns,—these all came in on the town part, and the thither side of innocence. Man found out inventions.

From my den I return you condolence for your decaying
sight; not for anything there is to see in the country, but
for the miss of the pleasure of reading a London newspaper.
The poets are as well to listen to; anything high may, nay
must, be read out; you read it to yourself with an imaginary
auditor; but the light paragraphs must be glid over by the
proper eye; mouthing mumbles their gossamery substance.
'Tis these trifles I should mourn in fading sight. A newspaper
is the single gleam of comfort I receive here; it comes from
rich Cathay with tidings of mankind. Yet I could not attend
to it, read out by the most beloved voice. But your eyes do
not get worse, I gather. O for the collyrium of Tobias in-
closed in a whiting's liver, to send you with no apocryphal
good wishes! The last long time I heard from you, you had
knocked your head against something. Do not do so; for your
head (I do not flatter) is not a knob, or the top of a brass
nail, or the end of a nine pin,—unless a Vulcanian hammer
could fairly batter a "Recluse" out of it; then would I bid
the smirched god knock and knock lustily, the two-handed
skinker. What a nice long letter Dorothy has written! Mary
must squeeze out a line *propriâ manu*, but indeed her fingers
have been incorrigibly nervous to letter writing for a long
interval. 'Twill please you all to hear, that though I fret like
a lion in a net, her present health and spirits are better than
they have been for some time past. She is absolutely three
years and a half younger, as I tell her, since we have adopted
this boarding plan.

Our providers are an honest pair, dame W[estwood] and
her husband. He, when the light of prosperity shined on
them, a moderately thriving haberdasher, within Bow bells,
retired since with something under a competence; writes
himself parcel gentleman; hath borne parish offices; sings fine
old sea songs at threescore and ten; sighs only now and then

when he thinks that he has a son on his hands, about fifteen, whom he finds a difficulty in getting out into the world, and then checks a sigh with muttering, as I once heard him prettily, not meaning to be heard, "I have married my daughter, however;" takes the weather as it comes: outsides it to town in severest season; and o'winter nights tells old stories not tending to literature (how comfortable to author-rid folks!) and has *one anecdote*, upon which and about forty pounds a year he seems to have retired in green old age. It was how he was a rider in his youth, travelling for shops, and once (not to balk his employer's bargain) on a sweltering day in August, rode foaming into Dunstable upon a mad horse, to the dismay and expostulatory wonderment of inn-keepers, ostlers, etc., who declared they would not have be-strid the beast to win the Derby. Understand, the creature galled to death and desperation by gad-flies, cormorant-winged, worse than beset Inachus's daughter. This he tells, this he brindles and burnishes on a Winter's eve; 'tis his star of set glory, his rejuvenescence, to descant upon. Far from me be it (*dii avertant*) to look a gift story in the mouth, or cruelly to surmise (as those who doubt the plunge of Cur-tius) that the inseparate conjuncture of man and beast, the centaur-phenomenon that staggered all Dunstable, might have been the effect of unromantic necessity; that the horse-part carried the reasoning, willy nilly; that needs must when such a devil drove; that certain spiral configuration in the frame of Thomas Westwood's unfriendly to alighting, made the alliance more forcible than voluntary. Let him enjoy his fame for me, nor let me hint a whisper that shall dismount Bellerophon. Put case he was an involuntary martyr, yet if in the fiery conflict he buckled the soul of a constant haber-dasher to him, and adopted his flames, let accident and him share the glory.

You would all like Thomas Westwood. How weak is painting to describe a man! Say that he stands four feet and a nail
high by his own yard measure, which, like the sceptre of Agamemnon, shall never sprout again, still you have no adequate idea; nor when I tell you that his dear hump, which I
have favoured in the picture, seems to me of the buffalo—
indicative and repository of mild qualities, a budget of kind-
nesses—still you have not the man. Knew you old Norris
of the Temple? sixty years ours and our father's friend? He
was not more natural to us than this old W., the acquaintance of scarce more weeks. Under his roof now ought I to
take my rest, but that back-looking ambition tells me I might
yet be a Londoner! Well, if we ever do move, we have in-
cumbrances the less to impede us; all our furniture had faded
under the auctioneer's hammer, going for nothing, like the
tarnished frippery of the prodigal, and we have only a
spoon or two left to bless us. Clothed we came into Enfield,
and naked we must go out of it. I would live in London
shirtless, bookless. Henry Crabb is at Rome; advices to that
effect have reached Bury. But by solemn legacy he bequeathed
at parting (whether he should live or die) a turkey of Suffolk to be sent every succeeding Xmas to us and divers other
friends. What a genuine old bachelor's action! I fear he will
find the air of Italy too classic. His station is in the Harz
forest; his soul is be-Goethed. Miss Kelly we never see; Talfourd not this half-year: the latter flourishes, but the exact
number of his children (God forgive me!) I have utterly
forgotten. We single people are often out in our count there.
Shall I say two? . . . We see scarce anybody. . . .

Can I cram loves enough to you all in this little O? Excuse
particularising.

C. L.

The death of Coleridge in July, 1834, gave Lamb's heart a blow from which he could not recover. Before five months had passed, Lamb, himself, had gone to join his life-long friend. On a cold December day, as Lamb was walking along the London road from Edmonton, he stumbled and fell, slightly wounding his face. Erysipelas set in shortly afterward, and on December 29, 1834, he died, "murmuring in his last moments, the names of his dearest friends." The last piece of writing from his pen was the following letter, written to Mrs. Dyer, on the day he became ill. Curiously enough, its references to good eating and its solicitude about a certain old book, betray two of Lamb's ruling passions, strong to the last.

LETTER TO MRS. DYER

Dec. 22nd, 1834.

Dear Mrs. Dyer,—I am very uneasy about a *Book* which I have either lost or left at your house on Thursday. It was the book I went out to fetch from Miss Buffam's, while the tripe was frying. It is called Phillip's Theatrum Poetarum; but it is an English book. I think I left it in the parlour. It is Mr. Cary's book, and I would not lose it for the world. Pray, if you find it, book it at the Swan Snow Hill, by an Edmonton stage immediately, directed to Mr. Lamb, Church-street, Edmonton, or write to say you cannot find it. I am quite anxious about it. If it is lost, I shall never like tripe again. With kindest love to Mr. Dyer and all,

Yours truly,

C. LAMB.

An appropriate leave-taking of Lamb's personality is through the essay *New Year's Eve*. Though written some fourteen years before his death, it indicates the attitude he held toward the "Arch Fear." Of this essay and its melancholy scepticism,

Lamb's first publisher, Ollier, said, "Hamlet himself would have recognized as in his subtlest vein the weird humorous sadness, the tragic jesting of Lamb's remarks on death in the essay on *New Year's Eve*. Lamb himself, however, felt that his essay was merely an attempt at describing "the feelings of the merely natural man, on a consideration of the amazing change which is supposable to take place on our removal from this fleshly scene."

NEW YEAR'S EVE

Every man hath two birthdays: two days, at least, in every year, which set him upon revolving the lapse of time, as it affects his mortal duration. The one is that which in an especial manner he termeth *his*. In the gradual desuetude of old observances, this custom of solemnizing our proper birthday hath nearly passed away, or is left to children, who reflect nothing at all about the matter, nor understand anything in it beyond cake and orange. But the birth of a New Year is of an interest too wide to be pretermitted by king or cobbler. No one ever regarded the First of January with indifference. It is that from which all date their time, and count upon what is left. It is the nativity of our common Adam.

Of all sound of all bells—(bells, the music nighest bordering upon heaven)—most solemn and touching is the peal which rings out the Old Year. I never hear it without a gathering-up of my mind to a concentration of all the images that have been diffused over the past twelvemonth; all I have done or suffered, performed or neglected, in that regretted time. I begin to know its worth, as when a person dies. It takes a personal colour; nor was it a poetical flight in a contemporary, when he exclaimed—

I saw the skirts of the departing Year.

It is no more than what in sober sadness every one of us seems to be conscious of, in that awful leave-taking. I am sure I felt it, and all felt it with me, last night; though some of my companions affected rather to manifest an exhilaration at the birth of the coming year, than any very tender regrets for the decease of its predecessor. But I am none of those who—

Welcome the coming, speed the parting guest.

I am naturally, beforehand, shy of novelties; new books, new faces, new years,—from some mental twist which makes it difficult in me to face the prospective. I have almost ceased to hope; and am sanguine only in the prospects of other (former years). I plunge into foregone visions and conclusions. I encounter pell-mell with past disappointments. I am armour-proof against old discouragements. I forgive, or overcome in fancy, old adversaries. I play over again *for love,* as the gamsters phrase it, games for which I once paid so dear. I would scarce now have any of those untoward accidents and events of my life reversed. I would no more alter them than the incidents of some well-contrived novel. Methinks, it is better that I should have pined away seven of my goldenest years, when I was thrall to the fair hair, and fairer eyes, of Alice W[interto]n, than that so passionate a love adventure should be lost. It was better that our family should have missed that legacy, which old Dorrell cheated us of, than that I should have at this moment two thousand pounds *in banco,* and be without the idea of that specious old rogue.

In a degree beneath manhood, it is my infirmity to look back upon those early days. Do I advance a paradox when I say, that, skipping over the intervention of forty years, a man may have leave to love *himself* without the imputation of self-love?

If I know aught of myself, no one whose mind is introspective—and mine is painfully so—can have a less respect for his present identity, than I have for the man Elia. I know him to be light, and vain, and humoursome; a notorious . . . ; addicted to . . . ; averse from counsel, neither taking it, nor offering it;— . . . besides; a stammering buffoon; what you will; lay it on, and spare not; I subscribe to it all, and much more, than thou canst be willing to lay at his door —but for the child Elia—that "other me," there, in the background—I must take leave to cherish the remembrance of that young master—with as little reference, I protest, to his stupid changeling of five and forty, as if it had been a child of some other house, and not of my parents. I can cry over its patient small-pox at five, and rougher medicaments. I can lay its poor fevered head upon the sick pillow at Christ's, and wake with it in surprise at the gentle posture of maternal tenderness hanging over it, that unknown had watched its sleep. I know how it shrank from any the least colour of falsehood.— God help thee, Elia, how art thou changed!— Thou art sophisticated.—I know how honest, how courageous (for a weakling) it was—how religious, how imaginative, how hopeful! From what have I not fallen, if the child I remember was indeed myself,—and not some dissembling guardian, presenting a false identity, to give the rule to my unpractised steps, and regulate the tone of my moral being!

That I am fond of indulging, beyond a hope of sympathy, in such retrospection, may be the symptom of some sickly idiosyncrasy. Or is it owing to another cause: simply, that being without wife or family, I have not learned to project myself enough out of myself; and having no offspring of my own to dally with, I turn back upon memory, and adopt my own early idea, as my heir and favourite? If these speculations seem fantastical to thee, Reader—(a busy man, perchance), if I tread out of the way of thy sympathy, and am singularly conceited only, I retire, impenetrable to ridicule, under the phantom cloud of Elia.

The elders, with whom I was brought up, were of a character not likely to let slip the sacred observance of any old institution; and the ringing out of the Old Year was kept by them with circumstances of peculiar ceremony.—In those days the sound of those midnight chimes, though it seemed to raise hilarity in all around me, never failed to bring a train of pensive imagery into my fancy. Yet I then scarce conceived what it meant, or thought of it as a reckoning that concerned me. Not childhood alone, but the young man till thirty, never feels practically that he is mortal. He knows it indeed, and, if need were, he could preach a homily on the fragility of life; but he brings it not home to himself, any more than in a hot June we can appropriate to our imagination the freezing days of December. But now, shall I confess a truth?—I feel these audits but too powerfully. I begin to count the probabilities of my duration, and to grudge at the expenditure of moments and shortest periods, like misers' farthings. In proportion as the years both lessen and shorten, I set more count upon their periods, and would fain lay my ineffectual finger upon the spoke of the great wheel. I am not content to pass away "like a weaver's shuttle." Those metaphors solace me not, nor sweeten the unpalatable draught of mortality. I care not to be carried with the tide, that smoothly bears human life to eternity; and reluct at the inevitable course of destiny. I am in love with this green earth; the face of town and country; the unspeakable rural solitudes, and the sweet security of streets. I would set up my tabernacle here. I am content to stand still at the age to which I am arrived; I, and my friends: to be no younger, no richer, no handsomer. I do not want to be weaned by age; or drop, like mellow fruit, as they say, into the grave.—Any alteration, on this earth of mine, in diet or in lodging, puzzles and discomposes me. My household gods plant a terrible fixed foot, and are not rooted up without blood. They do not willingly seek Lavinian shores. A new state of being staggers me.

Sun, and sky, and breeze, and solitary walks, and summer holidays, and the greenness of fields, and the delicious juices of meats and fishes, and society, and the cheerful glass, and candlelight, and fireside conversations, and innocent vanities, and jests, and *irony itself*—do these things go out with life?

Can a ghost laugh, or shake his gaunt sides, when you are pleasant with him?

And you, my midnight darlings, my Folios: must I part with the intense delight of having you (huge armfuls) in my embraces? Must knowledge come to me, if it come at all, by some awkward experiment of intuition, and no longer by this familiar process of reading?

Shall I enjoy friendships there, wanting the smiling indications which point me to them here,—the recognisable face—the "sweet assurance of a look"?

In winter this intolerable disinclination to dying—to give it its mildest name—does more especially haunt and beset me. In a genial August noon, beneath a sweltering sky, death is almost problematic. At those times do such poor snakes as myself enjoy an immortality. Then we expand and burgeon. Then we are as strong again, as valiant again, as wise again, and a great deal taller. The blast that nips and shrinks me, puts me in thoughts of death. All things allied to the insubstantial, wait upon that master feeling; cold, numbness, dreams, perplexity; moonlight itself, with its shadowy and spectral appearances,—that cold ghost of the sun, or Phœbus' sickly sister, like that innutritious one denounced in the Canticles:—I am none of her minions—I hold with the Persian.

Whatsoever thwarts, or puts me out of my way, brings death unto my mind. All partial evils, like humours, run into that capital plague-sore.—I have heard some profess an indifference to life. Such hail the end of their existence as a port of refuge; and speak of the grave as of some soft arms, in which they may slumber as on a pillow. Some have wooed death——but out upon thee, I say, thou foul, ugly phantom! I detest, abhor, execrate, and (with Friar John) give thee to six score thousand devils, as in no instance to be excused or tolerated, but shunned as an universal viper; to be branded, proscribed, and spoken evil of! In no way can I be brought to digest thee, thou thin, melancholy *Privation*, or more frightful and confounding *Positive!*

Those antidotes, prescribed against the fear of thee, are altogether frigid and insulting, like thyself. For what satisfaction hath a man, that he shall "lie down with kings and emperors in death," who in his lifetime never greatly coveted the society of such bedfellows?—or, forsooth, that "so shall the fairest face appear"?—why, to comfort me, must Alice W—n be a goblin? More than all, I conceive disgust at those impertinent and misbecoming familiarities, inscribed upon your ordinary tombstones. Every dead man must take upon himself to be lecturing me with his odious truism, that "Such as he now is, I must shortly be." Not so shortly, friend, perhaps, as thou imaginest. In the meantime I am alive. I move about. I am worth twenty of thee. Know thy betters! Thy New Years' days are past. I survive, a jolly candidate for 1821. Another cup of wine—and while that turncoat bell, that just now mournfully chanted the obsequies of 1820 departed, with changed notes lustily rings in a successor, let us attune to its peal the song made on a like occasion, by hearty, cheerful Mr. Cotton.

THE NEW YEAR

Hark, the cock crows, and yon bright star
Tells us, the day himself's not far;
And see where, breaking from the night,
He gilds the western hills with light.
With him old Janus doth appear,
Peeping into the future year,
With such a look as seems to say
The prospect is not good that way.
Thus do we rise ill sights to see,
And 'gainst ourselves to prophesy;
When the prophetic fear of things
A more tormenting mischief brings,
More full of soul tormenting gall
Than direst mischiefs can befall.
But stay! but stay! methinks my sight,
Better informed by clearer light,
Discerns sereneness in that brow
That all contracted seem'd but now.
His revers'd face may show distaste,
And frown upon the ills are past;
But that which this way looks is clear,
And smiles upon the New-born Year.
He looks too from a place so high,
The year lies open to his eye;
And all the moments open are
To the exact discoverer.
Yet more and more he smiles upon
The happy revolution.
Why should we then suspect or fear
The influences of a year,
So smiles upon us the first morn,
And speaks us good so soon as born?

Plague on't! the last was ill enough,
This cannot but make better proof;
Or, at the worst, as we brush'd through
The last, why so we may this too;

And then the next in reason shou'd
Be superexcellently good:
For the worst ills (we daily see)
Have no more perpetuity
Than the best fortunes that do fall;
Which also bring us wherewithal
Longer their being to support,
Than those do of the other sort:
And who has one good year in three,
And yet repines at destiny,
Appears ungrateful in the case,
And merits not the good he has.
Then let us welcome the New Guest
With lusty brimmers of the best;
Mirth always should Good Fortune meet,
And renders e'en Disaster sweet:
And though the Princess turn her back,
Let us but line ourselves with sack,
We better shall by far hold out,
Till the next Year she face about.

How say you, Reader—do not these verses smack of the rough magnanimity of the old English vein? Do they not fortify like a cordial; enlarging the heart, and productive of sweet blood, and generous spirits, in the concoction? Where be those puling fears of death, just now expressed or affected?—Passed like a cloud—absorbed in the purging sunlight of clear poetry—clean washed away by a wave of genuine Helicon, your only Spa for these hypochondries. And now another cup of the generous! and a merry New Year, and many of them, to you all, my masters!

NOTES

NOTES

AUTOBIOGRAPHICAL SKETCH (Page xiii)

teste suâ manu—witness his hand.

complexional—constitutional.

production of the juniper berry—gin.

Leadenhall Street—the location of the East India House where Lamb worked as accountant for thirty-three years.

THE OLD BENCHERS OF THE INNER TEMPLE (Page 1)

London Magazine, September, 1821.

"The essay on The Old Benchers of the Inner Temple is one of the most varied and beautiful pieces of prose that English literature can boast. Eminently, moreover, does it show us Lamb as the product of two different ages,—the child of the Renaissance of the sixteenth century and of that of the nineteenth." (Ainger.)

Bencher—one of the members of an inn of court, as an association of lawyers is called in England, who on account of seniority has a voice in the government of the society.

Temple—in the fourteenth century two of the English legal societies, called inns of court, acquired the buildings formerly belonging to the Knights Templars. The buildings used by one were called the Inner Temple, and those of the other the Middle Temple.

There when, etc.—from Spencer's *Prothalamion.*

Naiades—water nymphs; the allusion is to the fact that Twickenham, being higher up the river, was more suited to be the abode of the Naiades.

Elizabethan Hall—the hall of the Middle Temple.

nice—imperceptible.

Ah! yet, etc.—from Shakespeare's Sonnet CIV.

carved it, etc.—from *Henry VI,* Part III.

What wondrous, etc.—from a copy of verses entitled *The Garden.* (Lamb's note.)

South-Sea House—the office of the South Sea Company.

exploded—rejected.

winged horse—the badge of the Inner Temple.

Elisha bear—II Kings ii.

rappee—dark brown material.

chamber practice—giving private advice as a lawyer.

Lovel—an alias for Lamb's father.

Miss Blandy—a woman hanged in 1752 for poisoning her father.

hic currus, etc.—here was his chariot and his arms. (Virgil's *Aeneid*.)

Elwes—a famous eighteenth century miser.

flapper—prompter; in *Gulliver's Travels*, Swift had described the absent-minded Laputians as always accompanied by such a functionary.

Susan P[ierson]—a sister of the Peter Pierson mentioned below.

Garrick—the famous eighteenth century actor.

Bayes—a character in Buckingham's play, *The Rehearsal*.

philanthropist—probably Howard, the prison reformer, who was a friend of Lamb's.

Friar Bacon—Roger Bacon, the pioneer of science in the thirteenth century.

Moses—the famous statue in the Sistine Chapel, the head of which shows two horns.

old men, etc.—I Samuel xxviii. 14.

Goshen—the portion of Egypt in which the Hebrews lived while in bondage.

N[orris]—sub-treasurer and librarian of the Inner Temple.

Elia—the following is a quotation from a letter from Lamb to his publishers in 1821, explaining the *nom de plume* under which he hid for a while his identity: "Poor ELIA the real (for I am but a counterfeit), is dead. The fact is, a person of that name, an Italian, was a fellow-clerk of mine at the South Sea House, thirty (not forty) years ago, when the characters I described there existed [see the essay the *South-Sea House*] . . . and I having a brother now there, and doubting how he might relish certain inscriptions . . . clapt down the name of Elia to it . . . I went the other day (not having seen him for a year) to laugh over with him at my usurpation of his name, and found him, alas! no more than a name, for he had died of consumption eleven months before, and I knew not of it."

Urban's obituary—in the *Gentleman's Magazine*, the editor of which signed himself "Sylvanus Urban."

ye yourselves, etc.—*King Lear* II, vii.

Hooker, Selden—prose writers of the 17th century, both of whom had connections with the Temple.

illustrate—glorify.

CAPTAIN STARKEY (Page 14)

The Everyday-Bay Book, July 21, 1825.

to what, etc.—*Hamlet*, V, i.

Cato—Addison's tragedy.

MY FIRST PLAY (Page 19)

London Magazine, December, 1821.

Old Drury—The famous Drury Lane Theatre, first opened in 1663.

John Palmer—an actor.

Mary Linley—a noted singer.

Brinsley's easy autograph—the dramatist, Richard Brinsley Sheridan, was also manager of Drury Lane Theatre.

Seneca . . Varro—Roman writers.

landed property—this is perhaps a bit of humorous fabrication on the part of Lamb.

nonpareils—a kind of apple sold in the theatre.

pro—for.

fair Auroras—from the first song in *Artaxerxes*.

Artaxerxes—an opera by Arne.

St. Denys—the patron saint of France, about whom was the legend that he was beheaded, and so in old paintings he was shown as holding his head in his hands.

Harlequin—a clown.

Lady of the Manor—a comic opera.

Lun's Ghost—Rich, the actor, had taken the part of Lun.

Way of the World—one of Congreve's plays.

was nourished, etc.—probably an echo from Izaak Walton's *Compleat Angler*.

BLAKESMOOR IN H[ERTFORD]SHIRE (Page 32)

London Magazine, September, 1824.

puts us by—turns us away from.

Ovid—the Roman poet who related so many of the old myths and legends.

Acteon—in mythology, a hunter who was changed into a stag by the goddess Diana because he came upon her when bathing.

Dan Phoebus—Master Phoebus.

Marsyas—Phoebus entered into a musical contest with Marsyas, a satyr, Phoebus using a lyre, Marsyas a flute. The contest was close, Phoebus winning. He, however, punished Marsyas for his presumption by flaying him alive.

Mrs. Battle—a creation of Lamb's own who appears more at full length in the essay *Mrs. Battle's Opinions on Whist*.

garden-loving poet—Marvell on *Appleton House, to the Lord Fairfax*. (Lamb's note.)

Mowbray, De Clifford—famous noblemen of the Wars of the Roses time.

Blakesmoor—Lamb's disguise for Blakesware.

Resurgam—I shall arise again.

Damoetas—a common name for a shepherd in Greek pastoral poetry.

Aegon—a shepherd in Greek poetry.

W——s—Lamb's disguise for the name Plumer.

Alice—the early sweetheart so frequently mentioned by Lamb, usually as Alice W——n. See note, page 323.

Twelve Caesars—this collection of busts made an indelible impression on Lamb, judging by the frequent reference to them in his letters and essays.

Pan. . Sylvanus—a Roman wood-deity.

CHRIST'S HOSPITAL FIVE AND THIRTY YEARS AGO (Page 38)

London Magazine, November, 1820.

Mr. Lamb's "Works"—the first collection of Lamb's writings representing the pre-Eliana period of his literary work was published 1818. Among this material was an essay entitled Recollections of Christ's Hospital, in which Lamb paid a fine tribute of praise to this charitable institution for the education and support of the young. In the present essay, however, he presents another side of the picture, showing the grievances, real and imaginary, of the scholars, together with some of the humorous aspects of the regulations and traditions of the school. Coleridge in *Biographia Literaria* has drawn a companion picture of the better side of Christ's Hospital discipline, and Leigh Hunt, who was a scholar two or three years later than Lamb, has also described in his *Autobiography* the life and ideals of the famous school.

sub-treasurer—Randall Norris; see page 346.

banyan days—vegetable days.

caro, etc.—horseflesh.

relative—in a letter to Coleridge, January, 1797, Lamb writes: "My poor old aunt, whom you have seen, the kindest, goodest creature to me when I was at school; who used to toddle there to bring me good things, when I, schoolboy like, only despised her for it, and used to be ashamed to see her come and sit herself down on the old coal-hole steps as you went into the grammar school, and open her apron, and bring out her bason, with some nice thing she had caused to be saved for me."

regale—banquet.

cates—dainties.

the Tishbite—the prophet Elijah; see I Kings xvii.

friendless boy—Lamb writes as though he were Coleridge.

Calna—a masquerade for Coleridge's home, Ottery St. Mary, in Devonshire.

Lions—the royal menageries was kept in the Tower in Lamb's time.

L's governor—Samuel Salt (see *The Old Benchers of the Inner Temple*).

Nero—the Roman emperor famous for his inhumanity.

Caligula's minion—the horse of this Roman emperor, which was fed from a golden manger and afterwards made a consul.

waxing fat, etc.—Deuteronomy xxxii. 15.

Jericho—Joshua vi. 20.

blue-coat boys—nickname for the boys of Christ's Hospital, derived from their school dress.

Trojan—Aeneas.

To feed, etc.—Virgil's *Aeneid,* Book I.

'Twas said, etc.—*Antony and Cleopatra,* I, iv.

Bedlam—the insane asylum of South London.

subject him to—one or two instances of lunacy or attempted suicide, accordingly, at length convinced the governors of the impolicy of this part of the sentence, and the midnight torture to the spirits was dispensed with.—This fancy of dungeons for children was a sprout of Howard's brain; for which (saving the reverence due to Holy Paul) methinks I could willingly spit upon his statue. (Lamb's note.)

auto-da-fé—literally, "act of the faith"; applied to executions under the Inquisition.

Watchet-weeds—blue clothes.

in Dante—in the *Inferno.*

Ultima, etc.—extreme punishments.

San Benito—a short linen dress, worn by heretics on trial before the Inquisition.

Like, etc.—*Anthony and Cleopatra.*

insolent Greece, etc.—Ben Jonson's *Lines on Shakespeare.*

Peter Wilkins—a Robinson Crusoe-like story, *Life and Adventures of Peter Wilkins.*

Rousseau..Locke—Lamb refers to the pedagogical theories of these two philosophers, the one French and the other English.

Phaedrus—Roman writer of fables.

Helots—slaves among the ancient Spartans.

Xenophon..Plato—the Greek historian and the Greek philosopher.

The Samite—Pythagoras, the Greek philosopher, is said to have forbidden his pupils to speak until they had heard his lectures for five years.

Goshen—see note, page 316.

Gideon's miracle—Judges vi. 37.

our fleece, etc.—Cowley. (Lamb's note.)

Ululantes—howlers.

Tartarus—the infernal regions.

rapid pedant—in this and everything B. was the antipodes of his coadjutor. While the former was digging his brains for crude anthems, worth a pig-nut, F. would be recreating his gentlemanly fancy in the more flowery walks of the Muses. A little dramatic effusion of his, under the name of Vertumnus and Pomona, is not yet forgotten by the chroniclers of that sort of literature. It was accepted by Garrick, but the town did not give it their sanction.—B. used to say of it, in a way of half-compliment, half-irony, that it was *too classical for representation.* (Lamb's note.)

scrannel pipes—Milton's *Lycidas.*

Flaccus—Horace, the Roman poet; for the quibble about *Rex,* see *Satires* I.

tristis severitas, etc.—stern severity of his countenance.

inspicere in patinas—to look upon the plates.

Terence—a Roman dramatist.

vis—strength.

caxon—a wig.

rabidus furor—mad rage.

Debates—in Parliament.

literary life—*Biographia Literaria,* Chapter I.

Country Spectator—a periodical of Lamb's time.

First Grecian—the highest class, composed of boys who were considered suitable for university training with a view ultimately to the ministry.

Cicero, etc.—Cicero's book on Friendship.

regni novitas—newness of the rule (*Aeneid*).

Jewel..Hooker—noted English theologians.

Finding some, etc.—from Prior's poem *Carmen Seculare* for the year 1700.

fiery column—Exodus xi. 34-38.

Mirandula—Lamb applies to Coleridge the name of the famous Italian scholar of the 15th century.

Jamblichus..Plotinus—Greek philosophers.

Homer..Pindar—Greek poets.

Grey Friar's—another designation of Christ's Hospital.

Fuller—Thomas Fuller, 17th century prose writer, whose quaintness made his writing congenial to Lamb.

which two, etc.—an adaptation of Fuller's account of the tradition about wit combats between Shakespeare and Ben Jonson.

Nireus, etc.—beautiful Nireus, said to have been the handsomest Greek at the siege of Troy (*Iliad*).

the junior Le G[rice]—Samuel Le Grice, who was a great friend of Lamb. He had gone into the army and died in the West Indies.

F[lavell]—the "poor W——" of Lamb's essay *Poor Relations.*

MODERN GALLANTRY (Page 54)

London Magazine, November, 1822.

Dorimant—A genteel, witty libertine in one of Etheridge's comedies.

Prèux Chevalier—a valiant knightly defender.

Sir Calidore—a character in the *Faerie Queene* typifying courtesy. *Sir Tristran*—one of the knights of King Arthur's Round Table.

THE SOUTH-SEA HOUSE (Page 59)

London Magazine, August, 1820.

annuitant—Lamb did not hold such a position until 1825, when he was an employ of the East India House.

the Flower Pot—A London inn.

Balclutha—I passed by the walls of Balclutha, and they were desolate—Ossian. (Lamb's note.)

unsunned heap—Milton's *Comus*.

Bubble—the South Sea Bubble of 1720, a disastrous speculative scheme.

superfoetation—double layer.

plot—the Gunpowder Plot (1605), Guido Vaux being an Italianate form of Guy Fawkes.

Herculaneum—the Roman city destroyed in the Vesuvian eruption, A.D. 79.

pounce-boxes—boxes holding the powder used as a substitute for blotting paper.

Humourists—the word is used in its older sense of peculiarities, eccentricities.

Cambro-Briton—Welshman.

Pennant—a naturalist and antiquarian, author of an *Account of London* (1790).

Hogarth—an English painter and engraver; see Lamb's essay *On the Genius and Character of Hogarth*.

heroic confessors—Huguenots who fled from France in the 17th century.

Decus, etc.—honor and consolation (Virgil's *Aeneid*).

Orphean lyre—Orpheus, the great musician of mythology, whose music was irresistible. This phrase is an echo of *Paradise Lost*.

sweet breasts—musical voices.

Midas—in classical legend a king who judged a musical competition between Pan and Apollo, the god of music.

Fortinbras—in *Hamlet*.

new-born gauds—showy ceremonies; an echo of *Troilus and Cressida*.

Plumer—deputy secretary and master of the Hertfordshire mansion, with which essay *Mackery End in Hertfordshire* is connected.

Johnson's—Dr. Samuel Johnson.

Arden—the forest of Arden, the background for *As You Like It*.

fantastic—as a matter of fact these names are not fictitious but in each instance the man named "had a being."

Pimpernel . .Naps—names used in the introduction to *Taming of the Shrew*.

LETTER TO COLERIDGE (Page 69)

Mr. Norris—probably a different Norris from the sub-treasurer and librarian of the Inner Temple who was frequently mentioned in the Essays.

mine—a reference to four sonnets Lamb had contributed to Coleridge's projected volume of verse.

LETTER TO COLERIDGE (Page 70)

Sam LeGrice—see note, page 320.
Sara—Mrs. Coleridge.

MY RELATIONS (Page 76)

London Magazine, June, 1821.
an aunt—a sister of Lamb's father in whose honor, at her death, Lamb wrote a poem.
Brother or sister—clearly a literary fiction, since Lamb proceeds to describe his brother John and sister Mary under the thin disguise of cousins.
James and Bridget Elia—John and Mary Lamb.
Yorick—the *nom de plume* of Sterne in *Sentimental Journey* as well as a character in *Tristram Shandy*.
Domenichino—a painting by an Italian artist of that name.
upon instinct—an echo of Falstaff's explanation, *Henry IV, Part I*.
shall crow—an echo of *As You Like It*.
Christie's. .Phillips's—London art dealers.
Cynthia—the moon goddess; an echo of Pope's *Epistles I*.
Carricci—two cousins. Italian painters of the 17th century. Other mention of Italian artists occurs in the following sentences.
Hallowmass—All Saints' Day, November 1.
Clarkson—an English abolitionist.

MACKERY END, IN HERTFORDSHIRE (Page 83)

London Magazine, July, 1821.
rash king's offspring—Jephtha's daughter, Judges xi.
Margaret Newcastle—a maid of honor to Queen Henrietta Maria, noted for her faithfulness and love of literature. She wrote a life of her husband and an autobiography of which Lamb was fond.
speak to it—answer for, account for.
reading—Samuel Salt's library.
the poet—Wordsworth in *Yarrow Visited*.
two scriptural cousins—Luke i. 39-40.
B[arron] F[ield]—a lawyer and friend of Lamb's. The essay *Distant Correspondents* is addressed to him.

DREAM-CHILDREN: A REVERIE (Page 89)

London Magazine, January, 1822.
Norfolk—this should really be Hertfordshire.

John L————.—Lamb's brother John died in October, 1821.

Mary Field—she had been his housekeeper at Blakesware in Hertfordshire, in the house of the Plumers.

"Alice W[interto]n"—supposed to have been a Miss Ann Simmons, Lamb's early sweetheart, who married a pawnbroker named Bartram.

BARBARA S———— (Page 94)

London Magazine, April, 1825.

As usual, Lamb has made considerable change in the actual details of this incident, leaving it, however, substantially true to an experience of Miss Kelly.

young Arthur.—a part taken by Miss Kelly in Shakespeare's *King John.*

Richard—Richard III, iii.

Children in the Wood—see note, page 328.

principia—beginnings.

Mrs. Porter—this should be Mrs. Siddons, the actress.

Liston..Kemble..Macready—noted English actors.

punctuality—exactness.

Mrs. Crawford—the maiden name of this lady was Street, which she changed by successive marriages, for those of Dancer, Barry, and Crawford. She was Mrs. Crawford, and a third time a widow, when I knew her. (Lamb's note.) Lamb evidently intended this note to be misleading.

LETTER TO MISS KELLY (Page 102)

break no bones—seemingly a pun, the word "bones" being used, it is said, in theatrical slang for the bone or ivory tablets belonging to members of the company, who could lend them for an evening as a pass for a friend.

NEWSPAPERS THIRTY-FIVE YEARS AGO (Page 102)

The Englishman's Magazine, October, 1831.

Scaturient—gushing or springing out.

Brucian—explorer-like; James Bruce was a famous African explorer.

The Gnat..The Culex—a poem ascribed for many years to Virgil.

The Duck—The reference is to a bit of verse written by Dr. Samuel Johnson at the age of three.

> Here lies good master duck
> Whom Samuel Johnson trod on;
> If it had lived it had been good luck.
> For then we'd had an odd one.

The explanation of the last line is that the duck was the eleventh of a brood.

Cytherea—Venus.

Autolycus-like—the frolicsome rogue in *The Winter's Tale.*

Astraea—goddess of justice in the Golden Age.

Ultima, etc.—the last of the celestials has left the earth.

Basilian—pertaining to St. Basil the Great.

Capulets—one of the two factions in *Romeo and Juliet.*

revocare, etc.—to regain one's feet and go up out into the air.

Bel's Temple—one of the apocryphal books in the Bible is *Bel and the Dragon,* Bel being a Babylonian god.

Bob Allen—see essay, *Christ's Hospital Five and Thirty Years Ago.*

Astræan—see note above.

"Bigod"—John Fenwick, see note, page 325.

LETTER TO MANNING (Page 112)

The Mandarins—Manning had by this time been in China a long time.

two volumes—a collection entitled *Poetry for Children* that Lamb and his sister had prepared.

Holcroft—a dramatist and miscellaneous writer on friendly terms with Lamb, though of an entirely different temperament.

Hazlitt—the English essayist.

Tuthill—see page 346.

little book—so far as known purely an imaginary production.

OLD CHINA (Page 116)

London Magazine, March, 1823.

hays—an old-fashioned country dance.

Speciosa miracula—dazzlingly beautiful wonders (from Horace).

Bridget—Mary Lamb.

corbeau—tailor's slang for black goods.

Lionardo—Leonardo da Vinci; Mary Lamb had written a poem on this picture.

Izaak Walton—in *The Compleat Angler.*

Battle of Hexham, etc.—actual plays and actors of the time, favorites of Lamb.

Rosalind . . Viola—respectively the heroines of Shakespeare's *As You Like It* and *Twelfth Night.*

Mr. Cotton—seventeenth century poet.

R[othschild]—the famous banker, Nathan Meyer Rothschild (1777-1836).

LETTER TO WORDSWORTH (Page 124)

Joanna—a poem by Wordsworth in which he described the effect of laughter echoing among the mountains.

D.—Dorothy, Wordsworth's sister.

Barbara Lewthwaite—the girl in Wordsworth's poem *The Pet Lamb.*

LETTER TO MANNING (Page 126)

Allowance should be made for a degree of affectation in Lamb's disparagement of the charms of the scenery in the Lake country. His enthusiastic words in this letter to Manning counterbalance the disparagement in the preceding letter to Wordsworth.

you had left—Manning had gone to Paris early in 1802 to study Chinese in preparation for his trip to China.

Devil sits—a reference to a cave in Derbyshire.

Lloyd—Lamb's friend Charles Lloyd had recently settled in the Lake district.

to be married, etc.—Wordsworth's marriage to Mary Hutchinson took place October, 1802.

Clarksons—see note, page 322.

sacrifice the fat, etc.—Leviticus iii. 3-4, Isaiah xxv. 6.

The truth is......harpies, etc.—the sympathetic commentary of Ainger in his *Charles Lamb* on this shortcoming fittingly comes in at this point. "The tale is indeed a sad one, and we have no reason to suppose it less true than pitiful. There is no concealment on the part of Lamb himself, or his sister, or of those who knew him most intimately, of the fact that from an early age Charles found in wine, or its equivalent, a stimulus that relieved him under the pressure of shyness, anxiety, and low spirits, and that the habit remained with him till the end of his life. It is not easy to deal with this 'frailty' (to borrow Talfourd's expression) in Lamb, without falling into an apologetic tone, suggestive of the much abused proverb connecting excuse with accusation. But it is the biographer's task to account for these things, if not to excuse them, and at this period there is not wanting evidence of hard trials attending the life of the brother and sister which may well prompt a treatment of the subject, the reverse of harsh."

St. Gothard—Manning was at that time in Switzerland, where is the St. Gothard pass.

Fenwick—John Fenwick, editor of the *Albion,* for which Lamb wrote. See *Newspapers Thirty-Five Years Ago.*

Fell—one of Lamb's boon companions in his riotous moments.

Nam, etc.—here victorious I lay down my boxing gloves and my art (Virgil's *Aeneid*).

wife—Godwin's second wife, of whom Lamb said she was the only woman he hated. He drew her picture as Mrs. Priscilla Pry in the *Lupus Papers.*

Marshall—an actor and friend of Godwin's. See the essay *Old Actors.*

the Professor—William Godwin, the philosopher and novelist; his *Political Justice* appeared in 1793 and his *Caleb Williams* in 1794.

Holcroft—see note, page 324.

THE PRAISE OF CHIMNEY-SWEEPERS (Page 130)

London Magazine, May, 1822.

sweep—in Lamb's time small boys were used as chimney sweeps, their job being to climb up through the chimney and sweep out the accumulated soot. The system had much abuse and cruelty connected with it.

peep-peep—chimney-sweepers were required to signal the completion of their task by crying out "sweep," when their soot-covered faces emerged above the top of the chimney.

fauces, etc.—the jaws of Avernus (Virgil's *Aeneid*).

taster—sixpence.

The only Salopian house—the shop of the Mr. Read just mentioned. "Salop" was a drink made of sassafras and other ingredients.

fuliginous—sooty.

Hogarth—see note, page 321.

A sable cloud, etc.—Milton's *Comus*.

Noble Rachels—Jeremiah xxxi. 15.

the young Montagu—a lad who ran away and became a chimney-sweep.

Ascanius—the legend has it that Venus lulled Ascanius, son of Aeneas, to sleep, and sent Cupid to impersonate him, when the goddess plotted to have Dido fall in love with Aeneas. The story is found in Virgil's *Aeneid*.

incunabula—cradle clothes.

Jem White—James White, a schoolmate of Lambs at Christ's Hospital, and afterwards one of Lamb's intimates, especially on more convivial occasions.

fair of St. Bartholomew—the great national fair of England, held at Smithfield.

quoited—thrown, as one would a quoit.

wedding garment—Matthew xxii. 11-13.

Bigod—see note, page 324.

Rochester—the Earl of Rochester, a poet of the court of Charles II, who was noted for his madcap escapades.

old dame Ursula—perhaps an allusion to the name of the pig woman in Ben Jonson's play, *Bartholomew Fair*.

Golden lads, etc.—*Cymbeline*.

A COMPLAINT OF THE DECAY OF BEGGARS (Page 138)

London Magazine, June, 1822.

Alcides club—the club with which Alcides (Hercules) fought the Hydra.

Bellum, etc.—war to the death.

Dionysius—Dionysius the Younger, tyrant of Syracuse, who was finally expelled in 343 B.C.

Belisarius—a famous Byzantine general of the sixth century, in regard to whom there was a story that in his old age he became blind and had to beg.

obolus—a small Greek coin.

The Blind Beggar—the story recounted in an old popular ballad called *The Blind Beggar's Daughter of Bethnal Green.*

Margaret Newcastle—see note, page 322.

Lear—the old king in Shakespeare's tragedy of that name, who suffers at the hands of his unfilial daughters.

Cresseid—Cressida, the legendary daughter of the Trojan priest, Calchas.

Semiramis—the Assyrian queen who built Babylon.

King Cophetua—a legendary African king who wooed and won Penelophon, a beggar maid.

Spital sermons—Sermons preached specially for the boys of Christ's Hospital.

Look, etc.—*As You Like It.*

Old blind Tobits—Tobit is a character in the apocryphal book of the old Testament with that name.

Antæus—in mythology, a giant wrestler, who only gained more strength by being thrown to the earth.

Elgin marble—a collection of marbles that once adorned the Parthenon at Athens, which were brought to England by Lord Elgin in the early nineteenth century.

Lapithan—the Lapithæ were a people of Thessaly, who according to mythology engaged in a famous battle with the Centaurs. The occasion of the fight was the rude behavior of the Centaurs to the Lapithan women.

os sublime—upward-looking face.

Lusus, etc.—A freak, not of nature, but of accident.

Yorick—see note, page 322.

Bartimeus—Mark x.46.

It is good to believe, etc.—Compare this advice on alms-giving with that in *The Praise of Chimney-Sweepers.*

ON SOME OF THE OLD ACTORS (Page 147)

London Magazine, February, 1822.

Twelfth-Night—Shakespeare's comedy. A general knowledge of this play is indispensable to the understanding and appreciation of this essay, which is largely commentary upon it. The Malvolio interpretation is a notable piece of Shakespearean criticism.

Ophelia—in *Hamlet.*

Nells, etc.—Nell is a character in an old play *The Devil to Pay* by C. Coffey; Hoyden, a character in *The Relapse* by Vanbrugh.

Hotspur's famous rant—the gradiloquent speech by this character in *Henry IV,* Part I, I.iii.

Venetian incendiary—a reference to Otway's *Venice Preserved.*

Iago—the villain in *Othello.*

upon his straw—Lamb's note to this was the following quotation from *Twelfth Night:*

Clown. What is the opinion of Pythagoras concerning wild fowl?

Mal. That the soul of our grandam might haply inhabit a bird.

Clown. What thinkest thou of his opinion?

Mal. I think nobly of the soul, and no way approve of his opinion.

La Mancha—Don Quixote, a Spanish country gentleman, in Cervantes' romance.

Hyperion—the god of the sun, who in classical legends was overthrown by Apollo.

in, etc.—in its real nature.

Bacon—Sir Francis Bacon, jurist and philosopher, in the latter 16th and early 17th centuries.

Foppington—a character in Vanbrugh's comedy *The Relapse. Tattle* is a character in Congreve's *Love for Love; Backbite,* a character in Sheridan's *School for Scandal; Acres* a character in Sheridan's *The Rivals; Fribble* a character in Garrick's *Miss in Her Teens.*

Holy Paul—St. Paul's Cathedral.

put on, etc.—the distinctive garb of the Dominican friars.

Dodd—Dodd was a man of reading, and left at his death a choice collection of old English literature. I should judge him to have been a man of wit. I know one instance of an impromptu which no length of study could have bettered. My merry friend, Jem White, had seen him one evening in Ague-cheek, and recognising Dodd the next day in Fleet Street, was irresistibly impelled to take off his hat and salute him as the identical Knight of the preceding evening with a "Save you, *Sir Andrew*." Dodd, not at all disconcerted at this unusual address from a stranger, with a courteous half-rebuking wave of the hand, put him off with an "Away, *Fool*." (Lamb's note.)

pipe—voice.

Sir John—Sir John Falstaff in *King Henry IV.*

commerce, etc.—a paraphrase of a line in Milton's *Il Penseroso.*

Robin Goodfellow—the son of Oberon, king of the fairies.

Puck—a fairy, almost a parallel to Robin Goodfellow—mischievous.

force of nature, etc.—from Dryden's poem on Milton.

thorough brake, etc.—from Puck's speech in *A Midsummer Night's Dream.*

Children of the Wood—a comedy by Thomas Morton, a contemporary of Lamb.

Vesta's days—according to legend, Vesta was the mother of the gods, therefore Lamb intends to indicate the most primitive times.

sock or buskin—tragedy or comedy.

Servant—*High Life below Stairs* (Lamb's note); a farce by Townley, popular in the 18th century.

Captain Absolute.—a character in Sheridan's *The Rivals.*

Dick Amlet—a character in Vanbrugh's *The Confederacy.*

Wilding—a young gentleman from Oxford in Foote's *The Liar.*

Joseph Surface—a character in Sheridan's *School for Scandal.*

metaphrases—close translations.

Wapping—the quarter of London along the north bank of the Thames that was the congregating place of seamen.

PREFACE TO ELIA ESSAYS (Page 161)

London Magazine, January, 1823.

intimados—intimate friends.

toga virilis—the toga worn by Roman youth as an indication of having attained manhood.

THE OLD AND THE NEW SCHOOLMASTER (Page 165)

London Magazine, May, 1821.

Ortelius—a Flemish geographer of the 16th century.

Arrowsmith—an English geographer of Lamb's generation.

Euclid—the famous Greek geometrician.

"small Latin," etc.—Ben Jonson's *Lines on Master Shakespeare.*

tête-à-tête—face-to-face conversation.

Bishopsgate—one of the old gates in the northern wall of London.

Shacklewell—a suburb of London.

Smithfield—a locality in the city of London.

the Sirens—sea nymphs who fascinated mariners by their singing and then destroyed them.

Achilles—the brave Greek leader in the Trojan war.

Sir Thomas Browne—the 17th century English writer.

"wide solution"—*Urn Burial* (Lamb's note).

the North Pole Expedition—probably the second polar expedition of Lieutenant Parry in 1821.

Lily—the English grammarian of the 16th century.

Linacre—the famous classical scholar of the English Renaissance.

Flori...Spici-legia—anthologies.

King Basileus..Pamela, etc.—characters in Sidney's *Arcadia.*

Colet—an English classical scholar of the Renaissance.

Solon—the wise lawgiver of Athens.

Lycurgus—the famous legislator of Sparta.

cum multis aliis—with many other things.

Tractate on Education—Milton's.

mollia tempora fandi—pleasant times for speaking (Virgil's *Aeneid*).

Orrery—an astronomical contrivance to show the motions of the planets around the sun. It, as well as the panorama and the panopticon, were among the diversions of Londoners in Lamb's time.

Even a child, etc.—a free quotation from one of Lamb's own poems.
Gulliver—the hero of Swift's *Gulliver's Travels*.
Bridget—Mary Lamb.

IMPERFECT SYMPATHIES (Page 175)

London Magazine, August, 1821.
author—Sir Thomas Browne. The passage quoted is from Part II of *Religio Medici*.
notional, etc.—beings of fancy and conjecture.
admired—wondered at.
Standing, etc.—*Paradise Lost*, Book VII.
all people alive—I would be understood as confining myself to the subject of
  imperfect sympathies. To nations or classes of men there can be no direct
  antipathy. There may be individuals born and constellated so opposite to another individual nature, that the same sphere cannot hold them. I have met
  with my moral antipodes, and can believe the story of two persons meeting
  (who never saw one another before in their lives) and instantly fighting.

> —— We by proof find there should be
> 'Twixt man and man such an antipathy,
> That though he can show no just reason why
> For any former wrong or injury,
> Can neither find a blemish in his fame,
> Nor aught in face or feature justly blame,
> Can challenge or accuse him of no evil,
> Yet notwithstanding hates him as a devil.

The lines are from Old Heywood's "Hierarchie of Angels," and he subjoins a
curious story in confirmation, of a Spaniard who attempted to assassinate a king
Ferdinand of Spain, and being put to the rack could give no other reason for the
deed but an inveterate antipathy which he had taken to the first sight of the
king.

> —— The cause which to that act compell'd him
> Was, he ne'er loved him since he first beheld him.

(Lamb's note.)
Caledonia—poetic name for Scotland.
panoply—Minerva, Greek goddess of wisdom, was said to have sprung full-armed
  from the brain of Jupiter.
John Buncle—the hero of a book by Thomas Amory.
Leonardo da Vinci—Italian painter of the 15th century.
Swift—"There are some people who think they sufficiently acquit themselves, and
  entertain their company, with relating facts of no consequence, not at all out
  of the road of such common incidents as happen every day; and this I have observed more frequently among the Scots than any other nation, who are very

careful not to omit the minutest circumstances of time or place; which kind of discourse, if it were not a little relieved by the uncouth terms and phrases, as well as accent and gesture, peculiar to that country, would be hardly tolerable."
—*Hints towards an Essay on Conversation.* (Lamb's note.)

Thomson—a Scotch poet of the 18th century.

Smollet—a Scotch novelist.

Hume—a Scotch philosopher and historian.

Stonehenge—a prehistoric monument in Salisbury Plain.

Hugh of Lincoln—there were many ballads and stories recounting the murder of this little Christian boy by the Jews of Lincoln in the 13th century.

B[raham]—a popular tenor singer of Lamb's period.

Shibboleth—Judges xii. 1-6.

Kemble—a great tragic actor.

Jael—Judges iv. 18-22.

Fuller—see note, page 320.

Desdemona—*Othello,* I, iii.

the salads, etc.—*Paradise Lost,* Book V.

Evelyn—author of a book called *Complete Gardener.*

to sit, etc.—adapted from *Paradise Regained,* Book II.

I was travelling, etc.—this incident did not really occur in Lamb's presence. It was related to him, as he said, by Sir Anthony Carlisle, an eminent surgeon of Lamb's day, who was an eyewitness of the incident.

A CHAPTER ON EARS (Page 184)

London Magazine, March, 1821.

no ear—this confession is applicable to Lamb in only a limited degree.

Defoe—author of Robinson Crusoe. For writing a certain political pamphlet, he had his ears cropped and was placed in the pillory.

Alice W[interto]n—see note, page 318.

A[yrton]—a well-known musical critic.

Sostenuto...adagio—directions as to musical time, meaning slowly.

Baralipton—a term used in logic.

Jubal—Genesis iv. 21.

Hogarth—see note, page 321.

Party, etc.—lines in first version of Wordsworth's *Peter Bell.*

long a-dying—King Charles II is said to have begged his courtiers to excuse him for being "so unconscionable a time in dying."

disappointing book—Revelation x. 10.

Burton—the 17th century prose writer.

amabilis, etc.—pleasing madness.

mentis, etc.—most pleasant natural aberration.

subrusticus, et.—Awkward bashfulness.

Nov[ello]—an English musician and composer of Lamb's time.

minor heavens—

> I have been there, and still would go.—
> 'Tis like a little heaven below.—DR. WATTS.

that or that other—Psalms liv and xviii.

rapt, etc.—Walton's *Compleat Angler*, Part I.

Arions—in classical mythology, this famous musician was forced to cast himself overboard to escape mariners who wished to rob him. The beauty of his music brought around the ship a number of dolphins, one of whom carried Arion to land on his back.

Haydn, etc.—The four musicians mentioned are well-known European musicians and composers.

Tritons—water deities, usually represented with "wreathed horns."

malleus, etc.—hammer of heretics, a title given to Johan Faber on account of his vigorous opposition to the Reformation.

Marcion, etc.—the three founders of certain heretical sects in the early days of the church.

Gog and Magog—Revelation xx. 7-9; enemies who shall fight against the church towards the end of the world.

LETTER TO MANNING (Page 190)

Caius—Caius College, Cambridge, in which Manning was a lecturer.

salamander—a circular iron plate, heated and placed over a dish to brown the contents.

As Wordsworth sings—in the poem *A Poet's Epitaph*.

nuts, etc.—a reference to Moore's poem *A Case of Libel, Odes on Cash, Corn, etc.*

It will be wooed, etc.—*Paradise Lost*, Book VIII.

David. . Titian. . Corregio—famous painters all.

praesens, etc.—present though absent.

LETTER TO COLERIDGE (Page 192)

This gustatory letter probably has a close connection with the writing of the essay *A Dissertation upon Roast Pig*, which appeared in the *London Magazine* for September, 1822.

dredge—sprinkle with flour.

Oedipean avulson—violent tearing out. There is a reference to the legend that Oedipus, King of Thebes, put out his eyes in a passion of grief.

Owen—Lamb's landlord.

Highgate—the section of London where the Gilmans lived with whom Coleridge was staying.

tame villatic things—from Milton's *Samson Agonistes;* "villatic" means of, or pertaining to, a villa or farm.

char—a delicious fish, somewhat like a trout.

smack—taste.

old aunt—see note, p. 318.

LETTER TO CHAMBERS (Page 194)

John Dory—a jocose name for a variety of fish.

Quin—the actor of Lamb's time.

Apicius—a famous Roman epicure.

Heliogabalus—one of the Roman emperors.

sapor—taste.

Pope—the poet Pope was deformed.

Dr. Parr—a famous scholar and conversationalist of Lamb's period.

Epicurus—the Greek philosopher whose doctrine was that pleasure was the chief good. The phrase a "true son of Epicurus" has in it a suggestion of Chaucer's prologue to the *Canterbury Tales.*

MRS. BATTLE'S OPINIONS ON WHIST (Page 197)

London Magazine, February, 1821.

Sarah Battle—the weight of opinion seems to make Mrs. Battle purely an imaginary character.

Pope—in his *Rape of the Lock* occurs an elaborate account of the old card game, ombre.

Bowles—an English clergyman of antiquarian tastes who wrote a collection of sonnets which greatly influenced Coleridge.

Spadille—the ace of spades.

Sans, etc.—playing without a partner and endeavoring to take all the tricks.

Machiavel—Machiavelli, the Italian statesman and author.

Vandyke—a famous Flemish painter.

Potters—a noted Dutch portrait painter.

Pam—the knave of clubs.

Ephesian journeyman—Acts xix. 24-41.

Walter Plumer—see note, page 321.

Bridget Elia—Mary Lamb.

DETACHED THOUGHTS ON BOOKS AND READING (Page 205)

London Magazine, July, 1822.

his Lordship—Lord Foppington, a character in Vanbrugh's play *The Relapse.*

Shaftesbury—an English moralist and writer of the 17th century.

Jonathan Wild—Fielding's novel.

Gibbon. . Robertson—two 18th century historians.

Josephus—a Jewish historian.

Adam Smith—a Scotch political economist, author of *The Wealth of Nations*.

Paracelsus—a celebrated European scholar of the 16th century.

Raymond Lully—a Spanish scholar of the 13th century who wrote a treatise on logic.

Tom Jones. . Vicar of Wakefield—famous novels, the first by Fielding, the second by Goldsmith.

We know, etc.—from *Othello*.

Life of the Duke of Newcastle—the life of her husband by Margaret Newcastle. See note, page 322.

Anatomy of Melancholy—Burton's remarkable book.

pro, etc.—for the public benefit.

Candide—Voltaire's novel which sneers at "vulgar optimism," and paints this world of weal and woe with cool, philosophical indifference.

Cythera—an island sacred to Venus.

Pamela—Richardson's novel.

snatch, etc.—from Gray's *Ode on a Distant Prospect of Eton College*.

Martin B[urney]—the son of Captain Burney Lamb wrote of him:

> Free from self-seeking, envy, low design,
> I have not found a whiter soul than thine.

poetess—Mary Lamb.

LETTER TO MRS. WORDSWORTH (Page 215)

Plato's double animal—Plato's theory was that man and woman were originally one animal; after separation each yearns for reunion.

Miss Burrell—Fanny Burrell, a musician of Lamb's time.

Fanny Kelly—The actress and friend of Lamb.

Lalla Rookh—Tom Moore's poem.

what Coleridge said—Coleridge was at the time in London lecturing on poetry and Shakespeare.

Ante-Cadmeans—people who lived before Cadmus and the invention of the alphabet.

Hazlitt—Burney—see note, page 324.

Morgan—John Morgan, another friend of Lamb.

Demi-gorgon—some commentators think this a reference to Godwin. The name is an echo of *Paradise Lost*.

human faces, etc.—*Paradise Lost*, Book III.

Bishop—the composer of *Home Sweet Home*.

That fury, etc.—*Paradise Lost*, Book II.

Christabel's father—Coleridge's poem *Christabel*, Part II.

late visitation—the Wordworths had visited Lamb in the previous December.

W. H.—Hazlitt.

Gilman—Dr. Gilman at Highgate, with whom Coleridge was living.

that gentleman—During the Wordsworths' visit to London, Haydon the painter, had a gathering to which he invited Lamb, Wordsworth, Keats, Monkhouse, and others. Among those present was a certain Comptroller of Stamps, whose presence rubbed Lamb the wrong way, and whose remarks Lamb made ridiculous. Haydon's diary gives the incident in detail, and the passage deserves quotation as an illustration of Lamb's hilarity.

When we retired to tea we found the Comptroller. In introducing him to Wordsworth I forgot to say who he was. After a little time the Comptroller looked down, looked up, and said to Wordsworth, "Don't you think, sir, Milton was a great genius?" Keats looked at me, Wordsworth looked at the Comptroller. Lamb who was dozing by the fire, turned round and said, "Pray, sir, did you say Milton was a great genius?" "No, sir, I asked Mr. Wordsworth if he were not." "Oh," said Lamb, "then you are a silly fellow." "Charles, my dear Charles!" said Wordsworth; but Lamb, perfectly innocent of the confusion he had created, was off again by the fire.

After an awful pause the Comptroller said. "Don't you think Newton a great genius?" I could not stand it any longer. Keats put his head into my books. Ritchie squeezed in a laugh. Wordsworth seemed asking himself, "Who is this?" Lamb got up and taking a candle, said, "Sir, will you allow me to look at your phrenological development?" He then turned his back on the poor man, and at every question of the Comptroller he chanted —

> Diddle, diddle, dumpling, my son John
> Went to bed with his breeches on.

The man in office finding Wordsworth did not know who he was, said in a spasmodic and half-chuckling anticipation of assured victory, "I have had the honor of some correspondence with you, Mr. Wordsworth." "With me, sir?" said Wordsworth, "not that I remember." "Don't you, sir? I am a Comptroller of Stamps." There was a dead silence; the Comptroller evidently thinking that was enough. While we were waiting for Wordsworth's reply, Lamb sung out—

> Hey diddle diddle,
> The cat and the fiddle.

"My dear Charles!" said Wordsworth.

> Diddle, diddle, dumpling, my son John.

chanted Lamb; and then rising, exclaimed, "Do let me have another look at that gentleman's organs." Keats and I hurried Lamb into the painting-room, shut the door, and gave way to inextinguishable laughter. Monkhouse followed and tried to get Lamb away. We went back, but the Comptroller was irreconcilable. We soothed and smiled, and asked him to supper. He stayed, though his dignity was sorely affected. However, being a good-natured man, we parted all in good humor, and no ill effects followed.

All the while, until Monkhouse succeeded, we could hear Lamb struggling in the painting-room and calling at intervals, "Who is that fellow? Allow me to see his organs once more."

the Scarlet—Revelation xvii. 3, 4.

red letter days—holidays or saints' days marked on the old calendars in red.

Ferdinand—a king of Naples and Sicily.

Nero—see note, page 318.

LETTER TO COLERIDGE (Page 220)

Luster's Tables—the maid had distorted the pronunciation of Martin Luther's *Table Talk*.

deodand—a gift; old legal phraseology for anything forfeited to the crown, and usually devoted to pious uses.

Proselytes, etc.—alien converts.

More's fine poem—*Psychosoia Platonica*, by Henry More, a mystical philosopher of the 17th century.

Hartley—Coleridge's son.

Polemical Discourses—by Jeremy Taylor, the noted 17th century divine.

THE TWO RACES OF MEN (Page 222)

London Magazine, December, 1820.

Parthians, etc.—Acts ii. 9.

Alcibiades, etc.—an Athenian statesman; *Falstaff*—a character in Shakespeare's *King Henry IV; Sir Richard Steele*—English essayist and dramatist of the 18th century; *Brinsley*—Richard Brinsley Sheridan, politician and dramatist of the 18th century.

than lilies—Matthew vi. 28.

Tooke—Horne, a noted philologist of the 18th century.

calleth, etc.—Luke ii. 1.

primitive community—Acts ii. 44.

obolary—impecunious.

Candlemas—February 2, the feast of the Purification of the Virgin Mary.

Feast of Holy Michael—September 29, in honor the Archangel Michael.

lene, etc.—gentle spur; an echo of Horace's Odes.

Propontic—the old name for the Sea of Marmora.

reversion promised—Proverbs xix. 17.

Lazarus and Dives—Luke xvi. 20-31.

Bigod—John Fenwick, editor of the *Albion:* one of Lamb's close friends.

To slacken, etc.—*Paradise Regained*, Book II.

Alexander—Alexander the Great.

Comus—in Milton's poem with that name.

Hagar's offspring—Genesis xxi.

fisc—royal treasury.

*cana, etc.—honor due to gray hairs (Virgil's *Aeneid*).

mumping—coinage from the old word "mumper" meaning a beggar.

visnomy—countenance.

Comberbatch—correctly, Comberback, the name under which Coleridge enlisted in a cavalry regiment in 1793.

Switzer-like—tall—like the men composing the Swiss Guard.

Guildhall giants—large wooden figures that stood at the entrance of the Guildhall in London.

Opera, etc.—The works of St. Bonaventura.

Bellarmine—Jesuit theologian.

Holy Thomas—St. Thomas of Aquinas, a scholastic philosopher and theologian.

Ascapart—a legendary giant whose height was given as thirty feet.

Dodsley's dramas—the collection *Old English Plays*, edited in the 18th century by Robert Dodsley.

Vittoria Corombona—Webster's tragedy, usually called the *White Devil*, one of the noblest of the later Elizabethan plays.

Anatomy of Melancholy—see note, page 334.

Complete Angler—Izaak Walton's book, of which Lamb said that reading it would sweeten one's disposition.

John Buncle—see note, page 330.

deodands—see note, page 336.

Spiteful K[enny]—James Kenney, a dramatist.

Margaret Newcastle—see note, page 322.

Fulke Greville—a poet and statesman of the 16th century.

Zimmerman—Johann G. v. Zimmerman, a Swiss physician of the 17th century, the author of several medical and philosophical works.

Daniel—Samuel Daniel of the 16th century, author of a great deal of prose and verse.

S.T.C.—Initials of Coleridge. Lamb is using even a third disguise to puzzle the reader the more.

LETTER TO DIBDIN (Page 228)

Ephesians, Galatians—the point is that these Epistles are both very short.

Peter—Matthew xvi. 18.

The Fourth Person—Daniel iii. 24-25.

the Lover's seat—At Hastings where Dibdin was convalescing from the lung trouble to which he succumbed a few years later.

Juan Fernandez—the island on which Alexander Selkirk lived alone for four years.

Loretto—a famous shrine in Italy.

Caledonian Chapel—a reference to the London crowds that flocked to hear the Scotch preacher, Edward Irving.

two, etc.—Matthew xvii, 20.

grain, etc.—Matthew xiii, 31.

First fruits—Exodus xii, 29.

strait, etc.—Matthew vii, 13.

still, etc.—I Kings x. 12.

headless bear—mentioned in the rhyming *Abstract of Melancholy,* prefixed to Burton's *Anatomy of Melancholy.*

thumb in dirt—Dibdin had taken a batch of Lamb's books with him on his convalescence.

Probitum, etc.—it has been proved: a phrase which physicians used formerly on prescriptions.

cut the Baker's—Dibdin was lodging over a bakery.

Rankings—one of Dibdin's employers.

Peter Fin—a character in a popular play to which Lamb thought Dibdin bore a resemblance.

Dry Salter—a dealer in salted meats, etc.

Tommy Hill—a famous busybody of Lamb's day.

Colebrooke—Lamb's residence by New River.

LETTER TO DIBDIN (Page 231)

Thetis—a sea-goddess, but here the word designates the sea itself.

Wrekin—a noted hill in Shropshire.

Ranking—see note *supra.*

Grimaldi—a famous clown whose *Memoirs* were edited by Dickens.

Thirty Tyrants—Sparta imposed a series of tyrants on Athens.

Bloxam—an old acquaintance of Lamb's.

Wyat—a comic singer attached to Sadler's Wells Theatre.

clerks defunct—the sketches in the essay *The South-Sea House.*

OXFORD IN THE VACATION (Page 234)

London Magazine, October, 1820.

Quis, etc.—who carved it?

Vivares—a French landscape painter living in London.

Woollet—an English engraver.

scrivener—a clerk. "Cropt" probably refers to short hair, and "notched" to the tallies by which accounting was done.

agnize—acknowledge.

red-letter days—see note, page 336.

Paul, etc.—saints in whose honor certain days were celebrated.

Baskett Prayer Book—an edition of the prayer-book edited by John Baskett, printer to George II.

holy Bartlemy—St. Bartholomew.

Marsyas—a painting of Apollo flaying the satyr Marsyas by an Italian artist.

Jude—St. Jude, the Apostle; distinguished from Judas Iscariot by Lamb's use of "better."

gaudy-day—a festal occasion or anniversary.

Epiphany—January 6, sometimes called Twelfth Day, because coming that length of time after Christmas.

Selden—English jurist of 16th century.

Usher—an Irish theologian, remembered mainly for his biblical chronology.

Bodley—the Bodleian Library.

ad eundem—to the same standing; an academic term indicating no loss of class standing in going from one university to another.

Sizar..Servitor..Gentleman Commoner—different classes of students in an English university, the differences being in respect to money or social standing.

Christ..Magdalen—colleges of Oxford University.

devoir—duty.

Chaucer—this is a supposition of Lamb's; there is no evidence that Chaucer was a student at Oxford.

Manciple—one responsible for the purchase of food for a college.

Janus—a Roman god represented with two faces, since he was the god of the rising and setting sun.

Januses of one face—Sir Thomas Browne. (Lamb's note.)

arride—gratify.

sciential—productive of knowledge. Lamb's references is to the apple Eve ate in the Garden of Eden.

variae, etc.—different readings.

Herculanean raker—the reference is to some charred rolls found in a buried library at Herculaneum.

witnesses—I John v. 7.

G. D.—George Dyer.

Oriel—a college at Oxford.

a tall Scapula—"tall" means a book whose leaves have not been cut down in binding. Scapula pirated a certain Greek lexicon.

in manu—in possession.

M[ontagu]—famous for an edition of Bacon.

Queen Lar—the chief of the domestic deities among the Romans.

A[nne] S[kepper]—Mrs. Montagu's daughter.

Sosia—a slave in Palutus' *Amphitryon*.

Mount Tabor—the scene of the Transfiguration.

Parnassus—the abode of the Muses.

co-sphered, etc.—absorbed in philosophical speculation.

Harrington—author of the treatise on civil government, *Commonwealth of Oceana*.

personal presence—in the first publication, this essay continued at this point with the following paragraphs on Dyer's peculiarities, which Lamb saw fit to omit from the 1823 edition of his essays:

D. commenced life after a course of hard study in the house of "pure Emanuel," as usher to a knavish fanatic schoolmaster at ————, at a salary of eight pounds per annum, with board and lodging. Of this poor stipend he never received above half in all the laborious years he served this man. He tells a pleasant anecdote that when poverty, staring at his ragged knees, has sometimes compelled him against the modesty of his nature to hint at arrears, Dr. ———— would take no immediate notice, but after supper, when the school was called together to evensong, he would never fail to introduce some instructive homily against riches, and the corruption of the heart occasioned through the desire of them—ending with "Lord, keep thy servants, above all things, from the heinous sin of avarice. Having food and raiment, let us therewithal be content. Give me Agur's wish"—and the like— which, to the little auditory, sounded like a doctrine full of Christian prudence and simplicity, but to poor D. a receipt in full for that quarter's demand at least.

And D. has been under-working for himself ever since:—drudging at low rates for unappreciating booksellers, wasting his fine erudition in silent corrections of the classics, and in those unostentatious services to learning which commonly fall to the lot of laborious scholars, who have not the heart to sell themselves to the best advantage. He has published poems, which do not sell, because their character is unobtrusive, like his own, and because he is too much absorbed in ancient literature to know what the popular mark in poetry is, even if he could have hit it. And, therefore, his verses are properly what he terms them, *crotchets:* voluntaries: odes to liberty and spring; effusions, little tributes and offerings, left behind him upon tables and windowseats at parting from friends' houses; and from all the inns of hospitality, where he has been courteously (or but tolerably) received in his pilgrimage. If his muse of kindness halt a little behind the strong lines in fashion in this excitement-loving age, his prose is the best of the sort in the world, and exhibits a faithful transcript of his own healthy, natural mind, and cheerful, innocent tone of conversation.

Cam. . Isis—the Cam flows by Cambridge; the Isis, by Oxford.
waters of Damascus—II Kings v. 12.
Muses' Hill—Helicon or Parnassus.
Delectable Mountains. . House Beautiful—allusions to Bunyan's *Pilgrim's Progress.* It is from the Delectable Mountains that the pilgrims see the Celestial City; the Interpreter, symbolizing the Holy Ghost, is the lord of a house beyond the wicket gate, which is called the House Beautiful.

LETTER TO MANNING (Page 241)

Pliny's letters—those of the younger Pliny, a cultivated Roman gentleman of the 1st century A.D.

Algebra—Manning had published *An Introduction to Arithmetic and Algebra* a few years before.

Black Arts—magic.

Trismegist—Hermes Trismegistus, a name given to the Egyptian god of wisdom.

Bell Letters—Lamb's comical spelling of *belles-lettres.*

mera, etc.—absolute trifles.

in, etc.—in the nature of things.

Frend—a mathematician and Unitarian reformer.

pericranick—Lamb's humorous word for "pericranium."

Clifford's Inn—Dyer's lodging place.

Longinus—a Greek critic.

Theocritus—a Sicilian poet.

rules—in Aristotle's *Poetics.*

Dodsley's Collection—see note, page 337.

Otway. .Rowe—poets and dramatists of the 18th century. Rowe was distinguished as the first editor and biographer of Shakespeare.

invitation—Lamb had previously sent Manning an invitation to come to London.

LETTER TO MANNING (Page 243)

Archimedes—a Greek mathematician.

Archimagus—a chief magician; Lamb may have had in mind Archimage in the *Faerie Queene.*

Tycho Brahé—a Danish astronomer of the 16th century.

Copernicus—a Polish astronomer of the early 16th century; he is regarded as the founder of modern astronomy.

the Nine—the Muses.

Attic—with simple refinement characteristic of Athens, the capital of the district of Greece known as Attica.

St. Clare—a London market.

the Heathen—one of Lamb's epithets for George Dyer.

Black Backs—Manning's algebra.

Shenstone—a poet of the 18th century.

Parnassus—the mountain fabled as the abode of the Muses.

ministers—ministers of state.

Wilkie—a Scotch poet, whose *Epigoniad* was based on one of the books of the *Iliad.*

strictures—in Johnson's essay on Gray in *The Lives of the Poets.*

LETTER TO MANNING (Page 245)

phrenitis—frenzy.

Professor—William Godwin, who was at this time preparing to write his play *Abbas, King of Persia*.

Bethlehem College—Bedlam, the lunatic asylum in South London. Lamb uses the original form of the name, which in current usage had become contracted to Bedlam.

Fenelon—a reference to the passage in Godwin's *Political Justice*, in which he considers whether in case of rescue from a burning house, it would be more desirable to rescue Fenelon, his mother, or a chambermaid.

Deo, etc.—God willing and the devil unwilling.

crush a cup—an echo from *Romeo and Juliet*, I, ii.

St. Mary's lighthouse—St. Mary's Church in Cambridge.

sensorium—brain.

Gonville—a college at Cambridge.

LETTER TO RICKMAN (Page 247)

Phillips—a London publisher.

Frend—see note, page 341.

his bookseller—Phillips.

LETTER TO MRS. HAZLITT (Page 250)

babbled, etc.—*Henry V*, II, iii.

our house—the house in Colebrook Row to which the Lambs had moved. The New River was close to it.

Mary Hazlitt—a niece of the essayist.

AMICUS REDIVIVUS (Page 252)

London Magazine, December, 1823.

Where, etc.—Milton's *Lycidas*.

Anchises—the reference is to Aeneas's carrying his father from burning Troy.

Monoculus—one-eyed.

Cannabis, Hemp—Lamb makes a joking reference to hanging.

Middleton's Head—an inn.

tremor, etc.—quivering of the heart.

Sir Hugh in *Merry Wives of Windsor*.

Sir Hugh Middleton—the person who fathered the New River water supply of London.

Abyssinian traveller—James Bruce, explorer of the source of the Nile.

Cam—the river on which is located Cambridge University, which Dyer had attended.

And could, etc.—from a poem by John Cleveland, contributed to the same memorial volume to which Milton gave *Lycidas.*

Euripus—the strait into which according to an old story Aristotle threw himself when he was unable to discover the cause of its irregular tides.

dipper—a nickname for the Baptists, referring to their belief in immersion.

Clarence—in *Richard II.*

Christian—the hero of Bunyan's *Pilgrim's Progress.*

I sink, etc.—*from Pilgrim's Progress,* near end of Part I.

Palinurus—the pilot of Aeneas's ship, who was drowned in a storm while steering Aeneas and his followers to Italy (Virgil's *Aeneid*).

watchet—blue.

Lazari—people, like Lazarus, brought back from the dead. Lamb's own invention, this plural form.

Pluto—God of the lower world.

Charon—the ferryman of the lower world.

Arion—see note, page 332.

Machaon—physician to the Greeks in the Trojan War.

Dr. Hawes—the founder of the Royal Humane Society.

Ophelia—*Hamlet.*

grim Feature—Death.

Tantalus—a mythological character whose punishment was to be immersed in water up to the neck and to be forever thirsty. Whenever he tried to drink, the water receded from his lips.

Asphodel—the flower of Elysium.

Markland—a classical scholar of the 18th century, and an old Christ's Hospital boy.

Tyrwhitt—Thomas Tyrwhitt, a noted Chaucerian scholar of the 18th century.

sweet lyrist—the poet, Thomas Grey.

earth—Graium tantum videt. (Lamb's note.) "Gray he only saw."

Askew—Anthony Askew, a physician and classical scholar of note in the 18th century.

Aesculapian—medical, from Aesculapius, the god of medicine.

LETTER TO GEORGE DYER (Page 257)

con, etc.—with love.

obrepens, etc.—the creeping of old age.

old eyes—Dyer in his old age was going blind.

Answerer—Milton hastened the completion of his blindness, by working on his

Defence of the People of England, a reply to a book by the French scholar, Salmasius.

Valpy—the publisher who was fathering the series of classics Dyer was editing.

Trophonius—a Greek architect reputed to have built the temple of Apollo at Delphi.

Variae—variant readings.

Of sun, etc.—Milton's second sonnet to Cyriac Skinner.

Dr. Parr—see note, page 333.

Mrs. Clarke—wife of Charles Cowden Clarke.

Miss Hayes—a friend of Godwin's first wife, Mary Wollstonecraft.

Mede-and-Persian—unaltering, as the laws of the Medes and Persians.

a Grecian—the students in the highest of Christ's Hospital and intending to study for the ministry were known as Grecians. Lamb's impediment of speech had kept him from winning this school distinction.

Whalley . . Boyer—masters in Christ's Hospital. See Lamb's essay, *Christ's Hospital.*

Great Erasmians—one of the forms, or classes, at Christ's Hospital.

Leadenhall—the East India House.

How, etc.—Isaiah xiv. 12.

DISTANT CORRESPONDENTS (Page 261)

London Magazine, January, 1822.

Munden—James Munden, an actor of Lamb's time. See the essay *On the Acting of Munden.*

flam—deception.

Habakkuk . . Daniel—two of the old Hebrew prophets.

lustring—lutestring.

Saint Gothard—bishop of Hildesheim about 1038.

melior, etc.—finer clay.

sol, et.—sun father.

viznomy—countenance.

Diogenes—the Greek philosopher of the 4th century B.C. who sought through Corinth with his lantern for an honest man. In this passage Lamb has in mind the penal colony at Botany Bay, five miles south of Sydney.

Delphic voyages—voyages to the Delphic oracle.

Ave me, etc.—Milton's *Comus.*

J[ohn] W[hite]—an old school fellow of Lamb's.

LETTER TO MANNING (Page 268)

Norfolcian—Manning came from Norfolk.

Struldbrug—a race of beings described in Swift's *Gulliver's Travels,* as having immortality but not eternal youth.

Maclaurin. .Euler—noted mathematicians.

Godwin—see note, page 325.

Coleridge—the poet had been planning an epic on the *Wanderings of Cain* for some years previous.

LETTER TO MANNING (Page 271)

Fanny—Fanny Holcoft.

Priscilla—Priscilla Lloyd, who married a brother of the poet Wordsworth.

Robert Lloyd—brother of Charles Lloyd, had died in 1811.

St. Dunstan's—a church in Fleet Street, London.

LETTER TO ROBINSON (Page 273)

Grimaldi—a famous clown of Lamb's time, whose *Memoirs* were edited by Charles Dickens.

LETTER TO BARTON (Page 276)

Tarpeian, etc.—the rock on the Capitoline Hill at Rome, from which were hurled persons convicted of treason.

Southey—although Southey wrote prodigiously, yet, as a matter of fact, he did not make a fortune out of his literary work.

mechanic pounces—*Antony and Cleopatra*, V, ii.

B[aldwin]—a member of the firm Baldwin, Cradock & Joy, publishers of the *London Magazine*, in which Lamb's essays first appeared.

Leadenhall—see note, page 315.

Fox—the founder of the Society of Friends, commonly called Quakers.

LETTER TO BARTON (Page 278)

day-mare—Lamb's own coinage, paralleling "nightmare."

lethargy—*Henry IV, Part I*. I, ii.

Judge Park—the judge who tried the murderer Thurtell.

Jack Ketch—a generic name for hangman, Jack Ketch having been the barbarous executioner of the 17th century.

Grub street—an old street in London, largely the abode of poor writers.

who shall, etc.—Romans vii. 24.

baiting at Scorpion—the meaning seems to be that Thurtell halts in his progress to the nether world at the constellation of the zodiac called Scorpion.

LETTER TO MANNING (Page 280)

Tuthill—a noted physician, friend to Lamb, who gave him the requisite certificate of disability with which to reinforce his application for pension.
To all, etc.—*Macbeth*, I, v.
imbecility—the meaning here is simply "weakness."
susurration—whisper.

LETTER TO WORDSWORTH (Page 281)

Monkhouse—a friend of both Lamb and Wordsworth, who had recently died.
Gilman—see note, page 335.
Rachel—Genesis xxix.
"Church"—a book by Southey.

THE SUPERANNUATED MAN (Page 285)

London Magazine, May, 1825.
words of course—formal phrases.
Esto, etc.—may it last forever.
that's born, etc.—Quoted from Middleton's *Mayor of Queens Borough*.
Gresham—founder of the Royal Exchange in the 16th century.
Whittington—three times Lord Mayor of London in the 15th century.
Aquinas—Thomas Aquinas, a medieval theologian.
Carthusian—a member of the Carthusian order of monks, noted for the strictness of its discipline.
Elgin marbles—see note, page 327.
Black Monday—Easter Monday, so called because of a severe storm that occurred on that day in 1360.
Lucretian—the Roman poet Lucretius in the opening of *De Rerum Natura*, Book II, speaks of the pleasure one on land has in beholding the distress of another amidst the waves of the sea.
as low, etc.—*Hamlet*, II, ii.
gardens—an echo of Milton's *Il Penseroso*.
cum, etc.—with dignity.
opus, etc.—my work is finished.

LETTER TO ROBINSON (Page 294)

Norris—Randall Norris was subtreasurer and librarian of the Temple. "Mine and my father's friend for nearly half a century," is Lamb's statement in another place about the connection between his family and Norris.
decies, etc.—ten times repeated.

bottoms—ships.

How shall we, etc.—from one of Lamb's own poems, *Lines Written after the Preceding Poem*.

the Benchers—of the Inner Temple.

plain statement—Robinson's efforts were successful and Mrs. Norris received an annual grant.

LETTER TO BARTON (Page 296)

Idumean palm—Isaiah xxxiv. 4.

these limitary specialties—dates.

Lucy—Barton's daughter.

my poor Lucy—a reference to Mary Lamb.

Emma—Emma Isola, the young woman adopted by the Lambs.

Enfield—a village about ten miles from London, where Lamb lived for several years.

Eliza—Barton's sister.

farce—*The Pawnbroker's Daughter*.

Hessey..Hunt and Clarke—publishers, who had been unable to make the *London Magazine* successful financially.

Vulgar Truths—Barton never published anything with this title, although he seems to have discussed it with Lamb.

inch-meal—by inches.

Anna—a Miss Knight, a Quaker schoolmistress, to whom Lamb had been introduced by Barton.

LETTER TO WORDSWORTH (Page 299)

Edmonton—a village about nine miles from London. The Lambs lived there after 1823.

punctum, etc.—a standing point.

hey-pass, re-pass—conjurer's jargon.

Baucis, etc.—it should be Baucis and Philemon. In the legend they were a couple living in Phrygia, who accorded hospitality to Jupiter and Mercury, when they had been refused elsewhere.

otium, etc.—leisure instead of dignity.

confiding ravens—Job xxxviii. 41.

Eloisa, etc.—an allusion to the story of Abelard and Heloise. After they were separated, Abelard retired to a monastery which was then called Paraclete.

Palmyra—the ruined city of Asia in the Syrian desert.

Seven Sleepers—Seven Christians, who according to tradition, slept unharmed by persecution for two hundred years.

Scotch novels—those of Sir Walter Scott.

passengers—passers-by.

calenture—a fever, characteristic of the tropics.

Promethean felicity—according to legend, Prometheus, the protector of mankind, brought fire to earth from heaven. In revenge Zeus sent all manner of sufferings and disease on mankind.

proper—belonging to the person himself.

collyrium of Tobias—in the *Book of Tobit,* Tobias restores his sight with eye-salve (collyrium) made from the gall of a fish.

a Recluse—an unfinished poem by Wordsworth.

skinker—a tapster. The allusion is to the banquet of the gods told in the *Iliad,* where Vulcan filled the cups.

propria, etc.—with her own hand.

parcel gentleman—half gentleman. A pun is intended on parcel and haberdasher.

outside it—rides on the top of the stage coach.

Inachus's daughter—Io, who was turned into a cow and tormented by a gadfly.

dii avertant—"The gods forbid!"

Curtius—the Roman youth, who, according to tradition, leaped on horseback into a gap which had opened into the Roman forum, and so saved the city.

spiral configurations—bowlegs.

Bellerophon—the rider of Pegasus, the winged horse.

Put case—suppose.

the sceptre of Agamemnon—in the quarrel between Achilles and Agamemnon, the latter swore by his staff, which would never more put forth leaf, that the Greeks would one day want his help.

Norris—see note, page 346.

Clothed, etc.—Job i. 21.

Henry Crabb—Henry Crabb Robinson.

be-Goethed—obsessed with the German writer, Goethe.

Miss Kelly—see note, page 334.

Talfourd—a friend who, after Lamb's death, published some of his letters and wrote an account of his life.

Can I cram—*Henry V,* Prologue to Act I.

NEW YEAR'S EVE (Page 305)

London Magazine, January, 1821.

a contemporary—Coleridge in his *Ode to the Departing Year.*

welcome, etc.—from Pope's translation of the *Odyssey.*

Alice W[interto]n—see note, page 323.

changed—an imitation of the exclamation of Quince in *A Midsummer Night's Dream,* III, i.

not fallen—see Lamb's sonnet on *Innocence.*

like, etc.—Job vii. 6.

reluct—show reluctance.

Lavinian shores—after Aeneas fled from Troy he settled on the Lavinian shore in Italy. Lamb has here adopted from Virgil's *Aeneid*.

sweet, etc.—an echo of Royden's *Elegy on Sir Philip Sidney*.

sister—the moon.

Canticles—The Song of Solomon VII.

Persian—Zoroaster, founder of the religion of Persia, sun worship being one of its features.

Friar John—a character in Rabelais' *Gargantua*.

lie down, etc.—from Sir Thomas Browne's *Hydrotaphia or Urn-Burial*.

Mr. Cotton—see note, page 324.

Helicon—mountain in Greece, the fabled home of the Muses.